'Tis my maxim to let the plain naked truth speak for itself.

ALEXANDER HAMILTON

Discovering Hamilton

New Discoveries in the Lives of Alexander Hamilton, His Family, Friends, and Colleagues

From Various Archives Around the World

MICHAEL E. NEWTON

Published by Eleftheria Publishing
Phoenix, AZ
www.eleftheriapublishing.com

ISBN-10: 0-9826040-4-1
ISBN-13: 978-0-9826040-4-5
Library of Congress Control Number: 2019905596

Cover image: Charles Willson Peale, Portrait of Alexander Hamilton, ca. 1780,
        Columbia University.
Photo credit: Michael E. Newton.

Table of Contents

Preface

One would think that after more than two hundred years and dozens if not hundreds of biographies, just about everything concerning a famous, important, and popular Founding Father would have already been discovered. But in researching the life and origins of Alexander Hamilton, this author noticed disagreements between previous writers regarding specific details of his life and those of his family, friends, and colleagues. As any decent historian would do, or should do, the relevant sources were examined in an attempt to discover the truth. In more than one case, it became clear that previous biographers had failed to report the facts correctly due either to transcription errors or because the information was taken out of context. In other cases, these biographers omitted pertinent details, perhaps because the author had not noticed them, had not realized their importance, or was trying to be concise.

At this point it was decided that not only would it be worthwhile to check every possible source[1] for accuracy, but also that a systematic examination of the available West Indian records pertaining to Hamilton, his family, friends, and colleagues would probably bear fruit. And it certainly has!

Thankfully, historical research is much easier now than it was when Gertrude Atherton first went to the West Indies in search of Hamilton information back in 1901, or when H. U. Ramsing researched Hamilton from 1902 until 1939, or when Broadus Mitchell added to their work in the 1950s. In fact, one can do historical research today that was not even possible when Ron Chernow wrote about Hamilton in 2004 or even just a few years ago when this author started delving into Hamilton and wrote a book about his formative years.

Undoubtedly, the biggest advance in the ability to research the lives of Hamilton, his family, friends, and colleagues comes from the Rigsarkivet (Danish National Archives), which has recently made millions of pages of original manuscripts from the Danish West Indies available for free on their website.[2] While this enables historians to do research from their homes and offices, it also poses an immense challenge because there is simply too much information for one person to read or even skim everything. Moreover, almost all of these documents are handwritten, so there is no optical character recognition and therefore no way to search these millions of pages for the few that might be relevant. Even more challenging, most of the eighteenth century Danish records are written in a Gothic script that few today can read. Nevertheless, these records are available and if one knows where to look, one can get a good start and then expand the search outward from there.

Beyond just the Rigsarkivet, although that is where most of the new Hamilton discoveries have been and probably will continue to be found, other archives have also made it easier to do research. A number offer online indexes that help one find relevant information. Many have digitized all or part of their collections. Others make it easy to request information and have it scanned and sent at a relatively low cost. Some provide user-friendly websites where such requests are processed automatically and sometimes instantaneously. Others make it easy to visit, and for historians there is nothing like actually holding an original document that may not have been touched in decades and finding something new in it that no one before had noticed.

Unfortunately, a number of archives have been slow in digitizing, are not very welcoming to researchers, or are simply inconvenient for U.S.-based historians to visit. Accordingly, plenty probably remains to be discovered in these locations.

As a result, this book is very much a work in progress. The author continues to research Hamilton's life within various archives, most especially but certainly not limited to the Rigsarkivet. Moreover, one hopes that the new details, locations, and names presented in this work will open up new avenues of research for others to explore.

Even though this book is a work in progress, waiting until all the research is completed would have resulted in unnecessarily delaying the dissemination of interesting and important information. Many of the new discoveries within this book disprove or alter what many currently believe to be true about Hamilton. In order to correct these errors and prevent others from repeating them, these new discoveries are being made available now.

Many of the essays, or chapters, within this book are based on blog posts written by the author for DiscoveringHamilton.com, but all of those have been edited for this volume and most of them have been updated and expanded with new information. Several entirely new essays have also been written, a few of which are among the most important Hamilton discoveries found in this work and indeed were the catalyst for this book's publication.

Notes

1. Some sources have been lost, damaged, or destroyed since their initial discovery.
2. For the Danish version of the Rigsarkivet's "Vestindien" collection, see https://www.sa.dk/ao-soegesider/da/collection/theme/8.
   The English version of "The West Indies" collection is located at https://www.sa.dk/ao-soegesider/en/collection/theme/8.

Alexander Hamilton's Birth, Early Biography, and More: Newly Discovered Legal Testimony from Alexander Hamilton, His Aunt, and Others

The debate over Alexander Hamilton's birthdate has been raging now for eighty years, with one camp arguing for January 11, 1755, and the other for January 11, 1757.

But the uncertainty regarding Alexander Hamilton's birth and early years is much greater than the single debate over his year of birth. Nearly nothing had previously been known about Hamilton's life prior to his arrival on St. Croix in 1765. In fact, barely anything was known about the lives of Hamilton's parents between 1750 and 1765, and clearly their story is important because anything that happened to Alexander Hamilton during this period was not by his own doing but rather was the result of his parents' circumstances, decisions, and actions.

Previous Sources for 1750–1765 Information

The few facts known about the lives of James Hamilton, Rachel Faucett, and their children for the fifteen-year period of 1750–1765 come from just a few sources. Many of these are secondary sources recorded decades after the fact and therefore their reliability is suspect. These previous sources are:

- In a letter written to William Jackson but sent to James McHenry, Alexander Hamilton said that his "mother afterwards went to St Kitts, became acquainted with my father and a marriage between them ensued, followed by many years cohabitation and several children." Hamilton also noted that his mother's "divorce" from her first husband, John Michael Lavien, "was not absolute but qualified" and as a result her "second marriage" to James Hamilton "was not lawful."[1]
- Alexander Hamilton told friends and family how old he was and apparently informed them that he had been born on January 11, 1757, on the island of Nevis. This can best be seen in a few examples:

- Alexander Hamilton wrote to a relative in Scotland, "Myself at about sixteen came to this country. . . . I was able, by the age of nineteen, to qualify myself for the degree of Bachelor of Arts in the College of New York. . . . The American Revolution supervened. My principles led me to take part in it. At nineteen I entered into the American army as Captain of Artillery."[2] Since Hamilton "came to this country" in October 1772,[3] saying that he arrived at "about sixteen" indicates that he was born in 1756 or 1757. Similarly, Hamilton said he qualified for a degree "by the age of nineteen" and became an artillery captain "at nineteen," both of which occurred in early 1776. This again indicates that he was born in 1756 or 1757.

- Nicholas Fish stated he was "certain" that Hamilton "when he wrote the political pieces . . . was about eighteen" because "we . . . compared and knew each other's age, he being about one year older than me."[4] Since Hamilton wrote his "political pieces," i.e., *A Full Vindication of the Measures of the Congress* and *The Farmer Refuted* in late 1774 and early 1775[5] and Fish was born on August 28, 1758,[6] this clearly indicates that Hamilton was born in 1756 or 1757.

- James Yard reported that Hamilton was born on Nevis,[7] probably based on information from Hamilton's good friend Edward Stevens, who was Yard's brother-in-law.

- Hamilton's son John C. Hamilton wrote in two different books that his father was born on January 11, 1757, on the island of Nevis.[8]

- Another son, James A. Hamilton, also wrote that his father was born on January 11, 1757.[9]

- Despite Hamilton giving out his age and apparently telling friends and family that he was born on January 11, 1757, the registration and appraisement of Rachel Faucett's estate by the St. Croix probate court, which was recorded on February 22, 1768, and later transcribed into the probate record, stated that Alexander Hamilton was thirteen, indicating a birth between February 23, 1754, and February 22, 1755. It also stated that James Hamilton Jr. was fifteen, indicating a birth between February 23, 1752, and February 22, 1753.[10]

- According to John C. Hamilton, his father Alexander Hamilton "rarely . . . alluded to his personal history" but "mentioned with a smile his having been taught to repeat the Decalogue in Hebrew at the school of a Jewess when so small that he was placed standing by her side upon a table."[11] No location was given for this school, nor did John C. Hamilton say how old his father was when he attended.
- On the island of St. Eustatius on October 1, 1758, "James Hamelton en Rachel Hamelton desselfs Huysvrouw [James Hamilton and Rachel Hamilton his housewife]" served as godparents at the baptism of four-month-old Alexander Fraser Jr., son of "Alexander Fraser en Elisabeth Thornton desselfs Huysvrouw [Alexander Fraser and Elizabeth Thornton his housewife]."[12]
- A summons issued by the divorce court on St. Croix on February 26, 1759, stated that Rachel "for 9 years has been absent from him [John Michael Lavien] and gone to another place, where she is said to have begotten several illegitimate children."[13]
- The divorce court's ruling of June 25, 1759, stated that "Rachel Lavien has been absent from him [John Michael Lavien] and lived on an English island for 7 to 8 years" and "also that she during that time has begotten two illegitimate children."[14]

In other words, only a few records concerning James Hamilton, Rachel Faucett, and their children had been found from this fifteen-year period. The primary sources were limited to one distinct record of James Hamilton and Rachel Faucett from 1758, two vague accounts from 1759 regarding Rachel's absence from St. Croix for the previous seven to nine years and of her giving birth to two or more children, and a legal record from 1768 mentioning the ages of James Jr. and Alexander. Subsequent accounts concerning this period included one statement by Alexander Hamilton about his parents, statements by Alexander Hamilton, his friends, and his family regarding his age, place of birth, and birthdate, and one secondhand tale about Alexander Hamilton attending "the school of a Jewess." As a result, while a general idea of what happened during this fifteen-year period had been established, the details necessary for a full and accurate narrative were missing. How much time James, Rachel, and their children spent on different islands was completely unknown. The birthplace of James Hamilton Jr. was unclear. Even the date of

Alexander Hamilton's birth has been a matter of debate ever since Rachel Faucett's probate record was discovered and published eighty years ago.[15]

Two New Primary Sources

Two newly discovered records provide additional and more accurate information about the lost years of 1750–1765 and more specifically about Alexander Hamilton's birth and early biography.

These two new records are (1) the 1759 divorce court proceedings of John Michael Lavien v. Rachel Faucett and (2) legal testimony by Alexander Hamilton in August 1771.

Full accounts of these newly discovered records can be found in the chapters "John Michael Lavien v. Rachel Faucett: The 1759 Divorce Court Proceedings" and "Alexander Hamilton Working for Nicholas Cruger on St. Croix: More Newly Discovered Records." The present chapter will focus on how these new discoveries effect the 1750–1765 Hamilton story. Please refer to those other chapters for additional details and complete citations.

Alexander Hamilton's Birthdate

As noted earlier, Alexander Hamilton provided his age to friends and family and apparently told them his birthdate as well.[16] Accordingly, Alexander Hamilton's sons John C. Hamilton and James A. Hamilton both wrote that their father was born on January 11, 1757.[17]

But the February 22, 1768, registration and appraisement of Rachel Faucett's estate by the probate court stated that Alexander Hamilton was thirteen years old, indicating a birth between February 23, 1754, and February 22, 1755.[18] Accordingly, many have argued that the January 11 birthday is "probably right" but that the 1757 year of birth must be wrong and that Hamilton was not born January 11, 1757, but rather on January 11, 1755.[19]

According to the newly discovered divorce court proceedings for John Michael Lavien v. Rachel Faucett, Rachel's sister Jemima Gurley testified on April 18, 1759, that "two years ago" she "had come to St. Eustatius" and "that her sister on St. Eustatius had two children," the younger one then being "about three years old."[20] Jemima's statement implies that Alexander Hamilton was born around April 1754. To be more precise, if one assumes that "two years ago" means 1½ to 2½ "years ago" and "about three years old" means the child was above 2½ years old but not yet four, one ends up with Alexander Hamilton being born between October 1752 and April 1755. While April 1754 is the best estimate of Hamilton's birth based on this record alone, January 11, 1755, remains a distinct possibility. A birth on January 11, 1757, would seem to be ruled out by Jemima Gurley's testimony.

In another newly discovered record, Alexander Hamilton testified in court on August 5, 1771, in a case involving his boss Nicholas Cruger. Because of his young age, Hamilton was asked for some biographical details to ascertain his suitability to provide legal testimony. Among the questions, Hamilton was asked "how old he was." Hamilton "answered he was 17 years old."[21] Thus, Hamilton himself indicated that he was born between August 6, 1753, and August 5, 1754. Not only would this preclude a 1757 year of birth, but would also seem to rule out 1755. A birthdate of January 11, 1755, would only be possible if Hamilton said he was in his seventeenth year of life, was almost seventeen, or about seventeen, but the court record does not say this and there is no reason to believe that the court recorder omitted those details.

"Witness answered he was 17 years old," August 5, 1771, in *Christiansted Tingsvidneprotokoller 1771–1772* 74v.

There are now three primary sources from St. Croix regarding Alexander Hamilton's birthdate. Unfortunately, none of them give a precise date, but they all agree regarding the general timeframe, and when evaluated together they give a clear indication of when Hamilton was born.

- In April 1759, Jemima Gurley testified that Hamilton "two years ago" was "about three years old," suggesting a birth around April 1754 but offering a wide range of possibilities from October 1752 to April 1755.
- A February 22, 1768, registration and appraisement of Rachel Faucett's estate by the probate court stated that Alexander Hamilton was thirteen at the time, indicating a birth between February 23, 1754, and February 22, 1755.
- On August 5, 1771, Alexander Hamilton testified that "he was 17 years old," placing his birth between August 6, 1753, and August 5, 1754.

Based on the overlapping dates provided in these three primary sources, it would seem that Alexander Hamilton was born between February 23 and August 5, 1754.

It is thus clear that Hamilton was not born on January 11, 1757, as he apparently told friends and family. Moreover, a birthdate of January 11, 1755, is possible only if the court recorder omitted some words from Hamilton's testimony. And if Hamilton indeed was born on January 11 but changed the year, a 1754 year of birth is just as likely as 1755 since each of these years has one primary source supporting it and one contradicting it.

Accordingly, the question is no longer whether Hamilton was born on January 11, 1755 or 1757. Rather, the question is whether Hamilton was born between February 23 and August 5, 1754, or on January 11, 1754 or 1755.

Seeing how Hamilton misrepresented his age and year of birth (more on that shortly) and there are no primary sources supporting a January 11 birthday, this author must follow the available evidence and conclude that Alexander Hamilton probably was born between February 23 and August 5, 1754.

Poetry by "A.H."

On April 6, 1771, some poetry appeared in St. Croix's *The Royal Danish American Gazette*. These verses were preceded by a note:

> Sir,
>
> I am a youth about seventeen, and consequently such an attempt as this must be presumptuous; but if, upon perusal, you think the following piece worthy of a place in your paper, by inserting it you'll much oblige
>
> Your obedient servant,
A.H.[22]

The initials "A.H." and the age of the author suggested to some that Alexander Hamilton composed this poetry.[23] This author previously argued that "there is reason to doubt Hamilton's authorship of these verses." One of the reasons was that "Hamilton at that time was just fourteen, if a 1757 year of birth is to be believed." Moreover, it was argued that "even if Hamilton had been born in 1755, he was still nine months shy of being seventeen."[24]

Now that it has been established that Hamilton probably was born between February 23 and August 5, 1754, it is more likely that he wrote this poetry because in April 1771 he would have been or was about to turn seventeen years old.

Why Did Alexander Hamilton Misrepresent His Age?

It is clear from his 1771 testimony that Hamilton knew how old he was and that he was born, according to his own statement, between August 6, 1753, and August 5, 1754. Accordingly, when he later gave out his age and apparently told friends and family that he was born on January 11, 1757, he could not have been simply confused or mistaken. It therefore appears that Hamilton misrepresented his age in later life.

If Alexander Hamilton was born in 1754, as appears likely, or even on January 11, 1755, one must ask why he misrepresented his age and apparently told friends and family he was born on January 11, 1757. Indeed, people have been asking this question ever since H. U. Ramsing discovered Rachel Faucett's probate record back in the 1930s and suggested a 1755 year of birth.[25]

Since Hamilton's age was well known on St. Croix, he must have changed it after he came to mainland North America in 1772. The rationale behind Hamilton's decision cannot be known with certainty but one plausible theory is that Hamilton altered his birthdate so that he would appear closer in age to his fellow students. Hamilton would have been among the oldest students, if not the oldest, if he entered grammar school in Elizabethtown, New Jersey, when he was eighteen years old and then entered college in New York City when he was nineteen.[26] Indeed, Hamilton must have started misrepresenting his age immediately upon arriving in mainland North America because once his teachers and friends in Elizabethtown knew his true age, it would have been nearly impossible for him to alter it later in life since people who had known him in Elizabethtown would have realized he changed it.

However, many people knew Hamilton on St. Croix and then again in mainland North America, including but not limited to Edward Stevens, Nicholas Cruger, David Beekman, Anne Lytton Venton, and George Codwise, and they must have known Hamilton's true age and perhaps even his birthdate.[27] Those who realized that Hamilton provided an incorrect age must have gone along with the deception and therefore approved of the ruse, or Hamilton convinced them that they remembered incorrectly and that he of course would know how old he was.

It is difficult to rectify Hamilton's long deception regarding his age against his well-known honesty. Hamilton frequently remarked on the importance of being honest.[28] He often spoke honestly even to his detriment.[29] His friends noted his "bold and inflexible adherence to truth" and that "no man ever more disdained duplicity or carried frankness further than he."[30] Even his enemies acknowledged that they "never knew him [to] disguise his intentions or deny their consequences. On his word I could rely equally as his oath."[31] Given this, it is hard to believe that Hamilton misrepresented his age for his entire adult life.

It is possible, however, that these two phenomena are related. Perhaps Hamilton's strict honesty in other matters was a direct result of his dishonesty in this one case. Perhaps Hamilton maintained a "bold and inflexible adherence to truth" to compensate for continuously misrepresenting his age.

Besides, Hamilton surely was not the only person to misrepresent his age. The birthdate of another Founding Father, James McHenry, "is usually given as November 16, 1753, but the family records give the year as 1752, and in a letter to Timothy Pickering in June, 1813, McHenry gave it as November 25, 1751."[32] Did McHenry purposely give out an incorrect birthdate? Hitting closer to home, Hamilton's mother may have also altered her age.[33]

While it is clear that Hamilton misrepresented his age and that his birthdate of January 11, 1757, is incorrect, it appears that taking liberties with one's age or birthdate may not have been as big a deal then as it would be considered today.

Alexander Hamilton's Birthplace

In addition to apparently giving his birthdate as January 11, 1757, Alexander Hamilton evidently also told friends and family that he was born on the British island of Nevis.[34] Unlike his birthdate, this fact has never been questioned, for there never was any reason to doubt it.

However, none of the witnesses who testified in the divorce proceedings of John Michael Lavien v. Rachel Faucett mentioned Rachel having been on Nevis during the 1750s. Both Jemima Gurley and James Ash put Rachel on St. Kitts and St. Eustatius while James Hendrie, who apparently stayed on St.

Croix, only testified that Rachel was "away from the island [St. Croix]."[35] This is especially interesting because Jemima testified that she "had herself resided on Nevis" before having "come to St. Eustatius" in or around 1757,[36] though it appears she had also lived on or been a frequent visitor to St. Eustatius between 1748 and 1756.[37]

This does not mean that Rachel and her family never lived on or visited Nevis. There is a gap in the timeline during which Rachel could have been on the island. After leaving St. Kitts for St. Eustatius in 1753, it is not known where Rachel was living until she is still or again found on St. Eustatius in 1756.[38] While it is possible that Rachel and her family lived on St. Eustatius during this entire period, there is no record of their whereabouts during these three or four years. This gave them plenty of time to return to St. Kitts or to go to Nevis. In fact, at some point after Alexander Hamilton's birth but before 1757, Rachel must have been on St. Kitts because Jemima testified that her sister had made a "declaration . . . to the judge on Sainte Christopher [St. Kitts]" regarding her "2 children."[39] Thus, Rachel must have been on St. Kitts sometime during the period in question and could have been on Nevis as well.

Since there is evidence that James Hamilton and Rachel returned to St. Kitts from St. Eustatius sometime between 1754 and 1757 and that they could have also spent time on Nevis during this period, there is little reason to question Hamilton's birth on Nevis because it is a distinct possibility that is not contradicted by any evidence.

One could argue, however, that if Hamilton misrepresented his age and birthdate, he could have done the same regarding his place of birth. If Hamilton had been born on the Dutch island of St. Eustatius, he would have been considered even more of a foreigner. By saying he was born on Nevis, Hamilton could claim to be a British citizen just like everyone else born in the thirteen colonies.

Without evidence one way or the other regarding his place of birth, one must assume that Hamilton was born on Nevis like he apparently told friends and family, but there remains some uncertainty about it.

Even if Hamilton was born on Nevis, as assumed, it would seem that Rachel and her family spent significantly less time on Nevis and more time on St. Eustatius than previously thought. Just how much time they spent on each island is not known and cannot be known until additional evidence is found.

The School of a Jewess

According to son John C. Hamilton, Alexander Hamilton "rarely . . . alluded to his personal history" but "mentioned with a smile his having been taught to repeat the Decalogue in Hebrew at the school of a Jewess when so small that he was placed standing by her side upon a table."[40]

Hamilton biographers often place this "school of a Jewess" on Nevis, but it is now clear that the Hamiltons were living on St. Eustatius in 1753, from 1756 to 1758, and perhaps much longer.[41] Perhaps this Jewish school was on St. Eustatius rather than Nevis.

By the time Alexander Hamilton was born, the Jewish community of Nevis had all but disappeared. Nevis's Jewish population peaked at about 75 individuals in 1724 but it was closer to zero by Hamilton's time.[42] In contrast, St. Eustatius had a thriving Jewish community. A new synagogue was built there in 1737 and about 350 Jews lived on the island in 1781.[43]

It would therefore make more sense for this "school of a Jewess" to be on St. Eustatius rather than Nevis.

The Birth of James Hamilton Jr.

With the addition of the record of the divorce court proceedings, there are now three pieces of evidence regarding the birthdate of James Hamilton Jr., all of which agree regarding the general timeframe of his birth.

According to the registration and appraisement of Rachel Faucett's estate by the probate court on February 22, 1768, James Hamilton Jr. was fifteen years old.[44] If this was an exact figure rather than an estimate, and the record does not include the word "about" or any such term, James Hamilton Jr. was born between February 23, 1752, and February 22, 1753.

In her testimony of April 18, 1759, Jemima Gurley stated that "two years ago" she "had come to St. Eustatius" and "that her sister on St. Eustatius had two children," the older one being "about 5 . . . years old."[45] This indicates a birth around April 1752. To be more precise, if one assumes that "two years ago" means 1½ to 2½ "years ago" and "about 5 . . . years old" means the child was above 4½ years old but not yet six, James Hamilton Jr. was born between October 1750 and April 1753.

James Ash testified at the same divorce hearing that "he knew Rachel

Lavien when the witness was on Sainte Christopher [St. Kitts] in the years 1751, 1752, and 1753 in which years she resided on St. Christopher" and that "when he knew her on Sainte Christopher [she] had one or two children." This means that the older child, i.e., James Hamilton Jr., must have been born in 1753 or earlier, consistent with the other two records of James's age.

Based on these three pieces of evidence, James Hamilton Jr. probably was born in 1752 or early 1753. It also appears that he had been born on the island of St. Kitts.

James Hamilton Known as Rachel's Partner

The name of Rachel Faucett's partner on St. Kitts and St. Eustatius is not mentioned in the record of the divorce court proceedings. Instead, this person is referred to as the "ustevnt [unsummoned] person."[46] In other words, this person was not summoned by the court, was not present during the hearings, and the court did not mean to prosecute him or hold him accountable for any action. Of course, this "ustevnt" person's alleged offense took place on the British and Dutch islands of St. Kitts and St. Eustatius, so even if the Danish authorities on St. Croix had any interest in prosecuting him, they could not. But this was a divorce court and the matter at hand was Rachel's infidelity, which would give John Michael Lavien grounds for divorce. The identity of this "ustevnt" person was not only unimportant, but the court clearly did not want to imply that this person should be held liable for any crime.

Nevertheless, the court record states that the "man's name the witness [Jemima Gurley] mentioned to the court, but which will not be entered in the protocol-book." James Ash also testified that Rachel "lived . . . with the same ustevnt person," that Rachel's children "passed as her and the ustevnte person's children," and that he had heard of "the ustevnte's common reputation."[47] It is thus clear that Jemima Gurley and James Ash knew the identity of James Hamilton and reported it to the court, which of course means that John Michael Lavien knew Hamilton's name as well. It is likely, however, that Lavien and others already knew that it was James Hamilton who had partnered with Rachel even before it was reported in court.

This should come as no surprise because a 1758 baptismal record from St. Eustatius listed them as "James Hamelton en Rachel Hamelton desselfs

Huysvrouw [James Hamilton and Rachel Hamilton his housewife]."[48] Thus, all the attendees at that baptism and society at large knew that James Hamilton and Rachel Faucett were together and that they acted like a married couple, who by this time had been with each other for many years and had two children together.

Did James Hamilton know about Rachel's Past?

There has been much debate regarding how much James Hamilton knew about Rachel Faucett's past. One popular story is that when James, Rachel, and their children arrived on St. Croix in 1765, James learned the truth of Rachel's previous marriage, affair, and imprisonment, and that this discovery prompted him to separate from her and eventually leave her and their children forever.[49]

The record of the divorce proceedings completely debunks this narrative. According to the two witnesses who knew Rachel on St. Kitts and St. Eustatius, Rachel's prior marriage was well known. Jemima Gurley testified that Rachel had made "a declaration . . . to the judge on Sainte Christopher, the contents of which were that the 2 children that Rachel Lavien then had had been raised outside of marriage with an ustevnt person who was not her husband." Although this "declaration" did not mention a husband living on another island, the only reason such a declaration would have been necessary was if Rachel was barred from marrying another man. Relationships between two unwed individuals were common and not cause for legal action. Rachel's relationship with this "ustevnt person" was only an issue because she was already married. Thus, on St. Kitts, Rachel's marriage to another man and her forbidden relationship with James Hamilton became a matter of public record. Likewise, James Ash testified that Rachel and other people told him "that she was married to John Michael Lavien and that she went both on Sainte Christopher and Sainte Eustatius under the name of Rachel Lavien although she in both places associated with an ustevnt person of another name." Ash added that Rachel "and the ustevnte's common reputation was that she was a publique whore," which means that the general public knew at least some details regarding her past.[50]

While Rachel's previous marriage was well known and everyone therefore knew that her relationship with James Hamilton was in violation of that marriage, no mention was made in witness testimony of her prior affair with Johan Cronenberg.[51] It is therefore possible that James did not know about Rachel's prior affair and imprisonment, but he certainly knew that she had been and still was married to Lavien and that their two children were therefore considered illegitimate according to the law.

Nevertheless, Rachel's affair and imprisonment probably were also common knowledge and James presumably knew about them. These matters were not brought up by the witnesses nor were they asked about them because they were not a party to those events and those events were already well established by previous courts.[52] In his divorce claim, John Lavien mentioned Rachel's affair with Cronenberg and her imprisonment, although he did not mention Cronenberg by name.[53] Also, Lavien's lawyer Soren Bagge mentioned "other evidence he had in his possession," which probably included the court record of the Cronenberg affair.[54] One assumes that Bagge and Lavien referred the court to previous records of that affair and thus it did not need to be raised in the proceedings. So the fact that it was not mentioned by the witnesses, does not mean they knew nothing about it. One assumes that they did and that James Hamilton did as well.

A Marriage Between Them Ensued?

According to Alexander Hamilton, "My mother afterwards went to St. Kitts, became acquainted with my father and a marriage between them ensued, followed by many years cohabitation and several children."[55] Ever since, the question of whether there was "a marriage between" Rachel and James Hamilton has been raised.

In fact, this question was introduced back in 1759. When asked, Jemima replied that "she had heard it said" that "Rachel Lavien had gotten married to another person," i.e., James Hamilton, but that she "did not know" if it was true. In contrast, James Hendrie answered that he had heard that another man was associating with her, but he had not heard that she had married this other man. Similarly, James Ash was asked if Rachel had married anyone else but Ash replied that he had not heard that.[56]

Thus, even in 1759, it was unclear by those who knew Rachel and James Hamilton whether they had gotten married. Some had heard that they had been while others had not heard that, but none knew with certainty one way or the other. The fact that Lavien's lawyer asked the question and the witnesses were uncertain shows that then as now it was not known whether James and Rachel had a wedding ceremony.

But it will be recalled that according to Jemima Gurley, Rachel had made "a declaration . . . to the judge on Sainte Christopher, the contents of which were that the 2 children that Rachel Lavien then had had been raised outside of marriage with an ustevnt person who was not her husband."[57] It would thus appear that James and Rachel knew that they were not married.

On the other hand, a 1758 record from St. Eustatius listed James and Rachel as "James Hamelton en Rachel Hamelton desselfs Huysvrouw [James Hamilton and Rachel Hamilton his housewife]."[58] The fact that Rachel used the Hamilton name at this time and was listed as James's "housewife" implies that they acted as and were treated like a married couple, even if they knew that such a marriage was legally prohibited.

Alexander Hamilton's Father?

Even though Rachel had a "common reputation" as a "publique whore," the witnesses who knew her on St. Kitts and St. Eustatius all testified that "she in both places" was "associated with" the same "ustevnt person." According to these people, from the time Rachel met James Hamilton on St. Kitts, perhaps in 1751, until they last saw her in 1757, Rachel had been with James the whole time. Moreover, James Ash stated that "when he knew her on Sainte Christopher" in 1751–1753, "[she] had one or two children, which everywhere passed as her and the ustevnte person's children." Although Rachel had only one child at this time, Ash knew her again on St. Eustatius in 1756 where he "saw that she lived there with the same ustevnt person that she had lived with from Sainte Christopher." Thus, according to the witnesses, Rachel was with the same person the entire time and her children "passed" as the children of this man.[59]

It is always possible that Rachel cheated on her partner, but none of the witnesses nor John Michael Lavien made or repeated such an allegation. Such rumors, if they existed, surely would have been introduced into the court as further evidence of Rachel's infidelity and as an example of her being a "publique whore." One can therefore conclude that everyone believed that from 1751 to 1757 Rachel "associated" only with James Hamilton.

If, as the record suggests, Rachel was with just one man during this whole period, that means that James Hamilton was indeed Alexander Hamilton's father. Alternatively, if one wishes to argue that James Hamilton was not the father of Alexander Hamilton, one would need to present more substantial evidence to support this claim than had been necessary before this new record was discovered.

Alexander Hamilton's Religion

It has been argued that Alexander Hamilton was Jewish.[60] The contention is that John Michael Lavien was Jewish, Rachel Faucett converted to Judaism to marry Lavien, and thus Alexander Hamilton was Jewish because his mother was Jewish.

In his testimony to the divorce court, James Hendrie remarked that he knew John Michael Lavien and Rachel Faucett had been married "although he had not seen the priest marry them."[61] By saying "priest," Hendrie surely referred to a Christian priest. If the wedding had been conducted by a rabbi, which a gentile might refer to as a priest, Hendrie surely would have said a "Jewish priest." If Lavien had been Jewish, and there is no evidence he was, he must have converted to Christianity or pretended to be Christian when a priest officiated his wedding to Rachel.

So yet again, there is no evidence that John Michael Lavien was Jewish and it would appear that people believed him to be a Christian. There is therefore no reason to believe that Rachel converted to Judaism to marry Lavien or that Alexander Hamilton was a Jew.

In his own testimony of August 1771, Alexander Hamilton declared that he "had been brought up in the Reformed religion as it was observed in the English Established Church." In other words, Alexander Hamilton's parents raised him as an Anglican. Hamilton did not say if he had been baptized, but he testified that "he had not yet received communion."[62]

The Hamilton Story: 1750–1765

With the newly discovered records of the 1759 divorce court proceedings and Hamilton's August 1771 testimony along with the above analysis and various other sources, a new narrative for the years 1750–1765 can be established. (For more sources and full citations for the timeline below, see chapters "John Michael Lavien v. Rachel Faucett: The 1759 Divorce Court Proceedings" and "Alexander Hamilton Working for Nicholas Cruger on St. Croix: More Newly Discovered Records.")

After being imprisoned for nearly eight months for her extramarital affair, Rachel Faucett Lavien was released from prison on May 4, 1750.[63] Although Mary Faucett, Rachel's mother, left St. Croix sometime between October 1750 and year's end,[64] it is not known whether Rachel left St. Croix with her mother or more likely had done so back in May or shortly thereafter.

Whether Rachel went straight from St. Croix to St. Kitts, where she would be living the following year, or perhaps went first to Nevis, her old home, is not known from the available records. Either way, by the end of 1751, Rachel was living on St. Kitts.

On St. Kitts, Rachel met James Hamilton. Rachel gave birth, probably on St. Kitts, to James Hamilton Jr. in 1752 or early 1753.

In 1753, James Hamilton "absented himself" from St. Kitts to St. Eustatius "on account of debt." Rachel followed him.

What happened to James and Rachel over the next three years is not clear. No known record or witness reveals where they were in 1754 or 1755. Alexander Hamilton evidently was born between February 23 and August 5, 1754, or less likely on January 11, 1754 or 1755, reportedly on Nevis.

At some point after Alexander Hamilton's birth, Rachel was on St. Kitts, where she made a "declaration . . . to the judge" regarding her "2 children." Whether she was visiting St. Kitts or had moved there is not known.

In the meantime, Rachel's mother Mary Faucett, who presumably moved from St. Croix to St. Kitts in 1750, was on St. Eustatius in July 1755.[65] Jemima Faucett gave birth in March 1755 and baptized her child on St. Eustatius that same month,[66] so perhaps Mary's trip to St. Eustatius was related to that. It appears that Mary Faucett was back on St. Kitts in May 1756.[67] Curiously, Jemima was living on Nevis around this time, according to her testimony. Perhaps Rachel had traveled between the islands with her mother, or her mother traveled with her, or perhaps not.

Either way, by the end of 1756, Rachel and James "lived" on St. Eustatius again. They are found there still, or again, in 1757 and in October 1758.

After 1758, James, Rachel, and their children disappear again from the known records until James arrived on St. Croix in April 1765 and the rest of the family apparently followed shortly afterwards.[68]

Did James Hamilton, Rachel Faucett, and their children stay on St. Eustatius from 1758 to 1765? Or did they move back to St. Kitts or Nevis? Where were they living immediately before coming to St. Croix in 1765?

Unfortunately, all this and more remains a mystery.

Notes

1. Alexander Hamilton, addressed to William Jackson but sent to James McHenry, August 26, 1800, in *The Papers of Alexander Hamilton* 25:89–90.

2. Alexander Hamilton to William Hamilton, May 2, 1797, in *The Papers of Alexander Hamilton* 21:77.

3. Newton, *Alexander Hamilton: The Formative Years* 59–60, 69.

4. Nicholas Fish to Timothy Pickering, December 26, 1823, in *Timothy Pickering Papers* 32:42.

5. *The Papers of Alexander Hamilton* 1:45 and 81.

6. Fish, *The Fish Family in England and America* 323–324.

7. Timothy Pickering's Memoranda, February 15 and June 29, 1822, in Lodge, *Alexander Hamilton* 287 and 289.

8. John C. Hamilton, *The Life of Alexander Hamilton* 1:1; John C. Hamilton, *History of the Republic* 1:42.

9. James A. Hamilton, *Reminiscences* 2n.

10. *Christiansted Registrerings og Vurderingsprotokoller for Borgere og Plantere 1761–68,* 359v; *Christiansted Skiftebrevsprotokoller for Borgere og Plantere* 20:386v; Ramsing, "Alexander Hamilton Og Hans Modrene Slaegt" 245; Ramsing, *Alexander Hamilton's Birth and Parentage* 24; *The Papers of Alexander Hamilton* 1:2 and 3 note 1.

11. John C. Hamilton, *The Life of Alexander Hamilton* 1:3; John C. Hamilton, *History of the Republic* 1:42. For a discussion regarding Alexander Hamilton's possible knowledge of Hebrew, see Newton, *Alexander Hamilton: The Formative Years* 42–43 and 536 note 66.

12. *Hollandske Kirke, Sint Eustatius, Kirkebog, Baptisms 1743–1765,* October 1, 1758; Mitchell, *Alexander Hamilton: Youth to Maturity* 11 and 476 note 80; Newton, "Why Were the Hamiltons on St. Eustatius in 1758?"

13. *St. Croix Panteprotokoller 1756–1772* 43r–44r; transcribed in Ramsing, "Alexander Hamilton Og Hans Modrene Slaegt" 232–234; translated in Ramsing, *Alexander Hamilton's Birth and Parentage* 8–10.

14. *Christiansted Skiftebrevsprotokoller for Borgere og Plantere* 20:391r–v; transcribed in Ramsing, "Alexander Hamilton Og Hans Modrene Slaegt" 234–235; translated in Ramsing, *Alexander Hamilton's Birth and Parentage* 11–12.

15. Ramsing, "Alexander Hamilton Og Hans Modrene Slaegt" 232–235; translated in Ramsing, *Alexander Hamilton's Birth and Parentage* 8–12.

16. See pages 4–5.

17. John C. Hamilton, *The Life of Alexander Hamilton* 1:1; John C. Hamilton, *History of*

the Republic 1:42; James A. Hamilton, *Reminiscences* 2n.

18. *Christiansted Registrerings og Vurderingsprotokoller for Borgere og Plantere 1761–68* 359v; *Christiansted Skiftebrevsprotokoller for Borgere og Plantere* 20:386v; Ramsing, "Alexander Hamilton Og Hans Modrene Slaegt" 245; Ramsing, *Alexander Hamilton's Birth and Parentage* 24; *The Papers of Alexander Hamilton* 1:2 and 3 note 1.

19. For instance, see Ramsing, "Alexander Hamilton Og Hans Modrene Slaegt" 247–248; Ramsing, *Alexander Hamilton's Birth and Parentage* 27; *Mitchell, Alexander Hamilton: Youth to Maturity* 1 and 12; Randall, *Alexander Hamilton: A Life* 17; Chernow, *Alexander Hamilton* 17.

    For a full discussion of the prior debate regarding Alexander Hamilton's year of birth, see Newton, *Alexander Hamilton: The Formative Years* 19–29.

20. See page 78; Divorce proceedings of John Michael Lavien v. Rachel Faucett Lavien, 14r–16r, in *Christiansted Retsdokumenter 1740-1759*.

21. See pages 189–190; *Christiansted Tingsvidneprotokoller 1771–1772* 74v–75r.

22. *The Royal Danish American Gazette*, April 6, 1771; reprinted in *The Papers of Alexander Hamilton* 1:6–7.

23. Mitchell, *Alexander Hamilton: Youth to Maturity* 13 and 27; Kline, *Alexander Hamilton: A Biography in His Own Words* 1:16–17; Flexner, *The Young Hamilton* 36–37; *The Papers of Alexander Hamilton* 1:7n; Randall, *Alexander Hamilton: A Life* 28–29; Chernow, *Alexander Hamilton* 17 and 34.

24. Newton, *Alexander Hamilton: The Formative Years* 21 and 53–54.

25. Ramsing, "Alexander Hamilton Og Hans Modrene Slaegt" 247–248; Ramsing, *Alexander Hamilton's Birth and Parentage* 27.

26. Miller, *Alexander Hamilton and the Growth of the New Nation* 8; Randall, *Alexander Hamilton: A Life* 17 and 122; Chernow, *Alexander Hamilton* 48. See, however, Newton, *Alexander Hamilton: The Formative Years* 26.

27. Newton, *Alexander Hamilton: The Formative Years* 24–25.

28. Alexander Hamilton to Edward Stevens, November 11, 1769, in *The Papers of Alexander Hamilton* 1:4; Alexander Hamilton's *A Full Vindication of the Measures of the Congress*, December 1774, in ibid. 1:45n and 65; Alexander Hamilton to George Clinton, March 12, 1778, in ibid. 1:441; Alexander Hamilton to John Laurens, September 12, 1780, in ibid. 2:428.

29. Hamilton's unabashed honesty to his own detriment can be seen most notably in his June 18 speech at the Constitutional Convention, in his pamphlet on the Maria Reynolds affair, during the presidential election of 1800, and in his many criticisms of Aaron Burr over the years.

30. *A Collection of the Facts and Documents Relative to the Death of Alexander Hamilton* 228 and 234; *Works of Fisher Ames* 283 and 288.

31. Quoted in John McDonald, *A Sermon on the Premature and Lamented Death of General Alexander Hamilton* 16.

32. Steiner, *The Life and Correspondence of James McHenry* 1.

33. See pages 117–118.

34. See pages 4–5.

35. See pages 78–80; Divorce proceedings of John Michael Lavien v. Rachel Faucett Lavien, 14r–27r, in *Christiansted Retsdokumenter 1740-1759*.

36. See page 78; Divorce proceedings of John Michael Lavien v. Rachel Faucett Lavien, 14r–16r, in *Christiansted Retsdokumenter 1740-1759.*

37. See pages 87–89.

38. See page 79; Divorce proceedings of John Michael Lavien v. Rachel Faucett Lavien, 24r–27r, in *Christiansted Retsdokumenter 1740-1759.*

39. See page 78; Divorce proceedings of John Michael Lavien v. Rachel Faucett Lavien, 14r–16r, in *Christiansted Retsdokumenter 1740-1759.*

40. John C. Hamilton, *The Life of Alexander Hamilton* 1:3; John C. Hamilton, *History of the Republic* 1:42. For a discussion regarding Alexander Hamilton's possible knowledge of Hebrew, see Newton, *Alexander Hamilton: The Formative Years* 42–43 and 536 note 66.

41. See page 19.

42. Stern, "A Successful Caribbean Restoration: The Nevis Story" 23; Terrell, *The Jewish Community of Early Colonial Nevis* 129, 130, 149.

43. Hartog, *History of St. Eustatius* 40–42, 56, 58–59.

44. *Christiansted Registrerings og Vurderingsprotokoller for Borgere og Plantere 1761–68,* 359v; *Christiansted Skiftebrevsprotokoller for Borgere og Plantere* 20:386v; Ramsing, "Alexander Hamilton Og Hans Modrene Slaegt" 245; Ramsing, *Alexander Hamilton's Birth and Parentage* 24; *The Papers of Alexander Hamilton* 1:2 and 3 note 1.

45. See page 78; Divorce proceedings of John Michael Lavien v. Rachel Faucett Lavien, 14r–16r, in *Christiansted Retsdokumenter 1740-1759.*

46. See pages 78–80; Divorce proceedings of John Michael Lavien v. Rachel Faucett Lavien, 14r–27r, in *Christiansted Retsdokumenter 1740-1759.*

47. See pages 78–80; Divorce proceedings of John Michael Lavien v. Rachel Faucett Lavien, 14r–27r, in *Christiansted Retsdokumenter 1740-1759.*

48. *Hollandske Kirke, Sint Eustatius, Kirkebog, Baptisms 1743–1765,* October 1, 1758; Mitchell, *Alexander Hamilton: Youth to Maturity* 11 and 476 note 80; Newton, "Why Were the Hamiltons on St. Eustatius in 1758?"

49. For a broder discussion of the various theories regarding how much James Hamilton knew about Rachel Faucett's past, see Newton, *Alexander Hamilton: The Formative Years* 36–38.

50. See pages 78–80; Divorce proceedings of John Michael Lavien v. Rachel Faucett Lavien, 14r–27r, in *Christiansted Retsdokumenter 1740-1759.*

51. See chapter "The Extramarital Affair of Rachel Faucett."

52. See chapter "The Extramarital Affair of Rachel Faucett."

53. See page 76; *St. Croix Panteprotokoller 1756–1772* 43r–44r; transcribed in Ramsing, "Alexander Hamilton Og Hans Modrene Slaegt" 232–234; translated in Ramsing, *Alexander Hamilton's Birth and Parentage* 8–10.

54. See page 80; Divorce proceedings of John Michael Lavien v. Rachel Faucett Lavien, 27r–28r, in *Christiansted Retsdokumenter 1740-1759.*

55. Alexander Hamilton, addressed to William Jackson but sent to James McHenry, August 26, 1800, in *The Papers of Alexander Hamilton* 25:89–90.

56. See pages 78–80; Divorce proceedings of John Michael Lavien v. Rachel Faucett Lavien, 14r–27r, in *Christiansted Retsdokumenter 1740-1759.*

57. See page 78; Divorce proceedings of John Michael Lavien v. Rachel Faucett Lavien,

14r–16r, in *Christiansted Retsdokumenter 1740-1759*.

58. *Hollandske Kirke, Sint Eustatius, Kirkebog, Baptisms 1743–1765*, October 1, 1758; Mitchell, *Alexander Hamilton: Youth to Maturity* 11 and 476 note 80; Newton, "Why Were the Hamiltons on St. Eustatius in 1758?"

59. See pages 78–80; Divorce proceedings of John Michael Lavien v. Rachel Faucett Lavien, 14r–27r, in *Christiansted Retsdokumenter 1740-1759*.

60. See Newton, *Alexander Hamilton: The Formative Years* 34–35.

61. See page 79; Divorce proceedings of John Michael Lavien v. Rachel Faucett Lavien, 21v–24r, in *Christiansted Retsdokumenter 1740-1759*.

62. See pages 189–190; *Christiansted Tingsvidneprotokoller 1771–1772* 74v–75r.

63. See page 65.

64. See page 71.

65. Common Records of Nevis, July 23, 1755, quoted in Mitchell, *Alexander Hamilton: Youth to Maturity* 8.

66. See page 88.

67. Deed of Trust, May 5, 1756, in the Common Records of St. Kitts, quoted in Atherton, "The Hunt for Hamilton's Mother" 237–238; Atherton, *The Conqueror* 49 and 538.

68. See chapter "James Hamilton Working as a Sailor, Coming to St. Croix, and a Legal Dispute."

John Faucett, the French Invasion of Nevis in 1706, His Losses and Relief, and a Signed Deposition

In March 1706, a fleet of about fifty French ships with three to five thousand soldiers descended upon the island of Nevis. With a mere three or four hundred men of fighting age, the vastly outnumbered Nevisians fled into the mountains and capitulated the following day. In violation of the terms of surrender, the French burned down most of the dwelling houses on the plantations, many of the boiling houses, and about half of the capital city of Charlestown before absconding with 3,187 of the island's 6,023 blacks "besides the greatest parts of our mills and coppers with other rich merchandizes, to the value of a great many scores of thousand pounds." As a result, "Nevis, which formerly seemed to be the Garden of the Caribbees," was in "a deplorable spectacle of ruin, her forts demolished, plantations burnt, as well canes as houses, their negroes, some taken, the rest fled to the mountains." Many inhabitants left the island, "some to New England, Pennsylvania, etc." According to a petition by the merchants and planters of Nevis and St. Kitts, "the damage done to Nevis, by a modest computation, amounts to a million of money."[1]

Losses and Relief

The proprietors and merchants of St. Kitts and Nevis requested half a million pounds sterling from the home government "for the relief of the islands."[2] Over the next few years, Britain sent "considerable quantities of stores and provisions" to Nevis.[3] In the meantime, "Her Majesty was graciously pleased to appoint commissioners in those islands to compute their losses," which they calculated to be £356,926, 10 shillings, and 1 pence. In April 1709, Parliament voted £103,203 11s 4d "for the use of such proprietors or inhabitants only of Nevis and St. Christophers who were sufferers by the late French invasion there and who shall resettle or cause to be resettled their plantations in the said islands."[4]

Six hundred sixty-nine people submitted claims for the recovery of "one third of [their] losses" and took "oaths to prove" their "re-settlement" on Nevis and St. Kitts.[5] Among the group was Alexander Hamilton's grandfather, John Faucett, who submitted a claim for a loss of £1,088 12s 1d, more than double the average and about ten times the median claim.[6] In 1713, the Commission for Trade and Plantations started paying these claims and many received their relief funds that year.[7] On April 1, 1713, more than seven years after the French invasion, the Commission for Trade and Plantations issued a debenture, a monetary claim on the government, to John Faucett for £362 17s 4d.[8]

Even with this substantial relief, John Faucett still suffered a total loss of £725 14s 9d, more than fifty times the average annual wage of an Englishman.[9] A loss of this magnitude could not easily be recovered.

The Deposition of John Faucett

Many years later, the British and French governments were still arguing about whether the residents of Nevis owed France what they had agreed to in their terms of surrender or whether France owed the Nevisians for the illegal seizure and destruction of their property. To make their case, a number of Nevisians in 1720 provided accounts of what had happened back in March 1706.[10] One such deposition was provided by John Faucett:

The Deposition of John Faucet Planter aged about six and thirty years taken before the Honourable John Pinney Esq' Chief Justice of the Court of Kings Bench and Common Pleas, and John Dasent Esq' one other judge of said courts, and members of the committee appointed to answer the memorial of the French envoy Monsieur D'Iberville relating to the invasion of this island in the year seventeen hundred and six.

Who being duely sworn, to the second article saith, that this deponent contrary to the said article was stripped of all his wearing apparel to his shirt, shoes and stockings, some days after the surrender of the island at the Dodan; To the fifth article this deponent saith, that some few days before the departure of the French under the command of Monsieur D'Iberville, his own dwelling house, boyling house, with about

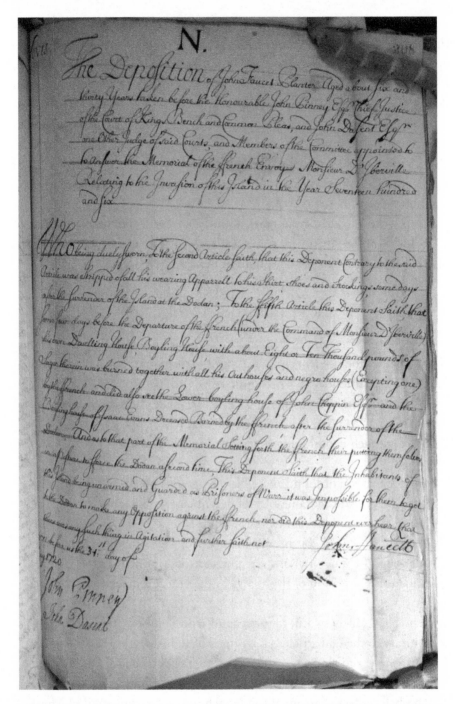

Deposition of John Faucett, May 31, 1720, in CO 152/13, page 208.

eight or ten thousand pounds of sugar therein was burned together with all his outhouses and negro houses (excepting one) by the French and did also see the lower boyling house of John Choppin Esqr and the boyling house of Isaac Evans deceased burned by the French after the surrender of the Dodan, And as to that part of the memorial setting forth the French their putting themselves in a posture to force the Dodan a second time, This deponent saith, that the inhabitants of this island being unarmed and guarded as prisoners of war it was impossible for them to get to the Dodan to make any opposition against the French nor did this deponent ever hear that there was any such thing in agitation and further saith not.   John Faucett
Sworn before us the 31st day of May 1720
John Pinney
John Dasent[11]

This deposition reveals much about John Faucett that was not previously known.

According to this deposition, John Faucett was "aged about six and thirty years" in May 1720. This means that he was born in "about" 1683 or 1684. It also means that he was "about" twenty-two years old when the French invaded Nevis in March 1706.

The deposition also shows that the "about" twenty-two-year-old John Faucett was already a "planter" on the island of Nevis in 1706, owning a sugar plantation complete with a "dwelling house," "outhouses," "negro houses" for his slaves, and a "boyling house" for converting the juice extracted from the raw sugar cane into molasses and crystallized sugar. The French, according to Faucett's statement, "burned" all this down, save for one negro house, and also burned "eight or ten thousand pounds of sugar." They also "stripped" him "of all his wearing apparel to his shirt, shoes and stockings." Even though the French absconded with 3,187 of the island's 6,023 blacks, John Faucett did not say how many of his slaves were seized by the French. Perhaps none of them were taken or they were seized prior to or as part of the surrender and therefore their loss was not in violation of the terms of surrender and thus not the subject of this deposition. According to the census of 1708 taken just two years after the French invasion, John Faucett is found with two white females, presumably a wife and a daughter, and seven slaves.[12] This paltry number of slaves was far too few to run a sugar plantation of any size, suggesting that the French had confiscated all or some of his slaves during their invasion.

John Faucett's deposition also mentions John Choppin and Isaac Evans as his close neighbors in 1706. Although it does not state where they lived at the time, all three would later be found in St. George's Parish.[13] This suggests that John Faucett in 1706 almost certainly owned a plantation and lived in St. George's Parish.

The deposition is signed by "John ffaucett," or "John Faucett" as the "ff" was at that time a common way to write a capital "F," as the deposition also features the words "ffrench" and "ffifth." A close analysis shows that this is an original John Faucett signature.[14] For years, there has been a debate over how to spell "Faucett." At least twenty-four different spellings of this name can be found in the records: Facet, Facett, Facit, Facy, Faecet, Falziet, Farcet, Fasitt, Fassett, Fassit, Fatzieth, Faucet, Faucett, Faucette, Faucit, Fauscett, Fauset, Fausset, Faussett, Faust, Fawcett, Fawsett, Fosseet, and Fossett. As this deposition contains the only known signature by a member of this family, the "Faucett" spelling used here must be considered the most authentic.[15]

Prior to these new discoveries, little had been known about John Faucett's life before 1714. In fact, the only pieces of information available were the previously mentioned census of 1708[16] and a statement by Alexander Hamilton that "my Grandfather by the mothers side of the name of Faucette was a French Huguenot who emigrated to the West Indies in consequence of the revocation of the Edict of Nantz and settled in the Island of Nevis and there acquired a pretty fortune. I have been assured by persons who knew him that he was a man of letters and much of a gentleman. He practiced as a Physician, whether that was his original profession, or one assumed for livelihood after his emigration is not to me ascertained."[17]

With these new discoveries, it is now known that:

- John Faucett, Alexander Hamilton's grandfather, was born in "about" 1683 or 1684.
- By the age of just twenty two, John Faucett was a wealthy planter on Nevis, owning a plantation that included a dwelling house, outhouses, slaves, negro houses, and a boiling house, all of which was valued in excess of a thousand pounds sterling.
- By 1706, John Faucett was living in St. George's Parish alongside John Choppin and Isaac Evans.
- The last name of Alexander Hamilton's mother and grandfather was spelled "Faucett."

These discoveries help fill in the gaps of John Faucett's biography. Nevertheless, most of his story remains a mystery. When did he move from France to Nevis? Did he come by himself as a young adult or as a child with his parents? How did he come to own a plantation at such a young age? Did he purchase it or inherit it from his father or another relative? Was he a doctor before he became a planter or did he take up this profession afterwards?

For now, these questions remain unanswered.

Notes

1. *Calendar of State Papers, Colonial Series, America and West Indies, 1706 – June 1708* 102, 108–110, 118, 141, 142–144, 146, 147, 180, and 184–185; ibid. *June 1708 – 1709* 8; ibid. *March 1720 – December 1721* 119–123. See also "The Case of the Poor Distressed Planters, and other Inhabitants of the Islands of Nevis, and St. Christophers, in America," London, 1709.
2. *Calendar of State Papers, Colonial Series, America and West Indies, 1706 – June 1708* 396.
3. *Calendar of State Papers, Colonial Series, America and West Indies, 1706 – June 1708* 411; ibid. *June 1708 – 1709* 91 and 92.
4. "The Case of the Poor Distressed Planters, and other Inhabitants of the Islands of Nevis, and St. Christophers, in America," London, 1709; *The History and Proceedings of the House of Commons from the Restoration to the Present Time* 4:63 and 129.
5. Affidavits of resettlement, in CO 243/6 and 7; Debentures issued by the Board of Trade, in CO 243/8; Index of losses claimed and debentures issued, in CO 243/9; *Journal of the Commissioners for Trade and Plantations, February 1709 – March 1715* 383–386, 387–388, 292–393, 394–395, etc.

6. Index of losses claimed and debentures issued, in CO 243/9, page 10, debenture #323. The 669 claims averaged £439 but the median claim was closer to £100. Most of the claims were for small losses of about £100 or less, but a few very large claims (the largest was for £8,525) skews the average upward.

7. Debentures issued by the Board of Trade, in CO 243/8; Index of losses claimed and debentures issued, in CO 243/9; *Calendar of State Papers, Colonial Series, America and West Indies, July 1712 – July 1714* 283; *Journal of the Commissioners for Trade and Plantations, February 1709 – March 1715* 406, 408, 410, etc.
   This process took years and the last of the relief funds was not "delivered" until 1743 (*Calendar of State Papers, Colonial Series, America and West Indies, July 1712 – July 1714* 283; *Journal of the Commissioners for Trade and Plantations, 1742–1749* 99).

8. Index of losses claimed and debentures issued, in CO 243/9, page 10, debenture #323; Debentures issued by the Board of Trade, in CO 243/8, folio 87r, #323.

9. "The Annual RPI and Average Earnings for Britain."

10. *Calendar of State Papers, Colonial Series, America and West Indies, March 1720 – December 1721* 119–123.

11. Deposition of John Faucett, May 31, 1720, in CO 152/13, page 208.

12. *Caribbeana* 3:179.

13. *Caribbeana* 2:267–272 and 3:218–221.

14. A comparison of the three signatures and the text of the document reveals four different hands. Compare, for instance, the "J" in all three signatures; the letter "n" in all three signatures and in the text; the "t" in Faucett, in Dasent, and in the text; the "ff" in Faucett versus the "ff" in the text; and the "a" in Faucett against those in Dasent and in the text. Susan Moore, the researcher who located and photographed this document at my request, concluded, "Yes, I am sure that the document is an original and that therefore the signature must be original as well." Mariana Oller, the Associate Curator of Special Collections at Wellesley College and Chair of the Alexander Hamilton Awareness Society, also inspected photographs of the deposition and determined that the document "is written in a skilled secretary hand, so it was prepared by someone whose job was to issue such documents, and it was then signed by the various parties."

15. In *Alexander Hamilton: The Formative Years*, this author conjectured, "Based on the available evidence, it appears that the name in the original French was Faucette and that it was anglicized to Fawcett upon arrival in the West Indies. It also appears that Fawcett was the spelling favored by those who bore the name. Accordingly, Fawcett is the spelling used in this book." (Newton, *Alexander Hamilton: The Formative Years* 10.) Obviously, this newly discovered document disproves that conjecture.

16. *Caribbeana* 3:179. A "John Fawcett, Junr" and a "Mr. John Fossett" resided on Nevis in 1678 (*Caribbeana* 3:78 and 80), but Alexander Hamilton's grandfather had not yet been born and, according to Hamilton, his grandfather did not leave France until after the revocation of the Edict of Nantes in 1685 (Alexander Hamilton, addressed to William Jackson but sent to James McHenry, August 26, 1800, in *The Papers of Alexander Hamilton* 25:89).

17. Alexander Hamilton, addressed to William Jackson but sent to James McHenry, August 26, 1800, in *The Papers of Alexander Hamilton* 25:89.

The Will of John Lytton:
James Lytton and his Siblings

James Lytton is well known among those who have studied the life of Alexander Hamilton. James Lytton married Anne Faucett, the sister of Alexander Hamilton's mother Rachel Faucett.[1] When the Hamiltons arrived on St. Croix, James Lytton helped them by giving Rachel Faucett "six walnut chairs with leather seats."[2] When Rachel Faucett died, "James Lytton on behalf of Peter Lytton" was "present" for the Hamilton children and may have taken them into his home.[3] Much is known about James Lytton's life: his marriage and children, his purchase of a plantation on St. Croix, his successful management of it, his selling the plantation, and his death.[4]

But what about James Lytton's past? Who were his parents? Did he have any siblings?

On May 1, 1709, a "John Lytton of the island aforesaid [Nevis] planter being sick & weak in body but of sound and perfect memory" made out his will. According to this will, John Lytton left one-third of his estate to his "loving wife" Sarah Lytton. He also provided for the schooling of his five daughters—Sarah, Ann, Mary, Frances, and Parnal—and for their maintenance until they married, at which time each would receive "one hundred pounds current money." John Lytton bequeathed "all the rest and residue of my estate reall & personal goods & chattells in what nature or kind forever it be . . . to my son James Lytton." John Lytton also appointed a "Capt. John Brown of Figtree [Nevis] to be guardian to my children."[5]

Leaving five hundred pounds for his daughters, providing for their maintenance and education, giving one-third of his estate to his wife, and yet still having enough to bequeath the largest share of his estate to his only son, it is clear that John Lytton was quite wealthy and that James Lytton's inheritance was in the hundreds and probably thousands or even tens of thousands of pounds.

A power of attorney accompanied the above will, in which "John Browne & Sarah Lytton guardians of the bodys and estate of James, Sarah, Anne,

Mary, Parnall & Francis Lytton, orphans of John Lytton of the island afore-said [Nevis] planter lately deceased" appointed "John Mills of the City of London Merchant" to be their "true and lawfull attorney" to collect any relief funds that may be issued "for payment of the damage done the said John Lytton by the French invasion" of Nevis. This power of attorney was dated the "twelfth day of June in the thirteenth day [year] of the regime of our Sovereign Anne," i.e., June 12, 1714, and executed July 28, 1714. Thus, John Lytton passed away shortly before June 12, 1714. A few months later, on September 17, 1714, John Lytton's will was executed.[6]

After the French invasion of Nevis in 1706, John Lytton claimed a loss of £972 17s and in August 1713 was granted £324 5s 8d in relief, more than double the average and about ten times the median of all those submitting claims, making him one of Nevis's most prominent citizens. The relief funds were collected in September 1714 by the abovementioned John Mills, the attorney of Sarah Lytton and John Browne, guardians to the Lytton children.[7]

Thus, when James Lytton, at about twelve or thirteen years of age,[8] inherited his father's estate in 1714, he suddenly became one of Nevis's wealthiest citizens. And when Anne Faucett, Alexander Hamilton's aunt, married James Lytton "around 1729 or even earlier,"[9] it represented the combination of two of Nevis's leading families—the Faucetts and the Lyttons.

It should also be noted that John Lytton wrote in his will "my daughter," "my son," and "my six children." He never referred to his wife, Sarah Lytton, as the mother of these children. The power of attorney refers to Sarah Lytton as a guardian to the children, but not their mother. It would seem that the Lytton children were the offspring of John Lytton but not of Sarah, but it is possible that the document's use of legal terminology merely conceals Sarah Lytton's motherhood. Moreover, the eldest female child was named Sarah, suggesting she perhaps was named after her mother, but Sarah is too common a name for this to be considered proof.

Notes

1. For the marriage and Anne being Rachel's sister, see Newton, *Alexander Hamilton: The Formative Years* 513 note 15; complemented by *Christiansted Registrerings og Vurderingsprotokoller for Borgere og Plantere 1761–1768* 359v–360r; *Christiansted Skiftebrevsprotokoller for Borgere og Plantere* 20:386v.
2. *Christiansted Skiftebrevsprotokoller for Borgere og Plantere* 20:392r.

3. *Christiansted Registrerings og Vurderingsprotokoller for Borgere og Plantere 1761–1768* 359v–360r; *Christiansted Skiftebrevsprotokoller for Borgere og Plantere* 20:386v.

4. See the various essays in this volume about James Lytton in addition to Ramsing, "Alexander Hamilton Og Hans Modrene Slaegt"; Ramsing, *Alexander Hamilton's Birth and Parentage.*

5. Copy of the Will of John Lytton of Nevis, May 1, 1709, in CO 243/5, Item 400.

6. Copy of the Will of John Lytton of Nevis, May 1, 1709, in CO 243/5, Item 400.

7. Index of losses claimed and debentures issued, in CO 243/9, page 15, debenture #480; Debentures issued by the Board of Trade, in CO 243/8, folio 126v, #480.

8. According to James Lytton's burial record of August 12, 1769, he was 67 years old (*St. John's Anglican Church, Christiansted, St. Croix, Burial Registry 1761–1787* page 12) and thus born in 1701 or 1702.

9. For the marriage and Anne being Rachel's sister, see Newton, *Alexander Hamilton: The Formative Years* 513 note 15; complemented by *Christiansted Registrerings og Vurderingsprotokoller for Borgere og Plantere 1761–1768* 359v–360r; *Christiansted Skiftebrevsprotokoller for Borgere og Plantere* 20:386v.

Alexander Hamilton's Grandparents and Great Aunt Fight Over a Parcel of Land on Nevis

O n August 20, 1723, the High Court of Chancery on Nevis ruled "in favour of John Fossett and Mary his wife," Alexander Hamilton's grandparents, "about the moiety [portion] of a plantation called Clay Gutt."

A "Margaret Cressey of the island of Nevis widow" appealed this decision, explaining that her "bill brought in the said Court of Chancery was dismissed with costs" and that the "injunction" she had "obtained" for a "stay of the said Faucett's proceedings" was "dissolved."

"All the proceedings in the said case" were "transmitted" from Nevis to the Privy Council in Great Britain "under the seal of the said island," but unfortunately the original proceedings and the copy sent to the Privy Council have not been found and may no longer exist.

On July 4, 1724, the Privy Council at Whitehall in London "ordered . . . the said petition of appeal . . . be . . . referred to the Right Honourable the Lords of the Committee for hearing appeals from the plantations . . . and report their opinion thereupon to his Majesty at this Board."[1]

A few weeks later, a motion was made "for a day to be appointed to hear the appeal of Margaret Cressey widow against John Faucett and Mary his wife from the island of Nevis." The "Lordships" of the Privy Council agreed and the motion passed.[2]

On November 4, 1724, the Committee for Hearing Appeals convened and decided:

In obedience to Your Majestys order in Councill of the 4th of July last referring to this Committee the humble petition of appeal of Margaret Cressey of the island of Nevis widow from an order or decree made in the Court of Chancery there on the 20th day of August 1723 in favour of John Faussett and Mary his wife (which Mary is sister to the said Margaret Cressy) relating to the moiety of a plantation called Clay

Gutt. . . . Their Lordships this day took the said appeal into consideration and having fully heard all parties therein concerned by the Coun-
sell learned in the law, do agree humbly to report their opinion to your
Majesty that the said order or decree of the Court of Chancery in the
island of Nevis be affirmed and the said appeal of Margarett Cressey
dismissed.[3]

Three days later, the Privy Council read the Committee's report and affirmed the decision "that the said appeal of Margaret Cressey be dismissed:
Whereof the Governor or Commander in Chief of the Leeward Charibee Islands for the time being and all others to whom it may concern are to take
notice and govern themselves accordingly."[4]

Thus, Margaret Cressey lost her appeal. John and Mary Faucett, Alexander
Hamilton's grandparents, emerged victorious in this dispute over a moiety or
portion of the Clay Gutt plantation.

In all the legal technicalities of the case, a key phrase was slipped into the
committee's report which could easily be overlooked: "Mary is sister to the
said Margaret Cressy."

This piece of information is the first ever found regarding Mary Uppington outside of her connection to John Faucett. Nothing had previously been
known about Mary Uppington's origins or family. For the first time, it is now
known that Mary Uppington Faucett had a sister named Margaret who had
married a man with the last name of Cressey.

This is especially noteworthy because in St. George's Parish, Nevis, the
same parish where John and Mary Faucett lived, a "Margaret Uppington,
Spinster" married "Edward Evans, Mason" on December 26, 1721.[5] In *Alex-
ander Hamilton: The Formative Years*, this author speculated that Margaret
Uppington Evans "probably" was the sister of Mary Uppington Faucett.[6]
Now that a different Margaret has been identified as the sister of Mary Up-
pington Faucett, one must question whether Margaret Uppington Evans was
Mary's sister, but it is always possible that Mary had two sisters named Mar-
garet, which sometimes happens, especially with half-sisters. Either way, this
Margaret Uppington Evans almost certainly was related to Mary Uppington
Faucett and her sister Margaret Cressey, especially as all three are found in St.
George's Parish, Nevis.

Unfortunately, little is known about the personal life of Margaret Cressey.

In every record found regarding her, she is referred to as Margaret Cressey, Mrs. Cressey, Madame Cressey, or "the widow Cressey." No record of her earlier life has been found, nor has her maiden name or the first name of her deceased husband been determined. She may have been married to Thomas Cressey, who was on Nevis as early as 1697 and was married to an unidentified woman on Nevis by 1699,[7] suffered losses in the French invasion of Nevis in 1706,[8] and was buried in St. George's Parish, Nevis, on March 9, 1718.[9] An Anne Cressey, perhaps the daughter of Thomas and Margaret Cressey, also appears in the records of St. George's Parish marrying a "Mr. John Lane of the City of Cork in the Kingdom of Ireland" on December 21, 1718.[10] They had a child together, William Cressey Lane, on August 9, 1720,[11] but this son was buried less than a month later on September 2, 1720,[12] all of which took place in St. George's Parish, Nevis. Margaret Cressey is likely the "Mrs. Cressey (from Nevis) widow" who passed away on St. Kitts on April 27, 1734.[13] Cresseys are later found on Antigua in the 1740s through the 1770s,[14] but if and how these people were related to Margaret Cressey is not known.

Notes

1. Privy Council Register, July 4, 1724, in PC 2/88, page 565; *Acts of the Privy Council, Colonial Series* 3:71–72.

   Clay Gutt or Clay Ghaut was located in St. George's Parish, the same parish in which the Faucetts lived, where the current Clay Ghaut Estate exists. According to one work, "Clay Gut, or a major part of it amounting to 102 acres, had belonged to a Margaret Cressey before the Pinney family foreclosed on a mortgage in 1728. It was smaller than, and seems to have bordered on, Upper Gingerland." (Eickelmann, *Montpelier Estate* 23.) Clay Gutt reportedly adjoined the Faucett plantation (Mitchell, *Alexander Hamilton: Youth to Maturity* 4 and 470 note 14).

2. Privy Council Register, in PC 2/88, page 594.

3. Privy Council Register, in PC 2/89, page 6.

4. Privy Council Register, in PC 2/89, page 13; *Acts of the Privy Council, Colonial Series* 3:72.

5. *Caribbeana* 2:270.

6. Newton, *Alexander Hamilton: The Formative Years* 530 note 154.

7. *Calendar of State Papers, Colonial Series, America and West Indies, October 1697 – December 1698* 581, 594; ibid. *1699* 40, 45–46.

8. Index of losses claimed and debentures issued, in CO 243/9, page 11, debenture #342.

9. *Caribbeana* 2:270.

10. *Caribbeana* 2:269.

11. *Caribbeana* 2:268.
12. *Caribbeana* 2:271.
13. *Caribbeana* 1:142.
14. Oliver, *The History of the Island of Antigua* 1:cii, ciii, 104, 3:6.

Questioning the Order and Years of Birth for
James Hamilton and His Siblings

G eorge Robertson published the family tree of "Hamilton of Grange" in 1820 in his *Topographical Description of Ayrshire*.[1] A portion of this tree is devoted to "Alexander Hamilton of Grange" and his eleven children, one of whom was James Hamilton, the father of Alexander Hamilton, the Founding Father.[2] (From this point forward in this chapter, the Founding Father will be referred to as Alexander Hamilton while his grandfather will be called Alexander Hamilton of Grange.)

> X. ALEXANDER HAMILTON of Grange, who succeeded him, and married Elisabeth Pollock, daughter of Sir Robert Pollock of that Ilk, by Annabella, daughter of Walter Stewart of Pardovan, by whom he had issue, nine sons and two daughters:
>
> 1. John, } successively Lairds of Grange,
> 2. Robert, }
> 3. Alexander, of whom afterwards.
> 4. James, a proprietor in the West Indies, and father of General Hamilton, the celebrated Statesman, and Patriot in the United States, who fell, greatly regretted, in a duel with a Mr Burr.
> 5. Walter; 6. George—both died unmarried.
> 7. William, married Jean, daughter of Robert Donald, Esq. and had issue,
> 8. Joseph; and 9. William who died in infancy; one of the daughters also died in infancy; the other, Elisabeth, was married to Alexander Blair, Esq. surveyor of the Customs at Port-Glasgow, and son of William Blair of Blair, and had issue.

According to this genealogical table, which has been the basis for all subsequent Hamilton genealogies, it appears that James Hamilton was the fourth child and fourth son of Alexander Hamilton of Grange and Elizabeth Pollock. Accordingly, Alexander Hamilton's son John C. Hamilton wrote that James Hamilton was the fourth son of Alexander Hamilton of Grange.[3]

Questioning the Order of Births

However, one problem and one possible difficulty are readily apparent in the above genealogical table:

- The William who "married Jean . . . and had issue" is listed seventh in the genealogy while a "William who died in infancy" is listed ninth. It is unlikely that the Hamiltons had a son William and then gave another child the same name when the first William was still living. More likely, the William listed ninth was born and died in infancy, after which the William listed seventh was born and given the same name as his deceased brother.
- The nine sons are listed followed by the two daughters. It is unlikely that Alexander Hamilton of Grange and Elizabeth Pollock had nine sons in a row followed by two daughters.

Based on these discrepancies, one suspects that the table may not be correct or was never intended to be one hundred percent accurate. Clearly, the author knew the order of the first three males since they or their heirs served "successively" as Lairds of the Grange, i.e., Robert took over when John died and Alexander's heir became laird when Robert passed away. Perhaps some of the others are also in their correct order, but it is clear that the William listed ninth was not born ninth and the two females probably were not born after all the males. Rather, the author not knowing the order of some of these children put the females last, the male who died in infancy before that, and the others either in their correct order or in an order that was convenient, such as putting Walter and George together just because they "both died unmarried." Accordingly, while the author may have done his best to present this genealogy in the correct order, it clearly is not one hundred percent accurate. The question remains as to which parts are correct and which are not.

Baptisms According to H. U. Ramsing

In his seminal essay on Alexander Hamilton's birth, parentage, and childhood in the West Indies, H. U. Ramsing wrote of the baptisms of four of the children of Alexander Hamilton of Grange that were found in the parish registers of Stevenston Parish, Ayrshire, Scotland, where the family lived:

- John Hamilton, baptized August 19, 1712.
- Robert Hamilton, born February 3, 1715, and baptized February 9, 1715.
- Alexander Hamilton, born February 6, 1717, and baptized February 12, 1717.
- William Hamilton (the one who had children), baptized October 7, 1721.[4]

Ramsing provided no dates for the births or baptisms of the other seven children.

However, it is known that Alexander Hamilton of Grange and Elizabeth Pollock married June 15, 1711,[5] which means that John born in August 1712 must be the firstborn child. It is also known that Alexander Hamilton of Grange died in April 1732,[6] so no child can be born much after that.

Based on these dates and the genealogical table, H. U. Ramsing asserted that the year of birth of James Hamilton, Alexander Hamilton's father, "can without much doubt be presumed to be 1718." This has been the narrative ever since. For example, Ron Chernow wrote, "Born around 1718, he was the fourth of eleven children."[7] The present author had also written that "James Hamilton was born in Scotland about 1718" and was "the fourth son."[8]

Ramsing also asserted that the two sons "Walter and George . . . presumably were twins"[9] because that was the only way in which they could have been born after James's birth in 1718 but before William's birth in 1721.

The Baptismal Records

The parish records from Stevenston Parish, Ayrshire, Scotland, contain baptismal information not just for John, Robert, Alexander, and William Hamilton, as Ramsing reported, but also for Elizabeth Hamilton. However, some of these records are missing vital information that would help determine years of birth for the children and therefore possibly confirm or alter the order of births given in the family tree.

As H. U. Ramsing wrote, John Hamilton was baptized on August 19, 1712.[10]

Robert Hamilton was born on February 3, 1715, and baptized February 9, 1715, as Ramsing said.[11]

Alexander Hamilton was born February 6, 1717, and baptized February 12, 1717, as Ramsing wrote.[12]

Unlike the three baptismal records above, those of William and Elizabeth Hamilton come from "a list of the baptisms" copied out of a "Mr. Thomas Brown's manuscripts," where they were "irregularly set down by him."[13]

Using this "list," H. U. Ramsing wrote that William Hamilton was baptized on October 7, 1721.[14] While the baptismal record clearly has October, the day of the month is ambiguous and the year is missing most of the final digit. According to the National Archives of Scotland, the baptismal date is October 4, 1722. To this author, it looks more like October 21, 1724.[15]

H. U. Ramsing did not write about the baptism of Elizabeth Hamilton, either because he did not see it on the same page as William Hamilton's baptism or more likely because it was not relevant to what he was writing about, which was an effort to determine the year of birth of James Hamilton. Elizabeth Hamilton was baptized on August 7, but unfortunately only the first digit of the year is visible and there is no way to determine the year of her baptism.[16]

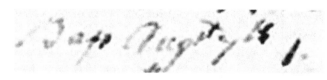

So instead of further clarifying the order and dates of birth, the baptismal records have only muddied the water by calling into question the date given by Ramsing for William Hamilton's baptism.

Baptismal Record for which William Hamilton?

H. U. Ramsing wrote "that the seventh son, William, who had children, was baptized on Oct.7, 1721."[17] This clearly was based on the assumption that the above genealogical table was presented in the correct order and also that the baptism took place in 1721. But it has already been seen that the year of William's baptism cannot be determined with certainty and that the William Hamilton who died in infancy almost certainly was born before the William who "married Jean . . . and had issue." Accordingly, it is not known which of the two Williams was the one found in the baptismal record.

The University of Glasgow

Four of the sons of Alexander Hamilton of Grange and Elizabeth Pollock attended the University of Glasgow. The dates of their matriculations (entrances) can help narrow down the years of their births.

- John Hamilton entered the University of Glasgow in November 1727.[18] His date of birth is already known to be in or just before August 1712, making him 15 when he entered the university.
- Robert Hamilton entered the University of Glasgow in November 1727 alongside his older brother.[19] It has already been seen that he was born on February 3, 1715, making him 12 when he entered the college.
- Walter Hamilton entered the University of Glasgow in November 1737, alongside the great Adam Smith (born June 1723).[20]
- George Hamilton entered the University of Glasgow in November 1743. In 1745, he received the Snell Exhibition scholarship for postgraduate studies at Balliol College, Oxford, the same award Adam Smith won five years earlier, but there is no record of George studying at Oxford.[21]

Based on the ages of John Hamilton, Robert Hamilton, and Adam Smith, it would appear that students entered the University of Glasgow when they were between 12 and 16 years old. Accordingly, it would seem that:

- Walter Hamilton, who entered the University of Glasgow in November 1737, was probably born between 1722 and 1725.
- George Hamilton, who entered the University of Glasgow in November 1743, was probably born between 1728 and 1731.

One will recall that the genealogical table listed Walter fifth and George sixth and that H. U. Ramsing thought they were twins. Given that they entered the University of Glasgow six years apart, it is almost certain that they were not twins. Moreover, it adds to the evidence that the genealogical table does not give an accurate order of births because Alexander Hamilton of Grange and Elizabeth Pollock had eleven children in twenty years, or on average one about every two years, so a large gap between two children of at least three years and probably about six years is unlikely.

Deducing James Hamilton's Birth from His Biographical Data

In February 1737, James Hamilton entered into a four-year apprenticeship in which he served as an "apprentice and servant" to a Glasgow businessman. After the expiration of his term of service in February 1741, James Hamilton spent the next few months buying goods and then sailed to the British West Indian island of St. Kitts to become a merchant.[22]

Unfortunately, none of the records related to James Hamilton's apprenticeship or career, nor any other known record of his life, gives his age or year of birth, but one can use the above dates to arrive at an estimate of James Hamilton's year of birth.

Given that James Hamilton entered into an apprenticeship in February 1737 and there is no record of him attending college, it would seem that he had previously been in primary school and at this time was around the age to either enter college as some of his brothers did or enter into a business apprenticeship. Therefore, one would conjecture that James probably was around 12 to 16 years old and thus born between 1720 and 1725.

On the other hand, James Hamilton became a merchant in the West Indies in 1741. The age of majority was twenty-one,[23] which suggests a birth in 1720 or earlier, but it is possible that John Hamilton acted as security for his brother and thus James need not have been twenty-one at the time.

Given these facts, the best guess is that James Hamilton was born around 1720.

Thus, the assertion that James Hamilton was born in 1718 and was the fourth child or the fourth son of Alexander Hamilton of Grange may be true, but there is no evidence in support of it. James Hamilton could have been born in 1718 or early 1719 and been the fourth child. Indeed, the second and third children were born in February 1715 and February 1717, so perhaps an early 1719 birth would make sense. Alternatively, James could have been born in 1720 or 1721 and be the fifth child, with perhaps the William who died in infancy or one of the daughters being born before him. It is even possible, though less likely, that James was born in 1721 or a bit later, in which case he could have been the sixth child.

As is so often the case, what has been presented by historians and biographers as fact or, as Ramsing wrote, "without much doubt," must indeed be questioned and doubted. The genealogical table is clearly wrong in parts, but to what extent and which parts are not certain. The claim that James Hamilton was born in 1718 may be true but it is not a certainty and it is just as likely, perhaps more likely, that he was born in 1719, 1720, 1721, or a bit later. Moreover, it is possible that James Hamilton was not the fourth child or son, as has been asserted. Although this does little to change James Hamilton's biography, "honesty is the best policy" and one should "never expect any good from a systematical deviation from it," as Alexander Hamilton himself said,[24] and that includes expressing uncertainty and providing other possibilities where they exist.

Notes

1. Robertson, *Topographical Description of Ayrshire* 168–172.
2. Robertson, *Topographical Description of Ayrshire* 170.
3. John C. Hamilton, *The Life of Alexander Hamilton* 1:1; John C. Hamilton, *History of the Republic* 1:41.
4. Ramsing, "Alexander Hamilton Og Hans Modrene Slaegt" 232; Ramsing, *Alexander Hamilton's Birth and Parentage* 7.
5. Old Parish Registers, Stevenston, Scotland, Marriages, 615/20, page 10; Marriage Contract between Alexander Hamilton and Elizabeth Pollock, June 15, 1711, with annotated transcript, in *Alexander Hamilton Papers*.
6. George Hamilton, *A History of the House of Hamilton* 221.
7. Chernow, *Alexander Hamilton* 12.
8. Newton, *Alexander Hamilton: The Formative Years* 16.
9. Ramsing, "Alexander Hamilton Og Hans Modrene Slaegt" 232; Ramsing, *Alexander Hamilton's Birth and Parentage* 7.
10. Old Parish Registers, Stevenston, Scotland, Baptisms, 615/10, page 20, #263.
11. Old Parish Registers, Stevenston, Scotland, Baptisms, 615/10, page 26, #234.
12. Old Parish Registers, Stevenston, Scotland, Baptisms, 615/10, page 32, #304.
13. Old Parish Registers, Stevenston, Scotland, Baptisms, 615/10, page 39.
14. Ramsing, "Alexander Hamilton Og Hans Modrene Slaegt" 232; Ramsing, *Alexander Hamilton's Birth and Parentage* 7.

15. Old Parish Registers, Stevenston, Scotland, Baptisms, 615/10, page 39.
16. Old Parish Registers, Stevenston, Scotland, Baptisms, 615/10, page 39.
17. Ramsing, "Alexander Hamilton Og Hans Modrene Slaegt" 232; Ramsing, *Alexander Hamilton's Birth and Parentage* 7.
18. *Munimenta Alme Universitatis Glasguensis* 3:235.
19. *Munimenta Alme Universitatis Glasguensis* 3:235.
20. *The Matriculation Albums of the University of Glasgow from 1728–1858* 18.
21. *The Matriculation Albums of the University of Glasgow from 1728–1858* 18, 30; Addison, *The Snell Exhibitions* 45–46; Foster, *Alumni Oxonienses* 593.
22. See chapter "The Early Business Career of James Hamilton."
23. According to British law, "Full age in male or female, is twenty one years . . . who till that time is an infant, and so stiled in law" (Blackstone, *Commentaries on the Laws of England* 1:451).
24. Alexander Hamilton to George Clinton, March 12, 1778, in *The Papers of Alexander Hamilton* 1:441.

The Ivy of Kerelaw Castle

In 1685, Alexander Hamilton's great-grandfather, John Hamilton of Grange, acquired a large estate in Stevenston Parish, Ayrshire County, Scotland. He removed from the Grange at Kilmarnock and took up residence in Kerelaw Castle, which had been built on the property centuries earlier and sat just north of the town of Stevenston. It was here that Alexander Hamilton's grandparents, Alexander Hamilton of Grange and Elizabeth Pollock, lived and raised their large family, which included Alexander Hamilton's father, James Hamilton.[1]

Descriptions of Kerelaw Castle and its Ivy

In his "reminiscences" published in 1869, Alexander Hamilton's son, James A. Hamilton, wrote of his visit to Kerelaw Castle in 1837:

My most interesting visit was to Grange, in Ayrshire, the residence of Alexander Hamilton, who was a cousin of my father. My grandfather, James Hamilton, had lived on this place—not in the house the Laird now occupied, but in a large stone house of which the ruins still remained, covered with ivy.[2]

Ever since, Alexander Hamilton biographers have written about Kerelaw Castle and its ivy-covered walls. For example, Alexander Hamilton's grandson, Allan McLane Hamilton, quoting a book published in 1876, wrote of "the ivy-mantled ruins of Kerilaw Castle."[3] James T. Flexner described James Hamilton's "childhood home" as "partly habitable, partly a ruin," with "thick masonry, almost hidden by ancient ivy."[4] Willard Sterne Randall likewise wrote, "Alexander Hamilton's father grew up in this romantic ruin, its thick stone walls, covered with ivy."[5] And Ron Chernow stated, "In 1685, the family took possession of ivy-covered Kerelaw Castle."[6]

Contemporary Descriptions

Despite the oft-repeated statement, either implicitly or explicitly, that Kerelaw Castle had ivy-covered walls when the Hamiltons purchased it in 1685 and when James Hamilton lived there as a youth, no contemporary source has been found mentioning the ivy. Timothy Pont described the castle in the early 1600s as:

> Karylaw castell, or Steuinstoune [Stevenston] castell, a faire stronge bulding, belonging to the earls of Glencairne, quho [who] had the said castell, barroney, parisch, and lordschipe by the mariage of the Douglass, heritrix therof. It belonged in anno 1191 to the Lockarts.[7]

The 1820 *Topographical Description of Ayrshire* also failed to remark upon Kerelaw's ivy-covered walls,[8] but this work did not describe any part of the already ruined building, so this omission does not allow the drawing of a conclusion regarding whether the ivy existed at that time.

Thus, the earliest source found regarding Kerelaw's ivy-covered walls, at least in a Hamilton-related book, appears to be James A. Hamilton's 1837 visit to the ruined building.

Did Kerelaw Castle have ivy-covered walls when the Hamiltons purchased it in 1685? Did James Hamilton, Alexander Hamilton's father, grow up inside thick walls covered by ivy? Or did the ivy sprout up to cover the castle walls at a later date?

Planting the Ivy

Writing about the birds of Ayrshire in 1887, David Landborough, a resident of the area, shared an interesting story:

> My memories of Stevenston parish carry me back a few years farther, and I remember that I then knew of only one place where the starling was to be seen. This was at the striking old ivy-clad castle of Kerelaw, interesting to Glasgow people as associated with the distinguished divine, Dr. Love, of Anderston Church, who, in the year 1775 lived in the castle as tutor to the Hamilton family. It continued to be occupied by

this family till about the year 1787, when a new mansion was built and the old castle planted with ivy. The ivy became most luxuriant; and here it was that as a boy I was wont to listen to the pleasing and not unmusical chattering, and clear whistling, of the starling. Soon afterwards the bird had greatly increased and become so tame that it was only necessary to erect a suitable box for its selection as nesting quarters. These boxes, placed on the tops of chimneys, trees, or tall poles, were a source of much pleasure to almost all the boys in the neighbourhood.[9]

It is now clear that it was not until "a new mansion was built" and Kerelaw abandoned "about the year 1787" that "the old castle [was] planted with ivy." Thus, despite the assertions of many Hamilton biographers, the walls of Kerelaw Castle were not covered with ivy when the Hamiltons purchased it in 1685 or when James Hamilton grew up there. It was not until many decades later that ivy was planted at the old ruined castle, grew "luxuriant," and became worthy of mention by Hamilton biographers.

Notes

1. Robertson, *Topographical Description of Ayrshire* 167–168; Pont, *Topographical Account of the District of Cunningham, Ayrshire* 21–22 and 104–106; *Cuninghame, Topographized by Timothy Pont* 19 and 252–254; James A. Hamilton, *Reminiscences* 302; "Kerelaw House," *Kilmarnock Standard*, April 5, 1924.
2. James A. Hamilton, *Reminiscences* 302.
3. Allan McLane Hamilton, *The Intimate Life of Alexander Hamilton* 438–439. The first paragraph quoted by Allan McLane Hamilton appears in the original 1604–1608 text by Timothy Pont (Pont, *Topographical Account of the District of Cunningham, Ayrshire* 21–22), but the second paragraph, which mentions "the ivy-mantled ruins of Kerilaw Castle," belongs to the "continuations and illustrative notices" added by John Shedden Dobie in 1874 (*Cuninghame, Topographized by Timothy Pont* 253–254).
4. Flexner, *The Young Hamilton* 17.
5. Randall, *Alexander Hamilton: A Life* 16.
6. Chernow, *Alexander Hamilton* 13.
7. Pont, *Topographical Account of the District of Cunningham, Ayrshire* 21–22. The additional notes at the end of this published work, written about 1858, also make no mention of the ivy, even though James A. Hamilton had already seen it.
8. Robertson, *Topographical Description of Ayrshire* 167–168.
9. *Proceedings and Transactions of the Natural History Society of Glasgow, New Series, Volume II* 299.

The Early Business Career of James Hamilton

In his award-winning, best-selling Hamilton biography, Ron Chernow presents a captivating narrative of how James Hamilton, Alexander Hamilton's father, apprenticed for a businessman in Glasgow, moved to St. Kitts as a merchant, failed in this career, and consequently found other employment.[1] Although Chernow's description was probably the best and most complete discussion of the topic to date, there is at least one error in his narrative and a number of omitted details.

According to an agreement dated November 11, 1737, on "the fifth day of February last," i.e., February 5, 1737, "James Hamilton son to the deceased Alexander Hamilton of Grange with the special advice and consent of John Hamilton of Grange his brother," who apparently acted as James's legal guardian, entered into a four-year apprenticeship with Richard Allan, the Glasgow businessman who owned the Haarlem Linen and Dye Manufactory. James was to serve as Allan's "apprentice and servant" while receiving room and board and being taught about manufacturing and commerce. For this education, John Hamilton paid Allan the agreed upon sum of forty-five pounds. All three parties—Richard Allan, James Hamilton, and John Hamilton—signed the agreement.[2]

On February 18, 1741, four years and thirteen days after entering into his apprenticeship, James Hamilton was "discharged" by Richard Allan of his "indentures" after having "dutifully, faithfully, and assiduously implemented, fulfilled, and . . . performed" his "whole obligations."[3]

An addendum to the above indenture states that John Hamilton gave Richard Allan an additional "five Guineas" at the end of the apprenticeship as a "compliment" to Allan's wife, presumably in gratitude for her taking care of James during his apprenticeship.[4]

Uninterested in continuing to work in the textile industry in Scotland and noticing Glasgow's burgeoning trade with the West Indian sugar islands, James Hamilton decided to move to the Caribbean as a merchant.[5]

In March and April 1741, still in Glasgow, James Hamilton made numerous purchases on credit, presumably of goods to resell in the West Indies and necessities for his new home.[6]

Soon afterwards, James Hamilton departed Scotland and sailed to the British-controlled West Indian island of St. Kitts.[7]

In August 1744, James Hamilton was still operating as a merchant on St. Kitts and had his brother John "purchase goods" on credit in Glasgow "to the extent of fifty pounds Sterling," with John acting as guarantor for the debt.[8]

At some point over the next four years, James Hamilton either abandoned his mercantile business or required additional income to make ends meet. In July 1748, he took a job as a watchman or a weighman at the port of Basseterre, St. Kitts.[9]

The following year, James Hamilton's creditors back in Scotland were pestering John Hamilton about the money owed to them. John Hamilton wrote to one associate:

> I think the only way will be for you to write a letter to my brother acquainting him that the Gentlemen from whom he had his goods wanted payment. I would not have given you this trouble but my brother does not know I am engaged for him. Likewise, I desired the favour you'll write to the Gentlemen at Glasgow that you had wrote to my brother, hoping they would have patience till you had an answer. The last letter his mother had from him was some time ago where he writes he had bills but at that time they were not due.[10]

In 1753, James Hamilton abandoned the island of St. Kitts "on account of debt" and "absented himself" to St. Eustatius.[11]

Thus, James Hamilton had become "bankrupt as a merchant." Alexander Hamilton later explained that his father "failed in business" and his "affairs at a very early day went to wreck" because of "too generous and too easy a temper" combined with "too much pride and too large a portion of indolence." In consequence of his business failure, James "fell into indigent circumstances" and "was supported by his friends in Scotland." Nevertheless, James Hamilton's "character," according to Alexander Hamilton, "was otherwise without reproach and his manners those of a gentleman."[12]

Notes

1. Chernow, *Alexander Hamilton* 14–15.
2. Agreement between John Hamilton and Richard Allan regarding James Hamilton, November 11, 1737, in *Alexander Hamilton Papers*.
   Ron Chernow wrote, "In November 1737, John Hamilton took the affable but feckless James, then nineteen, and steered him into a four-year apprenticeship with an innovative Glasgow businessman named Richard Allan" (Chernow, *Alexander Hamilton* 14). Although the agreement between John Hamilton and Richard Allan was dated November 1737, the agreement states that the apprenticeship began on "the fifth day of February last," i.e., February 5, 1737.
3. Richard Allan's Discharge of James Hamilton from Apprenticeship, February 18, 1741, in *Alexander Hamilton Papers*.
4. Agreement between John Hamilton and Richard Allan regarding James Hamilton, November 11, 1737, in *Alexander Hamilton Papers*.
5. Alexander Hamilton to Robert Troup, July 25, 1795, in *The Papers of Alexander Hamilton* 18:505; Alexander Hamilton, addressed to William Jackson but sent to James McHenry, August 26, 1800, in ibid. 25:89.
6. James Hamilton's bills, orders, and receipts, March 31, 1741, to May 4, 1742, in *Alexander Hamilton Papers*.
7. Alexander Hamilton, addressed to William Jackson but sent to James McHenry, August 26, 1800, in *The Papers of Alexander* 25:89.
8. John Hamilton to Thomas Reid, August 4, 1744, in *Alexander Hamilton Papers*.
9. Chernow, *Alexander Hamilton* 15.
10. John Hamilton to Thomas Reid, 1749, in *Alexander Hamilton Papers*. The letter at the bottom reads "Kerelaw 21ʳ 1749." No month is given. The year appears to be "1749" but it is unclear and could be "1748."
11. See pages 19 and 79.
12. Alexander Hamilton to Robert Troup, July 25, 1795, in *The Papers of Alexander* 18:505; Alexander Hamilton to William Hamilton, May 2, 1797, in ibid. 21:77; Alexander Hamilton, addressed to William Jackson but sent to James McHenry, August 26, 1800, in ibid. 25:89.

Where did Mary Uppington Faucett Live on St. Croix?

Mary Uppington Faucett, Alexander Hamilton's grandmother, evidently came to St. Croix in 1745. She is not found in the matrikel (tax list) for 1744 but is listed in the 1745 volume and the next four as well.[1] The earliest notice of Mary Faucett on St. Croix is a record of her purchase of one length of bleached striped cloth or linen for twenty rigsdalers on July 5, 1745. In August, she purchased four hoes for three rigsdalers.[2] On November 21, she served as godmother at the baptism of Josia, son of James and Anne Lytton.[3] While this shows that Mary Faucett arrived on St. Croix in 1745, where she lived this year and the next four is less clear.

Mary Faucett in Company's Quarter

According to the matrikels for the years 1745 to 1749, covering her entire time on St. Croix, Mary Faucett lived in Company's Quarter.[4]

The matrikel of 1745 lists Mary in Company's Quarter as owning three slaves that were previously owned by Jan de Lanney and states that "Maria Facet boer paa James Lyttons land [Mary Faucett lives on James Lytton's land],"[5] i.e., No. 9 Company's Quarter. James Lytton had, of course, married Anne Faucett,[6] either the daughter or step-daughter of Mary Faucett.[7]

"Mary Faucett lives on James Lytton's land," in *St. Croix Matrikel 1745* 25.

The matrikels for 1746 to 1749 all show Mary Faucett living in Company's Quarter, but unlike the 1745 volume they fail to provide a more precise location.[8]

One assumes that Mary Faucett continued to live on James Lytton's plantation during these years. This, however, is not certain and it is possible she resided part of the time with her daughter Rachel and her husband John Michael Lavien at No. 12 Company's Quarter.

Living with Town Captain Bertrand Pieter De Nully?

According to H. U. Ramsing, "In 1747 and 1748 Mary Faucett, with 3 capable slaves, is listed among the residents of Kompagniets Kvarter (The Company's Quarter). Her residence is not further indicated but probably she did not stay with either Lytton or Lavien but instead with Town Captain Bertrand Pieter de Nully, who owned the plantation Cathrines Rest."[9]

Based on Ramsing's statement, numerous Hamilton biographers have repeated this information. Broadus Mitchell added that Mary Faucett "may have been living on De Nully's plantation" in 1750.[10] James Flexner remarked, "We know that Mary Faucett was living in St. Croix, but had no residence of her own. She might have been living at the town captain's and working there in some capacity."[11] Writing with a certainty not expressed by his predecessors, Ron Chernow reported that Mary Faucett "was living with one of St. Croix's overlords, Town Captain Bertram Pieter de Nully."[12]

In reality, Bertrand Pieter De Nully did not own any plantations in Company's Quarter until 1756 or early 1757.[13] As Mary Faucett lived in Company's Quarter while on St. Croix and then left the island in 1750,[14] long before De Nully purchased his Company's Quarter plantations, she never could have lived with De Nully at Catharine's Rest.[15]

What caused Ramsing to make this error and prompted others to repeat it? Most likely it was related to another error regarding Bertrand Pieter De Nully, i.e., the notion that Rachel Faucett lived with him in 1750.[16] If Rachel lived with De Nully in 1750, perhaps Mary did as well. But Rachel never did live with De Nully, as will be seen in the chapter "Where Did Rachel Faucett Go After Being Released from Prison Following Her Extramarital Affair?," and it is clear that Mary Faucett did not either.

Where did Mary Faucett live on St. Croix?

It is clear that Mary Faucett lived with James and Anne Lytton at No. 9 Company's Quarter when the 1745 matrikel was compiled in late 1745 or early 1746 and that she continued to live in Company's Quarter for the following four years until her departure from St. Croix in 1750. It is also clear that Mary Faucett never lived with Bertrand Pieter De Nully, who owned no plantations in Company's Quarter when Mary lived there.

Mary Faucett's location from early 1746 until her departure in 1750 thus remains uncertain, but she probably continued to live with James and Anne Lytton at No. 9 Company's Quarter, though it is possible she also spent some time with John and Rachel Lavien at No. 12 Company's Quarter.

Notes

1. *St. Croix Matrikel 1745* 25; ibid. *1746* 13; ibid. *1747* 14; ibid. *1748* 11; ibid. *1749* 14.
2. Vestindisk-Guineisk Kompagni, *Hovedbog paa St. Croix 1745* 24, 33, 177. The purchase of four hoes is dated August 9 in one place and August 29 in the other.
3. *Danske Folkekirke, St. Croix, Kirkebog, 1740–1753* page 34 and transcript 41b.
4. *St. Croix Matrikel 1745* 25; ibid. *1746* 13; ibid. *1747* 14; ibid. *1748* 11; ibid. *1749* 14.
5. *St. Croix Matrikel 1745* 25.
6. No record of the marriage of James Lytton and Anne Faucett exists. For evidence regarding their marriage and Anne being Rachel's sister, see Newton, *Alexander Hamilton: The Formative Years* 513 note 15; complemented by *Christiansted Registrerings og Vurderingsprotokoller for Borgere og Plantere 1761–1768* 359v–360r; *Christiansted Skiftebrevsprotokoller for Borgere og Plantere* 20:386v.
7. For a discussion of the possibility that John Faucett married two women by the name of Mary and thus that Anne Faucett may not be the daughter of this Mary Faucett, see Newton, *Alexander Hamilton: The Formative Years* 9.
8. *St. Croix Matrikel 1746* 13; ibid. *1747* 14; ibid. *1748* 11; ibid. *1749* 14.
9. Ramsing, "Alexander Hamilton Og Hans Modrene Slaegt" 231; Ramsing, *Alexander Hamilton's Birth and Parentage* 5–6.
10. Mitchell, *Alexander Hamilton: Youth to Maturity* 8.
11. Flexner, *The Young Hamilton* 14.
12. Chernow, *Alexander Hamilton* 12.
13. See page 73.
14. See page 71.
15. For more about Catharine's Rest, see page 72.
16. See chapter "Where Did Rachel Faucett Go After Being Released from Prison Following Her Extramarital Affair?"

Oaths of Allegiance on St. Croix, 1738–1746

The nations of Europe involved themselves in nearly continuous warfare during the eighteenth century. Their colonies in the West Indies were not immune to these conflicts.

Like all colonial powers, Denmark worried about the loyalty of its colonists, especially those who had immigrated from other nations. Accordingly, immigrants wishing to establish residence on St. Croix were compelled "to swear their allegiance to the Danish monarch in accordance with a directive from the Directors of the West India and Guinea Company."[1]

Although no comprehensive catalog of oaths of allegiance from St. Croix has been found, a couple of lists have been located and they include a number of persons of interest to the Alexander Hamilton story.

1745 List of Oaths of Allegiance

According to a list from 1745, various residents of St. Croix did "promise and swear" to "be faithfull and beare true allegiance to His Majesty the King of Danemarck and Norwegue" and to "the Honorable Royal Danisch Privileged Westindie and Guinea Compagnie." In the extant record, a Danish copy of this oath of allegiance is followed by an English translation because "most of the residents who had not previously sworn their oath of allegiance were of the English nation" and "the governor found it fitting, upon their request, to have this translated into English for them . . . whereupon each swore his oath."[2]

According to this list, Edward Evans, a close friend of the Faucetts and the Lyttons who had married one of Mary Uppington Faucett's relatives,[3] swore allegiance to the Danish king and the Company on June 15, 1739, while James Lytton swore his oath of allegiance on October 29, 1744.[4]

It is curious that Edward Evans swore allegiance to the Danish king and Company more than five years before James Lytton, even though they both moved to the island in 1738.[5] While the reason for this difference is not known, a couple of possible explanations come to mind:

- Edward Evans was a mason who may have offered his services to the Danish West India Company, which acted as St. Croix's government. If so, he may have been required to swear allegiance, especially if he helped build or repair the island's fortifications.
- Perhaps James Lytton continued to own land on Nevis, St. Kitts, or elsewhere and continued to consider himself a British citizen despite taking up residence on St. Croix. At some point, he may have sold his land on the British islands, or his St. Croix estate and slaves grew as a share of his total holdings, and thus his economic center and his loyalty shifted to St. Croix.

Also of note on this list is Bertrand Pieter De Nully, later Christiansted's town captain and the future father-in-law of Nicholas Cruger. De Nully swore allegiance on October 22, 1744.[6]

Also appearing on this list is John Michael Lavien, soon to be the husband of Rachel Faucett. Lavien established residence on St. Croix by May 1744[7] and swore allegiance on March 26, 1745.[8]

1746 List of Oaths of Allegiance

A second list of oaths of allegiance, employing nearly the same wording as the previous one, was recorded in 1746. In this list, the residents of St. Croix swore their oaths of allegiance in one of three different languages: Danish, Dutch, and English.[9]

Again, a number of people appearing in the Hamilton story are found on this list. Bertrand Pieter De Nully appears among those who swore their oaths of allegiance in Dutch. James Lytton, John M. Lavien, and Isaac Evans are among those who swore allegiance in English.[10]

A couple of things are worth pointing out about this list:

- John Michael Lavien is listed among those who swore allegiance in English. Alexander Hamilton had written that Lavien was Danish[11] and many historians repeated it,[12] but most now believe that Lavien had German origins.[13] By swearing his oath in English, Lavien indicated that he was more familiar with the English language than Dutch or Danish, but there was no German option. So regardless where he originated, it is clear that he was not Danish and that by this time he had become proficient in English.

- Edward Evans passed away in 1744,[14] but his nineteen-year-old son[15] Isaac Evans swore allegiance to the Danish government in 1746.

These two lists show that James Lytton, Edward and Isaac Evans, John Michael Lavien, and others had at least nominally shifted their allegiance from their countries of origin to the Danish monarchy and Company within months or a few years of moving to St. Croix.

Notes

1. *St. Croix Mandtal o.a. dokumenter vedk. plantagernes optagelse* image 198.
2. *St. Croix Mandtal o.a. dokumenter vedk. plantagernes optagelse* images 198–200.
3. See page 35.
4. *St. Croix Mandtal o.a. dokumenter vedk. plantagernes optagelse* images 200–201.
5. *St. Croix Matrikel 1738.*
6. *St. Croix Mandtal o.a. dokumenter vedk. plantagernes optagelse* image 201.
7. Vestindisk-Guineisk Kompagni, *St. Croix Rekognitionsbog 1744* 4v, 8r, 8v; Vestindisk-Guineisk Kompagni, *Hovedbog paa St. Croix 1744* 31, 64, and 143; *Christiansted Bytingsprotokoller 1744–1745* 110; Ramsing, "Alexander Hamilton Og Hans Modrene Slaegt" 229; Ramsing, *Alexander Hamilton's Birth and Parentage* 3.
8. *St. Croix Mandtal o.a. dokumenter vedk. plantagernes optagelse* image 202.
9. Vestindisk-Guineisk Kompagni, *Breve og Dokumenter fra Vestindien 1746* images 94–96.
10. Vestindisk-Guineisk Kompagni, *Breve og Dokumenter fra Vestindien 1746* image 96.
11. Alexander Hamilton, addressed to William Jackson but sent to James McHenry, August 26, 1800, in *The Papers of Alexander Hamilton* 25:89.
12. For example, John C. Hamilton, *The Life of Alexander Hamilton* 1:2, John C. Hamilton, *History of the Republic* 1:41; Atherton, *The Conqueror* 12–20; Allan McLane Hamilton, *The Intimate Life of Alexander Hamilton* 9; Emery, *Alexander Hamilton: An Intimate Portrait* 15; Chernow, *Alexander Hamilton* 10.
13. Ramsing, *Alexander Hamilton's Birth and Parentage* 15; Mitchell, *Alexander Hamilton: Youth to Maturity* 6; Flexner, *The Young Hamilton* 12; Randall, *Alexander Hamilton: A Life* 8 and 13.
14. *Christiansted Skiftebrevsprotokoller for Borgere og Plantere* 3:260v–262r; *St. Croix Matrikel 1744* 19; ibid. *1745* 24.
15. *Christiansted Skiftebrevsprotokoller for Borgere og Plantere* 3:261r.

The Extramarital Affair of Rachel Faucett

On February 26, 1759, in Christiansted, St. Croix, John Michael Lavien filed for divorce from his wife, Rachel Faucett Lavien. In his divorce claim, John Lavien asserted that:

- Rachel committed "such mistakes [that] among married people are indecent and very suspect," for which she had been subject to "jail and lawsuit."
- "For 9 years [Rachel] has been absent from him and gone to another place, where she is said to have begotten several illegitimate children."
- "She has shown herself to be shameless, rude and ungodly."
- "She has . . . given herself up to whoring with everyone, which . . . her own family and friends must hate her for it."
- Rachel should not "take possession of the estate and . . . acquire what she ought not to have . . . [and] give it to her whore-children what such a legitimate child alone is due."[1]

Finding in favor of John Lavien, the court on June 25, 1759, granted a divorce to Lavien and stipulated that "Rachel Lavien shall have no rights whatsoever as wife to either John Michael Lavien's person or means which he now owns or will come to own. Also, Rachel Lavien's illegitimate children are forfeited all rights or pretensions to the plaintiff's possessions and means." The divorce decree concluded, "This divorce shall not bar the plaintiff John Michael Lavien from entering into another marriage. . . . His Majesty is reserved the right to Rachel Lavien," thus barring Rachel from remarrying.[2]

The above records were discovered by H. U. Ramsing and first shared in his 1939 essay on Hamilton's parentage.[3] Until now, nothing had been found to confirm or refute John Michael Lavien's claim that Rachel had "given herself up to whoring with everyone" or that she had any affair besides her relationship with James Hamilton, which occurred after she left Lavien.

St. Croix Superior Court Records

While the municipal court records regarding Rachel Faucett's alleged affair, for which she had been subject to "jail and lawsuit," have not been found (the relevant volume is too damaged to be read), the case made its way up to St. Croix's superior court and was recorded in that court's register. Unfortunately, this register was not recorded in a nice clean hand and many of the pages have suffered what appears to be water damage. Nevertheless, there is enough legible text remaining to reveal the matter at hand and to decipher a significant portion of the relevant facts.[4]

Fortunately, due to the significance of this case, a copy of the superior court record was sent back to the authorities in Denmark. This copy was written much more legibly and has survived without damage.[5]

These records reveal the names of the parties involved and the dates of certain key events, which then leads to other related documents in which government officials discuss the matter. These additional records provide further details and context regarding Rachel Faucett's alleged affair.[6]

The Initial Affair

By October 1749, a romantic liaison between Rachel Faucett Lavien and a man named Johan Jacob Cronenberg had been going on for some time.

According to the newly discovered records:

- "Johan Michael Lavien . . . had been obliged to experience that his wedded wife, Rachel, who for a long time had absented herself from him, was residing with a bachelor Johan Cronenberg."[7]
- Lavien's "wedded wife" was accused "of having resided with him [Cronenberg] for a long time in fornication."[8]
- Rachel was "found" in Cronenberg's "lodging, well hidden behind locked doors, wherefrom her husband fetched her and drove her home."[9]
- Johan Cronenberg was "not only . . . seriously warned to keep away from this woman of loose morals but also punished with some days' incarceration."[10]
- "Despite this chastisement and admonishment," Cronenberg "again

had sexual relations with this woman and without feeling shame publicly kept her with him in his house and lived there with her."[11]

Thus, Rachel Faucett Lavien and Johan Cronenberg lived with each other "for a long time in fornication." They were caught together "well hidden behind locked doors" and Rachel was driven back to her husband. Cronenberg was warned and even imprisoned for a few days. Despite this, Rachel soon returned to live with Johan Cronenberg.

Arrest of Cronenberg and Rachel

On October 8, 1749:

- John Lavien, "through Procurator Reimert Haagensen, . . . requested the court's assistance to repair with him to Cronenberg's plantation house to seize and arrest Cronenberg and Rachel for further legal prosecution."[12]
- "This the agent of the court complied with, and at night at about 12 o'clock had come to said plantation and . . . the 2 accused persons were found in the bedroom taking their usual night's rest."[13]
- "The agents of the court . . . seized them both in their bedroom, undressed and with more debauched circumstances that sufficiently demonstrated their shameless intercourse and scandalous life" and "declared them both to be under arrest and had them brought . . . to Fort Christiansvaern" to be imprisoned.[14]

So Rachel and Cronenberg were caught by Lavien and one or more agents of the court in Cronenberg's "bedroom, undressed and with more debauched circumstances." They were arrested and jailed in Fort Christiansvaern.

Municipal Court

On October 10, 1749,[15] the case of Johan Cronenberg and Rachel Lavien was brought before the Christiansted municipal court. Both Rachel and Cronenberg were charged and the court ordered them imprisoned in Fort Christiansvaern.[16]

About Johan Cronenberg

So who was this Johan Jacob Cronenberg with whom Rachel Faucett had this affair?

Born around 1710,[17] Cronenberg was about fifteen to twenty years older than Rachel.[18] Cronenberg enlisted in the Danish military service in 1728[19] and was sent by the Danish West India Company from Copenhagen in early 1746 to serve as St. Croix's land surveyor and to draw an accurate, up-to-date map of the island.[20] He arrived on St. Croix by early 1747.[21] According to the 1748 matrikel, the only one in which he appears, Cronenberg lived in Christiansted with two slaves on "Torve eller Tver Gaden [Market or Cross Street]."[22] But the court record, as noted earlier, said that Cronenberg had been living with Rachel in a plantation house, presumably a different residence than his house in town.

By the time of his imprisonment, Cronenberg had surveyed the entire island "except the North Side, whose natural formation except in very few places does not allow any serious planting," and his map was either finished or nearly so.[23] The map that Johan Cronenberg produced, which measures 3.3 feet tall by 4.7 feet wide,[24] is extraordinarily detailed, colorful, and beautiful. Cronenberg demarcated the individual estates, houses, slave quarters, processing mills, land under cultivation, forest land, rivers, and roads. His map is far superior to any map of St. Croix produced beforehand or for many decades afterwards.[25] (See the map on the following two pages.)

Rachel and Cronenberg in Fort Christiansvaern

At Fort Christiansvaern, Rachel and Cronenberg each occupied one of the "arrest" rooms. Some of the arrest rooms were like prison cells and others more like apartments.[26] Johan Cronenberg surely stayed in one of the nicer arrest rooms devoted to gentlemen and arrested officers. Rachel's room probably was not as nice. If there were other white women in prison at the time, she probably had to share a room with them.

Rachel and Cronenberg probably spent most of their days cooped up in their rooms, though each probably was granted some time to wander through the yard. Living in the fort, even under confinement, probably involved many distractions as the fort was a hive of activity. Protecting the city and harbor

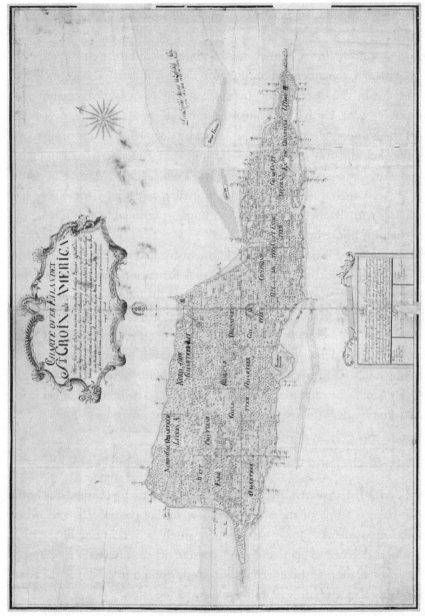

Cronenberg and Jaegersberg, *Charte Over Eilandet St. Croix.*

Company's Quarter with Christiansted and Fort Christiansvaern at top right, from Cronenberg and Jaegersberg, *Charte Over Eilandet St. Croix.*

of Christiansted, Fort Christiansvaern housed military personnel and equipment. Here in the fort, army soldiers regularly marched and trained, shooting
off noisy guns and even louder cannons. It also had a whipping post for con-
victed slaves[27] and acted as a prison for men and women, whites and blacks.[28]
The fort also served as a marketplace where the Danish West India Company
auctioned off slaves, mercantile goods, and household items of defaulting
borrowers, deceased residents, and cargo ships.[29] It was also the St. Croix
headquarters for the Danish West India Company, which acted as the island's
government and court system.[30]

Thus, Rachel had plenty to distract her during her imprisonment in Fort
Christiansvaern and she probably learned more than she ever wanted to know
about military, legal, and civil affairs just by observing all that occurred
around her. As for Cronenberg, he had even more to occupy his time as he
continued to work from prison, signing survey records and land certificates
from his cell,[31] and perhaps finishing his map during this time.

Nevertheless, both were undoubtedly eager to be released.

Privy Council Meeting

On January 7, 1750, about 3 months after Cronenberg and Rachel were
imprisoned in the fort, St. Croix's privy council met to discuss the matter of
Johan Cronenberg, "who because of a disgraceful case of shameless intercourse and association with a wedded husband's wife here in the country is
under arrest and prosecution by the same man." At this meeting, the governor
declared that Cronenberg had "dealt quite irresponsibly" and that "he has no
use for Cronenberg in regard to his extravagant and negligent behavior."[32]

Privy Council Report

Johan Cronenberg was still in jail on March 25, 1750, more than five
months after being imprisoned, when the privy council reported to officials
back in Denmark that Cronenberg was "under arrest here in the fort" on
"account of extravagance and unseemly deeds" in that John Michael Lavien
accused him "of having resided" with his "wedded wife" for "a long time in
fornication, and thus for this the matter is being prosecuted in the courts."
The council also reported, as noted earlier, that the governor asserted "that

with Cronenberg he can have nothing more to do, he being altogether too much given to extravagance and negligence."[33]

Cronenberg Auction

While Cronenberg sat "under arrest . . . in the fort," the Danish West India Company on April 27, 1750, auctioned off three of Cronenberg's slaves and two of his horses for 800 rigsdalers. The money was used to pay off an obligation of 630 rigsdalers owed by Cronenberg.[34]

Rachel Released and Cronenberg Exiled

Nearly eight months after having his wife and her paramour imprisoned, John Michael Lavien approached the municipal court and expressed his belief that Rachel had been sufficiently punished and requested that she be "freed . . . from jail and lawsuit, thinking that everything would change to the better and that she, as a wedded wife, [would] change her unholy way of life and . . . live with him."[35]

On May 4, 1750, the municipal court decided that Rachel, "in consideration of her long incarceration," was to be released so that she "might again betake herself to her husband and with him lead a better life."[36]

According to Danish law, "If a man and woman live together, so as to cause scandal, they . . . if they are single, shall be banished out of the town, village, or tribe, and sent different ways."[37]

Since Cronenberg was single and had caused a scandal by living with a married woman, the court ordered him to leave "the country within 15 days of the publication of the judgement, and in consideration of his long arrest and the loss of his position in the Company's service will be free of further fines and costs."[38]

Cronenberg Leaves St. Croix

Johan Cronenberg presumably left St. Croix in May 1750, before his fifteen days were up. He is next found on St. Thomas on August 12.[39]

On July 30, St. Croix's privy council wrote to officials back in Denmark to request a new land surveyor to replace Cronenberg because "a judgement of exile has been issued by the municipal court for his shameless intercourse with Lavien's wife."[40]

Cronenberg Appeals

At this point, one would think that the legal matter was settled. But the story continues, and thankfully so because if the story ended here it would not have been recorded in the registers of the superior court and perhaps no full and accurate record of this affair would exist.

On June 15, 1750, Johan Cronenberg's attorney Soren Bagge "submitted" an appeal to the superior court "against Johan Michael Lavien who sued the appellant Cronenberg for shameless association with his wife Rachel." Cronenberg's attorney argued "that none of the accusations laid against him have been legally proved" and "it therefore seems to him that the substance of the judgment against him is intolerable." Bagge requested that Cronenberg's expulsion be "disallowed" and "without effect" and that he be "completely relieved of the punishment laid upon him."[41]

After hearing these arguments, the Superior Court ordered John Lavien "to appear before" it on July 8 so that the court could "hear the appellant's claim with reference to the opposite proofs and to be subject to the judgment." It also ordered the members of the municipal court who issued the original order to appear "for the same purpose."[42]

On July 15, "the case was postponed" because "none of the individuals who had been called before the court appeared."[43]

As a result, on August 5, Cronenberg's attorney Soren Bagge presented "various documents and evidence" in his defense. What these were was not recorded. He also argued that "there is no proof against him to make him deserve such a punishment," that the judgement freeing Rachel from prison proves "Lavien's wife innocent of the accusations made against her," that "the most grave accusations were made" against Rachel rather than Cronenberg, and clearly that if Rachel was innocent so was he.[44]

Superior Court Ruling

After much delay, on February 3, 1751, the superior court ruled that Cronenberg, "for his shameless" and "scandalous" behavior, "with warning and admonishment, carrying on his life with the woman Rachel," was guilty and "liable for fines in accordance with the law" in addition to his previous incarceration. He was ordered to pay the "fine for fornication of 24 *lod* silver" and "further to submit to an open confession."[45]

According to Danish law, "If a man lies with a woman, he shall pay fine to his Lord two pound eight shillings sterling . . . and . . . shall do publick penance."[46] The 24 lod silver was equal to this prescribed £2 8s sterling, or 15 West Indian rigsdalers, a paltry sum considering the severity of the crime.

Thus, in appealing the case, Cronenberg was again found guilty. On top of his previous incarceration, the superior court added a fine and forced a confession, which was required by law but had not been dispensed by the municipal court. So Cronenberg not only lost his appeal, but he made it worse for himself.

Obviously, if Johan Cronenberg was deemed guilty, Rachel was considered so as well.[47]

Notes

1. *St. Croix Panteprotokoller 1756–1772* 43r–44r; transcribed in Ramsing, "Alexander Hamilton Og Hans Modrene Slaegt" 232–234; translated in Ramsing, *Alexander Hamilton's Birth and Parentage* 8–10.
2. *Christiansted Skiftebrevsprotokoller for Borgere og Plantere* 20:391r–v; transcribed in Ramsing, "Alexander Hamilton Og Hans Modrene Slaegt" 234–235; translated in Ramsing, *Alexander Hamilton's Birth and Parentage* 11–12.
3. Ramsing, "Alexander Hamilton Og Hans Modrene Slaegt" 232–235; Ramsing, *Alexander Hamilton's Birth and Parentage* 8–12.
4. *St. Croix Overretten Justitsprotokol 1736–1755* 175r, 177r, 178v–180v.
5. Extract from Overretten Justitsprotokol, enclosure to letter of Governor Peter Clausen, April 12, 1753, in Vestindisk-Guineisk Kompagni, *Breve og Dokumenter fra Vestindien 1753* (116) images 301–306.
6. *Afskrifter og Ekstrakter af St. Croix Sekrete Råd Sekretprotokoller* January 7, 1750, images 167–168; General letter, St. Croix, March 25, 1750, 11r–v, in Vestindisk-Guineisk Kompagni, *Breve og Dokumenter fra Vestindien 1750* (113) images 45–46; General letter, St. Croix, April 23, 1750, 2v–3r, in ibid. image 260a–b.
7. Extract from Overretten Justitsprotokol, enclosure to letter of Governor Peter Clausen, April 12, 1753, in Vestindisk-Guineisk Kompagni, *Breve og Dokumenter fra Vestindien 1753* (116) image 305a.
8. General letter, St. Croix, March 25, 1750, 11r–v, in Vestindisk-Guineisk Kompagni, *Breve og Dokumenter fra Vestindien 1750* (113) image 46a.
9. Extract from Overretten Justitsprotokol, enclosure to letter of Governor Peter

Clausen, April 12, 1753, in Vestindisk-Guineisk Kompagni, *Breve og Dokumenter fra Vestindien 1753* (116) image 305b.

10. Extract from Overretten Justitsprotokol, enclosure to letter of Governor Peter Clausen, April 12, 1753, in Vestindisk-Guineisk Kompagni, *Breve og Dokumenter fra Vestindien 1753* (116) image 305b.

11. Extract from Overretten Justitsprotokol, enclosure to letter of Governor Peter Clausen, April 12, 1753, in Vestindisk-Guineisk Kompagni, *Breve og Dokumenter fra Vestindien 1753* (116) image 305b.

12. Extract from Overretten Justitsprotokol, enclosure to letter of Governor Peter Clausen, April 12, 1753, in Vestindisk-Guineisk Kompagni, *Breve og Dokumenter fra Vestindien 1753* (116) image 305a.

13. Extract from Overretten Justitsprotokol, enclosure to letter of Governor Peter Clausen, April 12, 1753, in Vestindisk-Guineisk Kompagni, *Breve og Dokumenter fra Vestindien 1753* (116) image 305a.

14. Extract from Overretten Justitsprotokol, enclosure to letter of Governor Peter Clausen, April 12, 1753, in Vestindisk-Guineisk Kompagni, *Breve og Dokumenter fra Vestindien 1753* (116) images 305a–b.

15. Some records state that the court took up the case on October 10 but others say October 20. October 10 makes more sense given their arrest on October 8.

16. *St. Croix Overretten Justitsprotokol 1736–1755* 178v; Extract from Overretten Justitsprotokol, enclosure to letter of Governor Peter Clausen, April 12, 1753, in Vestindisk-Guineisk Kompagni, *Breve og Dokumenter fra Vestindien 1753* (116) image 304b; General letter, St. Croix, March 25, 1750, 11r–v, in Vestindisk-Guineisk Kompagni, *Breve og Dokumenter fra Vestindien 1750* (113) images 45b–46a; *St. Croix Panteprotokoller 1756–1772* 43r–44r; transcribed in Ramsing, "Alexander Hamilton Og Hans Modrene Slaegt" 232–234; translated in Ramsing, *Alexander Hamilton's Birth and Parentage* 8–10.

17. Johan Cronenberg wrote that he had joined the military service in 1728 (Johan Cronenberg, July 9, 1766, in Vestindisk-Guineisk Generaltoldkammeret, *Indkomne Vestindiske Breve 1760–1767* B815; see also *St. Croix Ordrer og Instruktioner til de Militære Afdelinger* image 49b). His widow said that he was seventy-something when he died in 1783 (Letter of Elisabeth Cronenberg, May 8, 1786, in Vestindisk-Guineisk Generaltoldkammeret, *Vestindiske (og Guineiske) Kongelige Resolutioner 1786* images 259–260). These facts indicate a birth around 1710.

18. For a discussion of Rachel Faucett's year of birth, see Newton, *Alexander Hamilton: The Formative Years* 10–12.

19. Johan Cronenberg, July 9, 1766, in Vestindisk-Guineisk Generaltoldkammeret, *Indkomne Vestindiske Breve 1760–1767* B815.

20. Vestindisk-Guineisk Kompagni Direktionen, *Protokoller 1741–1752* 78v; Vestindisk-Guineisk Kompagni Direktionen, *Amerikansk og Afrikansk Kopibog 1743–1746* 303v, 309v.

21. Vestindisk-Guineisk Kompagni, *Hovedbog paa St. Croix 1747* 185; *Cassa Bog for St. Croix 1747* 8b, in *Kassebog for St. Croix* image 291b.

22. *St. Croix Matrikel 1748* 26b. Another record shows that Cronenberg owned a "house and lot" on the south side of Queen's Street as of March 19, 1748 (*Udmålingsattester*

mm. for hele St. Croix 48.2.2 image 528), but whether this is the same house listed in the matrikel cannot be determined. It is possible that Cronenberg's house was on the corner of Queen's Street and Market or Cross Street. Alternatively, it is possible that he lived in one house and that the house and lot he owned was rented out or was vacant.

It is not known why Cronenberg fails to appear in the 1747 matrikel. Perhaps he lived in the fort with the other military officers and soldiers. At the time the 1749 matrikel was compiled, Cronenberg was in prison and thus not listed at his previous address, though perhaps he still owned or rented that same house.

23. General missive to St. Croix, December 16, 1749, in Vestindisk-Guineisk Kompagni Direktionen, *Amerikansk og Afrikansk Kopibog 1749–1750* 259r–260v; Hopkins, *The Danish Cadastral Survey of St. Croix* 247–248, 250.

24. Hopkins, "An Extraordinary Eighteenth-Century Map of the Danish Sugar-Plantation Island St. Croix" 57.

25. Hopkins, "An Extraordinary Eighteenth-Century Map of the Danish Sugar-Plantation Island St. Croix" 50; Hopkins, *The Danish Cadastral Survey of St. Croix* 251–254.

26. Giellerup and von Friis, *Grundtegning over Christiansværnsfort med narmeste Omgivelser.*

27. *Proceedings of the St. Croix Burgher Council, 1767–1780* 36.

28. In addition to Rachel's imprisonment, see also *St. Croix Overretten Justitsprotokol 1736–1755* 26r, 159v, 171v; *Proceedings of the St. Croix Burgher Council, 1767–1780* 335, 419, 438, 442, 444, 519, 520, 547.

    Many other white women besides Rachel were imprisoned in the fort over the years, at least one of whom was a "loose woman" who suffered a "long imprisonment" and another woman, or perhaps the same one, who committed the "crime [of] having had a child with a negro" (*Proceedings of the St. Croix Burgher Council, 1767–1780* 335, 438, 444).

29. For auctions during Rachel's time in prison at Fort Christiansvaern, see Danish West India Company, *St. Croix Auktionsprotokol 1748–1752* 27v, 28v, 32r, 41v, 42r.

30. For instance, see *St. Croix Overretten Justitsprotokol 1736–1755*; *Afskrifter og Ekstrakter af St. Croix Sekrete Råd Sekretprotokoller 1744–1754.*

31. *Udmålingsattester mm. for hele St. Croix* 48.2.1 images 23, 34, 48, and 48.2.2 images 274, 637. If it was not known that Cronenberg was in prison, one would think from these records that he continued to survey the island during this period.

32. *Afskrifter og Ekstrakter af St. Croix Sekrete Råd Sekretprotokoller* January 7, 1750, images 167–168.

33. General letter, St. Croix, March 25, 1750, 11r–v, in Vestindisk-Guineisk Kompagni, *Breve og Dokumenter fra Vestindien 1750* (113) images 45–46; Hopkins, "An Extraordinary Eighteenth-Century Map of the Danish Sugar-Plantation Island St. Croix" 49. See also *Afskrifter og Ekstrakter af St. Croix Sekrete Råd Sekretprotokoller* January 7, 1750, images 167–168.

34. Vestindisk-Guineisk Kompagni, *St. Croix Auktionsprotokol 1748–1752* 43r–v; Vestindisk-Guineisk Kompagni, *Hovedbog paa St. Croix 1750* 159.

35. *St. Croix Panteprotokoller 1756–1772* 43r–44r; transcribed in Ramsing, "Alexander

Hamilton Og Hans Modrene Slaegt" 232–234; translated in Ramsing, *Alexander Hamilton's Birth and Parentage* 8–10.

36. *St. Croix Overretten Justitsprotokol 1736–1755* 178v–179r; Extract from Overretten Justitsprotokol, enclosure to letter of Governor Peter Clausen, April 12, 1753, in Vestindisk-Guineisk Kompagni, *Breve og Dokumenter fra Vestindien 1753* (116) image 305a.

37. *The Danish Laws* 429.

38. *St. Croix Overretten Justitsprotokol 1736–1755* 178v–179r; Extract from Overretten Justitsprotokol, enclosure to letter of Governor Peter Clausen, April 12, 1753, in Vestindisk-Guineisk Kompagni, *Breve og Dokumenter fra Vestindien 1753* (116) image 305a.

39. General Letter from St. Thomas, August 12, 1750, in Vestindisk-Guineisk Kompagni, *Breve og Dokumenter fra Vestindien 1750* (113) 368b.

40. General letter, St. Croix, July 30, 1750, in Vestindisk-Guineisk Kompagni, *Breve og Dokumenter fra Vestindien 1750* (113) image 302a.

41. Extract from Overretten Justitsprotokol, enclosure to letter of Governor Peter Clausen, April 12, 1753, in Vestindisk-Guineisk Kompagni, *Breve og Dokumenter fra Vestindien 1753* (116) images 301a–302b.

42. Extract from Overretten Justitsprotokol, enclosure to letter of Governor Peter Clausen, April 12, 1753, in Vestindisk-Guineisk Kompagni, *Breve og Dokumenter fra Vestindien 1753* (116) images 302b.

43. *St. Croix Overretten Justitsprotokol 1736–1755* 175r; Extract from Overretten Justitsprotokol, enclosure to letter of Governor Peter Clausen, April 12, 1753, in Vestindisk-Guineisk Kompagni, *Breve og Dokumenter fra Vestindien 1753* (116) images 303a.

44. *St. Croix Overretten Justitsprotokol 1736–1755* 175v; Extract from Overretten Justitsprotokol, enclosure to letter of Governor Peter Clausen, April 12, 1753, in Vestindisk-Guineisk Kompagni, *Breve og Dokumenter fra Vestindien 1753* (116) images 303a–304a.

45. *St. Croix Overretten Justitsprotokol 1736–1755* 178v–180a; Extract from Overretten Justitsprotokol, enclosure to letter of Governor Peter Clausen, April 12, 1753, in Vestindisk-Guineisk Kompagni, *Breve og Dokumenter fra Vestindien 1753* (116) images 304b–306b.

46. *The Danish Laws* 428.

47. The court record makes no mention of Rachel paying a fine or doing public penance. The lower court had not punished Cronenberg with these penalties, so it likely did not do so for Rachel either. The superior court added these punishments to Cronenberg only because he appealed and lost. Rachel's case was not taken to the superior court, so it could not impose the same punishments upon her.

Where Did Rachel Faucett Go After Being Released from Prison Following Her Extramarital Affair?

After spending nearly eight months in prison for "fornication," Rachel Faucett Lavien, the future mother of Alexander Hamilton, was "freed . . . from jail and lawsuit" in May 1750 upon her husband John Lavien's request because he thought "that everything would change to the better and that she, as a wedded wife, [would] change her unholy way of life and . . . live with him."[1]

Despite her husband's expectations, Rachel apparently left the island of St. Croix by year's end. It is known that Rachel lived on St. Kitts by the end of 1751.[2] It is also known that Rachel's mother, Mary Faucett, left St. Croix in 1750 because in October of that year she sold a "negro boy" named Alexander for eighty pieces of eight,[3] announced her intention to leave the island, and requested both debtors and creditors to present their accounts for settlement.[4] By year's end, Mary was no longer on St. Croix as she failed to appear in the matrikel for 1750 as she had the previous five years.[5]

It is not known whether Rachel fled St. Croix immediately or shortly after her release from prison with Mary following later or if mother and daughter left together in late 1750. Either way, Rachel must have had some time, whether it be mere hours or several months, after her release from prison but before her departure from St. Croix.

So where did Rachel go after being released from prison but before leaving St. Croix?

1759 Divorce Summons

According to the record of the divorce court, a "consistorial summons for John Michael Lavien against his wife Rachel Lavien" was proclaimed on March 2, 1759, "on the plantation owned by the Town Captain, and also proclaimed in the Fort, where she was in jail, which were her two last places of residence."[6]

Bertrand Pieter De Nully

Based on the divorce summons, Hamilton biographers reported that Rachel Faucett Lavien went to live on the plantation of town captain Bertrand Pieter De Nully[7] after her release from prison.

H. U. Ramsing, who discovered the above divorce summons and first wrote about it in 1939, explained, "Rachel Lavien was summoned on her last places of residence in 1750, namely the prison in Christiansvaern Fort and on the plantation of Town Captain Bertrand Pieter de Nully, Cathrines Rest in Kompagniets Kvarter (The Company's Quarter)."[8]

Subsequent biographers have since asserted that Rachel in 1750 went to live with Bertrand Pieter De Nully at his Catharine's Rest plantation. For example, Broadus Mitchell in 1957 explained, "Though the Town Captain's (Bertram Pieter de Nully's) plantation ('Catharine's Rest' in Company's Quarter) was mentioned before the Fort, it may be that Rachael went there after she was released from jail. Possibly De Nully interceded for her. Her mother may have been living on De Nully's plantation at the time."[9] Similarly, James T. Flexner wrote that Rachel, after her release from prison, "fled to the mansion of the town captain, Bertram Peter de Nully."[10] Willard Sterne Randall noted that Rachel was "released to the custody" of De Nully, who Randall called "the fort's commandant" and "the island's highest ranking officer," even though neither of those things was true, and that she "went to live with him on his own plantation."[11] Ron Chernow stated that "after Rachel left the fort, she spent a week with her mother, who was living with one of St. Croix's overlords, Town Captain Bertram Pieter de Nully."[12]

Thus, based on the text of the divorce court summons, Hamilton biographers described how Rachel went to live "with" Bertrand Pieter De Nully on his plantation after her release from prison.

Town Captain Bertrand Pieter De Nully's Plantations in 1759

When the divorce summons was proclaimed in March 1759 "on the plantation owned by the Town Captain," Town Captain Bertrand Pieter De Nully owned two plantations, namely a 138-acre estate comprised of portions of Nos. 12, 20, and 21 Company's Quarter and also the 150-acre No. 35 Queen's Quarter.[13] The Catharine's Rest mentioned by Ramsing, Mitchell, etc., was the name for the estate comprised of "one and three quarter plantations" made up of land in Nos. 12, 20, and 21 Company's Quarter.[14]

No. 12 Company's Quarter in 1745–50

It just so happens that one of the properties owned by Bertrand Pieter De Nully in 1759, i.e., the 75-acre portion of No. 12 Company's Quarter, had been owned by John Michael Lavien, husband of Rachel Faucett, from 1745 to 1750.[15]

Thus, in proclaiming the summons in March 1759 "on the plantation owned by the Town Captain," the court did so on Bertrand Pieter De Nully's plantation No. 12 Company's Quarter because it had been the home of John Michael Lavien and Rachel Faucett Lavien back in the 1740s and thus was one of Rachel's "two last places of residence." The divorce court was not saying that Rachel had ever lived with Bertrand Pieter De Nully, but rather that her previous place of residence was now owned by that gentleman.

De Nully Acquires Catharine's Rest in Company's Quarter

According to the matrikel from 1755, compiled in March 1756, Bertrand Pieter De Nully did not yet own Nos. 12, 20, and 21 Company's Quarter.[16]

But the matrikel for 1756, compiled in April 1757, shows that by this time De Nully had acquired these properties.[17]

Thus, Bertrand Pieter De Nully did not acquire Nos. 12, 20, and 21 Company's Quarter until 1756 or early 1757. Accordingly, Rachel could not have stayed with Bertrand Pieter De Nully at his Catharine's Rest plantation back in 1750 when she was released from prison because he did not yet own that estate.

Bertrand Pieter De Nully as Town Captain

It should also be noted that most of the matrikels starting in 1758 list Bertrand Pieter De Nully as "Stadshauptmand" or "Town Captain," also frequently referred to as "militia commander."[18] But in the 1757 matrikel,[19] as in all previous matrikels, De Nully did not yet have that title. It thus appears, though one cannot be certain,[20] that Bertrand Pieter De Nully was not Town

Captain back in 1750 when Rachel was released from prison and therefore he could not have acted in any position of authority as some Hamilton biographers assert.

Correcting An Error

Hamilton biographers are therefore incorrect in stating that Rachel went to live with Town Captain Bertrand Pieter De Nully at his Catharine's Rest plantation, or any other plantation he may have owned, after her release from prison. Instead, the divorce summons was proclaimed on De Nully's plantation in 1759 because he had by that time acquired No. 12 Company's Quarter, which back in the 1740s had been owned by John Michael Lavien and therefore was one of Rachel's "two last places of residence." Rachel did not live with Bertrand Pieter De Nully after her release from prison and there was no connection between Rachel and De Nully back in 1750 or at any other time.

Where Did Rachel Go After Being Released from Prison?

While this debunks the story that Rachel lived with Bertrand Pieter De Nully after her release from prison, it does not answer the question of where Rachel went.

Regrettably, there is no positive evidence regarding where Rachel went after being released from prison on May 4, 1750. Perhaps she returned to her husband for a brief time, but that does not seem likely. Possibly she went to stay with her sister, Anne Lytton, at No. 9 Company's Quarter. Or maybe she stayed with a friend. Or she could have rented a room for a short time as she made arrangements to leave the island. Or perhaps she headed straight for the docks and took the first boat off of St. Croix. Unfortunately, where Rachel went and what she did upon her release from prison is not known.

Notes

1. See pages 65 and 76; *St. Croix Panteprotokoller 1756–1772* 43r–44r; transcribed in Ramsing, "Alexander Hamilton Og Hans Modrene Slaegt" 232–234; translated in Ramsing, *Alexander Hamilton's Birth and Parentage* 8–10.
2. See pages 19 and 79.
3. *Christiansted Panteprotokoller 1749–1752* 80r.

4. *Christiansted Panteprotokoller 1749–1752* 77r.
5. *St. Croix Matrikel 1750.*
6. *St. Croix Panteprotokoller 1756–1772* 43r–44r; transcribed in Ramsing, "Alexander Hamilton Og Hans Modrene Slaegt" 232–234; translated in Ramsing, *Alexander Hamilton's Birth and Parentage* 8–10.
7. Bertrand Pieter De Nully is usually referred to as "Bertram Pieter de Nully" in both contemporaneous records and in the histories, but he signed his name at times as "De Nully" and other times as "Bertrand P^r De Nully" (*St. Croix Indkomne skrivelser til Generalguvernøren og Det sekrete Råd 1760–1761* 173; ibid. *1770* 296, 310, 336, 372).
8. Ramsing, "Alexander Hamilton Og Hans Modrene Slaegt" 234; Ramsing, *Alexander Hamilton's Birth and Parentage* 11.
9. Mitchell, *Alexander Hamilton: Youth to Maturity* 7–8.
10. Flexner, *The Young Hamilton* 14 and 50.
11. Randall, *Alexander Hamilton: A Life* 14–15.
12. Chernow, *Alexander Hamilton* 12.
13. *St. Croix Matrikel 1758* 15 and 18; ibid. *1759* 19 and 24.
14. Last joint will and testament of Bertrand Pieter De Nully and Catharine Heyliger, in *Christiansted Skiftebrevsprotokoller for Kgl. Betjente 1771–1777* 2–3 and in *Christiansted Testamentprotokoller 1808–1815* 21; *St. Croix Matrikel for Plantagerne* Christiansted 3; Oxholm, *Charte over den Danske Øe St. Croix.*
15. *St. Croix Matrikel 1745* 27; ibid. *1746* 10; ibid. *1747* 11; ibid. *1748* 8; ibid. *1749* 11; ibid. *1750* 15.
16. *St. Croix Matrikel 1755* 41 and 46–47.
17. *St. Croix Matrikel 1756* 2 and 3.
18. *St. Croix Matrikel 1758* 15; ibid. *1759* 19.
19. *St. Croix Matrikel 1757* 58 and 72..
20. No one else in the older matrikels is listed as town captain and it is possible that such a position did not yet exist. Perhaps it was established after the crown took over control of the island from the Danish West India Company in 1754. Other records from as early as 1747 show that Bertrand Pieter De Nully was a captain, but this probably means he was a ship captain or a captain of militia rather than the town captain. Regardless, nothing has been found to suggest that Bertrand Pieter De Nully was the town captain back in 1750, before he had purchased the plantations in Company's Quarter and risen to greater prominence on St. Croix.

John Michael Lavien v. Rachel Faucett: The 1759 Divorce Court Proceedings

In 1759, in the city of Christiansted on the island of St. Croix, John Michael Lavien divorced Rachel Faucett. Previously, there were two known sources regarding this divorce.

The first source was a claim by John Michael Lavien and a summons issued by the divorce court on February 26, 1759. In his claim, John Lavien argued that a divorce should be granted because Rachel had made "such mistakes [that] among married people are indecent and very suspect," for which she was imprisoned. After she "was freed by him from jail and lawsuit," Rachel "for 9 years has been absent from him and gone to another place, where she is said to have begotten several illegitimate children, so that this is thought to be more than enough reason to obtain a divorce. . . . She has shown herself to be shameless, rude and ungodly, as she has completely forgotten her duty and left husband and child alone, and instead given herself up to whoring with everyone, which things the plaintiff says are so well known that her own family and friends must hate her for it. . . . Let her ungodliness be known." John Lavien claimed to have been "in this manner . . . insulted" and "for many years already to have taken care of this child and maintained it from what little he was able to earn." The purpose of the divorce, as stated in Lavien's claim, was that if he should die, Rachel should not "take possession of the estate and therefore not only acquire what she ought not to have but also take this away from his child and give it to her whore-children what such a legitimate child alone is due." Rachel and three witnesses who lived on St. Croix—Jemima Gurley, James Ash, and James Hendrie—were "summoned with 6 weeks' notice to appear . . . in person or by proxy in the Consistorial Court, which will be held in the morning at 9:00 o'clock sharp this first coming April 18," at which time "the plaintiff's evidence as well as summoned and unsummoned witnesses" are to be "produced" and a "final decision made." The court warned Rachel that if it found against her, she "shall have no rights whatsoever to the plaintiff's person or means which he now owns or hereafter will own" and that John Lavien "will be free" from her "in every way" and "if he so desires" could "marry again." As for Rachel, she would "be further punished (if seized) according to law and ordinances." The summons was "lawfully proclaimed" on March 2 in the court "for all the here mentioned persons" and also at "her two last places of residence here in the country," namely "the Fort, where she was in jail," and at the plantation No. 12 Company's Quarter, where she had lived with her husband but which was now "owned by the Town Captain [Bertrand Pieter De Nully]."[1]

The second previously known source for the divorce was the court's ruling of June 25, 1759. Having "legally proved that Rachel Lavien has been absent from him and lived on an English island for 7 to 8 years" and "also that she during that time has begotten two illegitimate children," the court granted a divorce to John Lavien. The terms of the divorce stipulated that "Rachel Lavien shall have no rights whatsoever as wife to either John Michael Lavien's person or means which he now owns or will come to own. Also, Rachel Lavien's illegitimate children are forfeited all rights or pretensions to the plaintiff's possessions and means." The divorce decree concluded, "This divorce shall not bar the plaintiff John Michael Lavien from entering into another marriage. . . . His Majesty is reserved the right to Rachel Lavien," thus barring her from remarrying.[2]

These two sources were found by H. U. Ramsing and first published in his 1939 essay on Hamilton's birth and parentage.[3] The information has since been included in Hamilton biographies. But the record of the divorce court proceedings with the testimony of the three witnesses had been lost until now.

Record of the Divorce Court Proceedings

In the Rigsarkivet in a collection of "legal documents" from Christiansted, St. Croix, there sits a 56-page booklet of the court proceedings for the divorce of John Michael Lavien v. Rachel Faucett,[4] which includes the court's record of the testimony of the three witnesses.

Narrative of the Divorce Court Proceedings

On February 16, 1759, John Michael Lavien approached the court seeking a divorce from his wife Rachel Lavien.[5] On February 26, John Michael

Lavien's attorney Soren Bagge, who in 1750 had acted as Cronenberg's lawyer[6] and therefore knew all about Rachel's extramarital affair, introduced a claim and the court issued its summons,[7] as described earlier.

On April 18, 1759, an "extra" divorce court was seated. Soren Bagge called for the witnesses.[8]

The first witness, Jemima Gurley, was sworn in. Bagge asked Jemima if she knew Rachel and that Rachel was married to Lavien, if she knew that Rachel "has for a long time absented herself from her wedded husband and lived in foreign places," that Rachel "with another man has raised illegitimate children," and if she knew "for how long" Rachel had "absented herself from her husband as well as how many bastard children she has had."[9]

Jemima replied that she knew Rachel, who was her sister, and knew that she was married to John Michael Lavien. "To the second question answered the witness that when the witness, two years ago, had come to St. Eustatius, Rachel Lavien was there, but as the witness had herself resided on Nevis, she did not know how long a time it was since Rachel Lavien had left St. Croix, but the witness knew that her sister on St. Eustatius had two children, the one about 5 and the other about three years old, which children her sister Rachel Lavien had explained to her that she had had with an ustevnt [unsummoned] person outside of marriage, although in that time she had been married to John Michael Lavien. Furthermore the witness had read a declaration that Rachel Lavien had made to the judge on Sainte Christopher, the contents of which were that the 2 children that Rachel Lavien then had had been raised outside of marriage with an ustevnt person who was not her husband, which man's name the witness mentioned to the court, but which will not be entered in the protocol-book, and it is about two years since the witness heard this declaration." Bagge then asked whether the witness "does not know that Rachel Lavien had gotten married to another person." Jemima replied that "she had heard it said but . . . did not know."[10]

The other two summoned witnesses, James Hendrie and James Ash, were then called but did not appear. Soren Bagge requested that they should be found liable for a fine for being in contempt of court and the court summoned them "under penalty of contempt" to appear on April 25 "to present their testimony in this case." Bagge similarly requested that Rachel Lavien should present herself at the next session of this special divorce court on the afternoon of June 6 and again the court agreed and summoned Rachel "either to respond in the case or to suffer judgement according to the law."[11]

On April 25, the "extraordinary divorce court" reconvened but the witnesses a second time failed to appear and they were summoned again.[12]

On June 6, or so it says in the record but this date is probably mistaken, the witness James Hendrie appeared before the court and was sworn in. Soren Bagge asked him the same three questions presented to Jemima Gurley. Hendrie answered that "he knew" Rachel "and had heard that she was married to John Michael Lavien, although he had not seen the priest marry them. To the 2nd question the witness answered that for as long as he had known both parties they had not lived together, and the witness did not know that Rachel Lavien had been away from the island for a matter of 7 to 8 years, in which time of 7 to 8 years, the witness never had heard that John Michael Lavien had been away from the island. But the witness knew no more than what he had heard commonly said that Rachel Lavien was said to have had two children since she departed from the island." These answers presumably were to establish that John Michael Lavien was not the father of Rachel's children born during this time. Bagge followed up by asking Hendrie if he knew that Rachel had married another man since she left the island, to which Hendrie answered that he had heard that another man was associating with her, but he had not heard that she had married this man.[13]

Soren Bagge then called the next witness, who is recorded as James Hendrich but must be the previously summoned James Ash, a relative of the Faucetts and Lyttons by marriage and a business associate of James Lytton,[14] because no James Hendrich had been summoned and no such man is known to have been on St. Croix at this time. Ash was sworn in and asked the same three questions. Ash answered that "he knew Rachel Lavien when the witness was on Sainte Christopher in the years 1751, 1752, and 1753 in which years she resided on St. Christopher but when an ustevnt Person with whom she associated on Sainte Christopher absented himself, on account of debt, to Sainte Eustatius, then Rachel Lavien also absented herself from Sainte Christopher and when the witness later himself in the year 1756 went to Sainte Eustatius, the witness saw that she lived there with the same ustevnt person that she had lived with from Sainte Christopher. As far as her marriage to John Michael Lavien was concerned, the witness had heard both from herself and others that she was married to John Michael Lavien and that she went both on Sainte Christopher and Sainte Eustatius under the name of Rachel

Lavien although she in both places associated with an ustevnt person of another name." Ash added that "when he knew her on Sainte Christopher [she] had one or two children, which everywhere passed as her and the ustevnte person's children, and the witness had heard that her and the ustevnte's common reputation was that she was a publique whore." Ash concluded "that he had been here on the island [St. Croix] for three years, thus he had also been [here] in the year 1756, but the witness had never seen Rachel Lavien here on the island in that time." Bagge asked Ash if Rachel had married anyone since she left St. Croix but Ash replied that he had not heard that.[15]

Bagge then stated that he had more witnesses "but as he was assured that the witnesses already heard, besides other evidence he had in his possession, was enough, so he did not intend to hear more witnesses unnecessarily, but requested that this case might be postponed" until the appointed time, "which was the 6th June in the afternoon at 2 o'clock, at which time he shall move the case to judgment." The case was accordingly postponed.[16]

On the afternoon of June 6, the divorce court sat again and proceeded with the case. Bagge produced some document of April 18 related to Rachel Lavien, probably the summons demanding she "respond in the case or . . . suffer judgement according to the law." And here the record of the divorce court proceedings ends abruptly.[17]

But it is known, as quoted earlier, that the court granted a divorce to John Lavien on June 25, 1759, stipulating that "Rachel Lavien shall have no rights whatsoever as wife to either John Michael Lavien's person or means which he now owns or will come to own. Also, Rachel Lavien's illegitimate children are forfeited all rights or pretensions to the plaintiff's possessions and means." The divorce decree concluded, "This divorce shall not bar the plaintiff John Michael Lavien from entering into another marriage. . . . His Majesty is reserved the right to Rachel Lavien," thus barring her from remarrying.[18]

This record of the divorce court proceedings has significant implications to the Hamilton story, most of which can be read about in the chapter "Alexander Hamilton's Birth, Early Biography, and More."

Notes

1. *St. Croix Panteprotokoller 1756–1772* 43r–44r; transcribed in Ramsing, "Alexander Hamilton Og Hans Modrene Slaegt" 232–234; translated in Ramsing, *Alexander*

Hamilton's Birth and Parentage 8–10.

The divorce court summons was "lawfully proclaimed" at Rachel's "two last places of residence" because Danish law required that the person "be cited in the last place dwelt or resided in." Danish law also required six weeks' notice if the summoned person "has no habitation in the Kingdom, and absconds." However, the law also stated that "if a person to be summoned is out of the Kingdom, or it is not known where he resides, the summons must be served in the same places, as before mentioned, requiring his appearance in the court within a year." (*The Danish Laws* 21–22.) Rachel, as the record shows, was "summoned with 6 weeks' notice to appear." There is no evidence Rachel received the summons, but if she had she probably would not have replied or tried to appear in court because she surely knew the facts, the law, and social custom were against her.

2. *Christiansted Skiftebrevsprotokoller for Borgere og Plantere* 20:391r–v; transcribed in Ramsing, "Alexander Hamilton Og Hans Modrene Slaegt" 234–235; translated in Ramsing, *Alexander Hamilton's Birth and Parentage* 11–12.

3. Ramsing, "Alexander Hamilton Og Hans Modrene Slaegt" 232–235; translated in Ramsing, *Alexander Hamilton's Birth and Parentage* 8–12.

4. *Christiansted Retsdokumenter 1740-1759* images 211–239.

5. Divorce proceedings of John Michael Lavien v. Rachel Faucett Lavien, 1v–4r, in *Christiansted Retsdokumenter 1740-1759.*

6. See page 66.

7. Divorce proceedings of John Michael Lavien v. Rachel Faucett Lavien, 4v–12r, in *Christiansted Retsdokumenter 1740-1759.*

8. Ibid. 12v–13r.

9. Ibid. 13r–14r.

10. Ibid. 14r–16r.

11. Ibid. 16r–18r. According to Danish law, "matrimonial causes are to be decided on the four Ember Days yearly" (*The Danish Laws* 17). June 6, 1759, was the Ember Day following Pentecost/Whitsunday.

12. Divorce proceedings of John Michael Lavien v. Rachel Faucett Lavien, 18v–21v, in *Christiansted Retsdokumenter 1740-1759.*

13. Ibid. 21v–24r. For the life of James Hendrie, see Newton, "Who was James Hendrie?"

14. For the life of James Ash and his connection to the Faucetts and Lyttons, see Newton, "The Story of James Ash."

15. Divorce proceedings of John Michael Lavien v. Rachel Faucett Lavien, 24r–27r, in *Christiansted Retsdokumenter 1740-1759.*

16. Ibid. 27r–28r.
    Generally speaking, Danish law "required two witnesses, agreeing in all things on the same point" (*The Danish Laws* 67).

17. Divorce proceedings of John Michael Lavien v. Rachel Faucett Lavien, 28r–28v, in *Christiansted Retsdokumenter 1740-1759.*

18. *Christiansted Skiftebrevsprotokoller for Borgere og Plantere* 20:391r–v; transcribed in Ramsing, "Alexander Hamilton Og Hans Modrene Slaegt" 234–235; translated in Ramsing, *Alexander Hamilton's Birth and Parentage* 11–12.

The Story of Jemima Faucett and Her Children

Nearly all Hamilton biographers write not just about Alexander Hamilton's mother, Rachel Faucett, but also about his aunt, Anne Faucett. Rachel Faucett married John Michael Lavien, left him, established a relationship with James Hamilton, and famously gave birth to Alexander Hamilton. Meanwhile, Anne Faucett married the wealthy James Lytton, became leaders of their community, and supported both Rachel Faucett and Alexander Hamilton on St. Croix.

While these two sisters are relatively well known and their lives well documented, John Faucett of Nevis fathered many children in addition to Anne and Rachel.[1] A number of the Faucett children died in childhood and appear in the burial records of St. George's Parish, Nevis, where the Faucetts lived, but several others simply disappear from the extant records, or so it was thought. Without explicitly saying so, Hamilton biographers assumed that these other children probably died young. Although no record of their deaths has been found, the burial records of St. George's Parish, Nevis, are incomplete, as are those of St. Croix. Historians simply forgot about these children, assuming that records of their lives and deaths were lost forever.

Thankfully, the above assumptions were without foundation. One of these other children of John Faucett has now been identified, and her story is worth telling because it is an interesting one.

Identifying Jemima Faucett

Only recently was it noticed that a Jemima Faucett lived in St. George's Parish, Nevis, and that John Faucett, the father of Anne and Rachel Faucett, and Jemima Faucett had both given their sons the uncommon name of Lillingston, leading to the conclusion that it was a "near certainty" that Jemima Faucett was John Faucett's daughter and thus the sister of Anne and Rachel. This author shared the discovery in a series of blog posts but admitted that "no positive evidence has yet been found to prove" this relationship.[2]

It was then discovered that Jemima Gurley, in her testimony before the divorce court, stated that Rachel Lavien was "her sister," referred to Rachel repeatedly as "her sister," and Lavien's lawyer Soren Bagge introduced Jemima as "Rachel's sister."[3] Jemima Gurley's testimony thus proves that she was the daughter of John Faucett and the sister of Anne and Rachel Faucett.

Now to the story of Jemima Faucett. . . .

The Birth of Jemima Faucett

No record of Jemima Faucett's birth has been found, but the date of her wedding (see below) and other evidence give some indication of when she was born.

In March 1708, John Faucett lived on Nevis with two white females, presumably a wife and a daughter.[4] As Anne Faucett married James Lytton sometime in the 1720s and had a son with him prior to April 15, 1730,[5] both of which occurred before Jemima married, one assumes that Anne was older than Jemima and that the daughter living with John Faucett in 1708 was Anne or possibly another unidentified daughter rather than Jemima.

The extant baptismal records of St. George's Parish, Nevis, where the Faucetts lived, start in May 1716.[6] Since Jemima does not appear in these records, one assumes she was born prior to that date.

It is thus reasonable and logical to conclude that Jemima Faucett was born to John Faucett between March 1708 and April 1716.

Jemima's mother has not been identified. John Faucett lived with two females according to the 1708 census, had a wife named Mary in 1714, and in June 1718 had another child, but then married Mary Uppington in August 1718. It is therefore uncertain whether John Faucett had been married to one or two women named Mary and also unclear whether Anne, Jemima, and Rachel had the same or different mothers.[7]

The Marriage of Jemima Faucett to William Iles

On April 19, 1730, Jemima Faucett married William Iles in St. George's Parish, Nevis.[8]

William Iles's family history has not been found but members of the Iles family were apparently among the early settlers of Nevis. In the Nevis census of 1678, there appears an "Edward Illes" along with one white woman and two white children but no slaves, a "William Iles & Wife" along with 2 white children and four slaves, and an "Edward Iles" with a white woman and two children.[9] In the census of March 13, 1708, there was a "John Iles" by himself and an "Anne Iles" along with three white children and seven blacks.[10] A "William Isles" claimed a loss of £483 3s 4d during the French invasion of Nevis of 1706 and in 1715 received £161 1s 1d in relief.[11]

The William Iles who married Jemima in 1730 presumably was not the one found in the above records but perhaps was the son of the William Iles of 1706 and grandson of one of the three Iles listed in the 1678 census.

William Iles appears to have been related to James Lytton through Lytton's sister Sarah, who had married a Thomas Iles in 1720.[12] Perhaps this Thomas Iles was William's brother, or maybe a cousin or an uncle. Another Iles, an Edward Iles, is also found in St. George's Parish, Nevis, in the 1720s and 1730s.[13] He is probably also related to William and Thomas.

Children Born to William and Jemima Iles

Nearly a year after their wedding, on April 15, 1731, William and Jemima Iles baptized a son and named him William, making him William Iles Jr.[14]

The next offspring of William and Jemima Iles found in the records was a daughter, who they baptized on September 16, 1733, and was named Jemima like her mother.[15]

Next, on April 9, 1735, William and Jemima Iles baptized a son and named him Lillingston.[16] Interestingly, John and Mary Faucett a few years earlier had given birth to a son, who they baptized and named Lillingston on July 19, 1731.[17] This Lillingston passed away and was buried on March 2, 1735.[18] Thus, barely a month after Lillingston Faucett's death, Jemima gave her son the same name.

In addition to those three children—William, Jemima, and Lillingston—a fourth was born to William and Jemima Iles prior to June 1739, as will be seen below. As there is a gap in the records of St. George's Parish, Nevis, between March 1737 and March 1738,[19] one assumes that this fourth child was born during that timeframe. As will be seen later, the evidence suggests that this son was named Charles Iles.

William Iles's Slaves Help Repair Saddle Hill Defenses

In 1735, the Nevis government repaired the fort on Saddle Hill. Between August 29 and November 11 of that year, William Iles made available 26 negro work days to service the defenses. An Edward Iles made available 17 negro work days while a Thomas Iles, perhaps the man who had married Sarah Lytton, made 10 negro work days available.[20]

Unfortunately, this reveals little about the wealth of each individual since providing ten to twenty-six days of slave work over a two and a half month period would not have been a significant allocation of resources.

The Death of William Iles and Jemima's Financial Troubles

William Iles died sometime before June 1739. His burial does not appear in the records of St. George's Parish, Nevis, and it may have occurred during the gap in the church records between March 1737 and March 1738.

By June 1739, Jemima was "in debt to the public of this island [Nevis] near sixteen pounds current money" and was "not in a condition to pay it, being in very deplorable circumstances and having four helpless children to provide for."[21] Despite her debt totaling less than sixteen West Indian pounds or about £9 sterling, she received either no or insufficient help from family and friends. Jemima's parents were unable or unwilling to help her as they suffered their own problems and would separate the following year.[22] Her wealthy sister Anne Lytton had already moved to St. Croix.[23] Edward Iles and Thomas Iles were still on Nevis[24] but their help, if they provided any, must not have been enough.

Jemima Faucett Iles petitioned the Assembly of Nevis in June 1739 to have her debt remitted.

Nevis

To the honorable the President & Council and the Gentlemen of the Assembly in the Island aforesaid.

The petition of Jemima Iles, humbly sheweth that whereas your poor petitioner hath fallen in debt to the publick of this Island near sixteen pounds current money, and is not in a condition to pay it being in very deplorable circumstances and having four helpless children to provide

for with but one negroe that is dutable, so that with her utmost industry she barely can get the necessaries of life and such a sum cannot be
greatly lost by a community. She therefore humbly implores your hon-
our & the gentlemen of both houses to commiserate her calamities by
remitting the debt. And your petitioner as in duty bound shall ever
pray etc.

Read at this Board & Referred to the Gentlemen of the assembly.
By Command
John Brodbelt

Nevis June 21ˢᵗ 1739. Read in the assembly & rejected.[25]

The Marriage of Jemima Faucett Iles to Richard Gurley

On May 23, 1740, Jemima Faucett Iles married a Richard Gurley in St.
George's Parish, Nevis.[26]

The family history of Richard Gurley is not known. It has been suggested
that the Gurleys may have derived from the Gurlings found on Nevis in 1674
and 1678,[27] but no Gurleys or Gurlings are listed in the Nevis census of March
1708 nor in the list of sufferers from the French invasion of Nevis in 1706. A
Thomas Gurley was on Nevis in October 1656 but he was bound for Jamaica.[28] All this suggests that Richard Gurley or his predecessors arrived on
Nevis after 1708 but before 1740.

Children Born to Richard and Jemima Gurley

On March 2, 1741, a John Gurley was both baptized and buried in St.
George's Parish, Nevis.[29] The name of the parents is not given in the record,
but as no other Gurleys appear in the parish registers, one assumes that this
was the son of Richard and Jemima Gurley.

On February 12, 1743, a son was born to Richard and Jemima Gurley. Six
months later, on August 19, the parents baptized the boy and named him
Richard, making him Richard Gurley Jr.[30]

It appears that Richard and Jemima Gurley had another child, a daughter
Elizabeth, born in about 1745.[31]

Richard Gurley Dies, Jemima Moves, Remarries, Gives Birth

No more records of Richard and Jemima Gurley on Nevis have been found. Richard Gurley must have passed away by 1747 because Jemima is next found on the island of St. Eustatius on December 18, 1748, married to a John Peters and baptizing a son named Richard, who had been born earlier in the month. A Peter Gurley acted as one of the godparents.[32] Although the parents are listed as "Johan Piterson en Syn Huysvrouw [and his housewife] Jumeyma Peeters" in this record, later records refer to the couple as "Jan Pieters en Jumeymy Gorly Syn Huysvrouw [John Peters and Jemima Gurley his housewife],"[33] clearly indicating that this was Jemima Faucett Iles Gurley.[34] The Peter Gurley who acted as godfather was apparently the brother of Richard Gurley.[35]

One assumes that Jemima attended the St. Eustatius wedding of the above Peter Gurley of St. Kitts to Jane Scrogkan, the widow of John Howard of Bermuda. Banns were read on March 19, 1750, and the couple was married on April 19.[36]

William Iles, Juror in the 1753 Trial of John Barbot on St. Kitts

On Friday, January 5, 1753, the court on St. Kitts met to try John Barbot, who was accused of killing Mathew Mills in a duel. An argument had commenced between the two, prompting Mills to say to Barbot, "Sir, you are an impertinent puppy."[37] This insult was grounds for a duel, at which Barbot shot and killed Mills. After a full day of court, the jury at about 11 p.m. found Barbot guilty.[38] He was executed by hanging on January 20.[39]

This case gained international attention, occupying the first four pages of *The London Magazine* in August 1753.[40] Being such a "sensational murder trial," Ron Chernow writes that "Nevis children such as Hamilton . . . would have savored every gory detail of this history."[41]

Among the jurors was one William Iles.[42] Jemima's son William Iles was, at this time, twenty-one years old. It could be that William Iles Jr., son of William Iles and Jemima Faucett, sat on the jury of this famous trial, but there were others named William Iles in the region, though it is impossible to know which were still alive and where they were living, and there may have been even more people with this name, so it is not certain.[43]

If "Nevis children such as Hamilton" did indeed savor hearing "every gory detail of this history," perhaps Alexander Hamilton heard the details from his first cousin William Iles.

Jemima Gurley Gives Birth to More Children on St. Eustatius

On March 3, 1753, Jemima Gurley gave birth to a daughter. On St. Eustatius on March 18, "Jan Pieters en Jumeymy Gorly Syn Huysvrouw [John Peters and Jemima Gurley his housewife]" baptized the infant and christened her Catharina.[44]

Two years later, on March 22, 1755, "Jan Pieters en Jumeymi Gorley Syn Huysvrouw [John Peters and Jemima Gurley his housewife]" baptized a daughter who had been born on March 5 and named her Sarah. A "Jan Gorley [John Gurley]" was among the godparents.[45] His relationship to Jemima is not known.

Iles Family Members on Nevis

While Jemima was on St. Eustatius and one assumes her children, or at least the younger ones, went with her, the Iles family remained firmly entrenched on Nevis. According to a 1755 tax list, five individual members of the Iles family plus the orphans of a John Iles paid taxes on 54 slaves while another 14 slaves were "written off." Most of these entries specifically mention the slaves or their owners being in St. George's Parish, where the Faucetts, Lyttons, and Iles were all found a generation earlier.[46]

None of the names on this list appear to be children of Jemima. One however is Thomas Iles Jr., who could be the Thomas Iles Jr. born to Thomas Iles and Sarah Lytton in 1721.[47]

Jemima Returns to Nevis then Moves Back to St. Eustatius

According to her April 1759 testimony in the divorce case of John Michael Lavien against Rachel Faucett Lavien, Jemima said that she "had herself resided on Nevis" before having "come to St. Eustatius" "two years ago."[48]

If the above St. Eustatius records had not been found, one would have assumed that Jemima had stayed on Nevis the entire time and only come to

St. Eustatius in 1757. But it is known that Jemima was on St. Eustatius by 1748. Appearing multiple times in the church records, it would appear that Jemima resided on St. Eustatius, but her testimony makes it sound like she was living on Nevis.

With Nevis and St. Eustatius being just thirty miles apart, it is possible that Jemima moved back and forth between the two islands. Since Jemima was a resident of Nevis and had children living there but her new husband John Peters was a denizen of St. Eustatius and presumably had family on that island, perhaps the couple split their time between the two islands.

Thus, in testifying that she "had herself resided on Nevis" before having "come to St. Eustatius" "two years ago," perhaps Jemima was referring only to her most recent move from Nevis to St. Eustatius as she travelled back and forth between the islands.

Either way, Jemima's testimony seems to indicate that she returned to Nevis sometime after baptizing her child in March 1755 but that in 1757 she left Nevis again and returned to St. Eustatius.

The Relationship of Jemima Gurley and Rachel Faucett

On St. Eustatius in 1757, Jemima reconnected with her sister Rachel Faucett. According to her 1759 testimony to the divorce court, it would appear that Jemima Gurley had not seen Rachel on St. Kitts, Nevis, or St. Eustatius until 1757.[49]

How likely is it that these sisters, who were probably on the same island and certainly in the same area for about seven years (1750–1757), did not see each other? All three islands—St. Kitts, Nevis, and St. Eustatius—were within a few dozen miles of each other and travel between them was relatively quick and easy. How is it possible that they never saw each other during these seven years despite living so close to each other?

One possible explanation is that Rachel and Jemima did not get along and therefore had no desire to see each other. As mentioned earlier, Rachel and Jemima may have had different mothers. Moreover, Jemima was about ten to twenty years older than Rachel. Jemima married her first husband in 1730,[50] when Rachel was at most five years old. Having lived together only briefly and perhaps Rachel not even remembering having lived with her much older sister, they may not have formed a close connection. Moreover, when their father John Faucett made out his will in 1743, he left everything to Rachel.[51] Jemima may have resented this action, and resented her sister for it. Furthermore, John Michael Lavien in his divorce claim stated that Rachel's "own family and friends must hate her" for her extramarital activities.[52] Perhaps Jemima was one who hated Rachel. It will be noted that Jemima was the only witness who promptly testified. The other two failed to appear on the appointed date and had to be summoned again and threatened with punishment.[53] Perhaps James Ash and James Hendrie supported Rachel, or maybe they just did not want to get involved, or perhaps they were busy with other matters. Either way, Jemima was the only one to testify promptly, perhaps because she resented and even hated her sister.

If Jemima and Rachel did not get along and therefore did not see each other for so many years, why did they get together in 1757, at which time Rachel told Jemima her recent history? Why would Rachel be so open with someone who resented and hated her and did not want to see her for the previous seven years?

Perhaps it was the death of Mary Faucett in 1756 or soon thereafter,[54] mother of Rachel Faucett and perhaps Jemima's mother as well, that brought the sisters together.

Alternatively, it is possible that the sisters had lost touch and were not aware that they lived so close to each other. Indeed, Jemima made no mention of having been aware of Rachel's presence on the same or nearby islands until she met her in 1757 on St. Eustatius. The other witnesses provided hearsay testimony about Rachel's location, but Jemima did not. It would seem that she did not know about her sister living nearby. Obviously, if they did not know about each other being so close, they could not have gotten together.

This lack of communication between Rachel and Jemima does not prove that they never were on the same island at the same time, but it does raise questions both about their whereabouts and also about their relationship.

Jemima Serves as Godmother on St. Eustatius

The following year, on February 1, 1758, "Jan Peeters en Jomimy Peeters Desselfs Huysvrouw [John Peters and Jemima Peters his housewife]" served as godparents at the baptism of a Martha, daughter of "James Simmons and Rebekka Leverock."[55]

Richard Gurley Jr. Stays on Nevis

In returning to St. Eustatius in 1757, it appears that Jemima left at least one and possibly more of her children on Nevis. Richard Gurley Jr., born in 1743, apparently stayed on Nevis and was there in November 1758.[56] With other Gurleys and Iles on Nevis and this Richard Gurley Jr. growing up, perhaps he was in the middle of school or an apprenticeship and it was decided that he should stay with family on Nevis.

Jemima Gurley and Some Children Move to St. Croix

After moving from Nevis to St. Eustatius in 1757 and still being there in February 1758, Jemima moved to Christiansted, St. Croix, by the end of 1758, at which time she was listed in the matrikel as "Jeahomie Gorly," living on Market Street with no man, one girl, and no slaves.[57]

The lack of a man living with her and the use of the name Gurley suggests that Jemima's third husband, John Peters, may have passed away between his appearing as a godfather on February 1, 1758, and the compilation of this matrikel on December 30, 1758.

The girl listed with Jemima may have been the previously mentioned daughter Elizabeth Gurley, born about 1745, or her daughter Sarah Peters, born in 1755.

Jemima's move to St. Croix may have been prompted by some of her older children.

Although Lillingston Iles, the son born in 1735, is not listed in the 1758 matrikel, he appears in multiple records on St. Croix. A record from July 1754 shows a "Lingston Iles" on St. Croix and subsequent records from August and September show this to be Lillingston Iles.[58] More interesting is an account between Lillingston Iles and the estate of Christian Leonard showing that Lillingston Iles was on St. Croix in 1758. Working as a mason, Lillingston billed Leonard for "building your boiling house," "hanging a still," "building a worm cistern," and "plastering and underpinning your boiling house."[59]

A William Iles also appears on St. Croix in 1758. According to the matrikel, he lived with a woman, presumably a wife, at the 38-acre No. 20 Queen's Quarter plantation, which he leased from the heirs of Henry Hodge. The neighboring 150-acre No. 21 Queen's Quarter plantation was being leased by William Hartman and Francis Pearce from Josiah Webbe. Iles, Hartman, and Pearce worked the land as one plantation and their 53 slaves are counted together in the matrikel.[60]

A Charles Iles appears in St. Croix's account books for the first time on December 31, 1757, being charged his annual taxes.[61] He is not found in the 1757 matrikel, perhaps because that volume has suffered damage and much of it is illegible. He does appear, however, in the 1758 matrikel living in Queen's Quarter with his wife and two children.[62] No specific location is given for him, so perhaps he lived with the above William Iles, who leased land and lived in the same quarter.

On November 6, 1758, "Lillingstone Iles and Charles Iles of the island aforesaid [St. Croix] masons" sold a "negro boy named Cuffey now in the possession of Richard Gurley in the island of Nevis." Charles Iles signed his name but Lillingston Iles merely left his mark, suggesting he was either illiterate or somehow incapacitated.[63]

It is noteworthy that Lillingston Iles and Charles Iles worked together as masons and sold a slave for a Richard Gurley on Nevis. Lillingston Iles is clearly the son of Jemima Faucett Iles Gurley Peters. Richard Gurley almost certainly was the Richard Gurley Jr. born in 1743. Accordingly, Charles Iles almost certainly was a son of Jemima, presumably the unnamed fourth child from Jemima's 1739 petition. And with William Iles arriving on St. Croix the same year as Jemima and living in the same quarter as Charles Iles, this probably was the same William Iles born to Jemima on April 15, 1731.

All told, Jemima Faucett Iles Gurley Peters and at least four children—the unnamed daughter in the matrikel, Lillingston Iles, William Iles Jr., and Charles Iles—were all on St. Croix in 1758.

Jemima Gurley Testifies in Lavien v. Faucett Divorce

In February 1759, John Michael Lavien filed for divorce from his wife Rachel Faucett. In addition to calling for Rachel to appear, the court summoned three others to serve as witnesses. One of them was Jemima Gurley. Thus, on April 18, 1759, Jemima appeared before the court and provided testimony regarding her sister Rachel's activities, as well as she knew them, over the past few years. The details of Jemima's testimony can be seen in the chapter "John Michael Lavien v. Rachel Faucett: The 1759 Divorce Court Proceedings."

Unfortunately, Jemima provided little information about her own life. The details she shared have already been noted in their proper places.

Jemima Gurley Visits or Returns to St. Eustatius

On November 21, 1759, "Jumeyma Pieters [Jemima Peters]" served as a godmother to the baptism of a daughter born to "Jan Boudewin en Helena Gordeley [Gurley]." How this Helena Gurley was related to the other Gurleys is not known. Other godparents included "Jan Gordeley [John Gurley]" and "Richard Gordeley [Gurley]," who perhaps was Jemima's son. The daughter, who had been born on November 3, was named Jemima, presumably after Jemima Faucett Iles Gurley Peters.[64]

Jemima Gurley Sells Two Slaves on St. Croix

On October 19, 1761, "Jemima Gurley of the island aforesaid [St. Croix] Widow" sold two slaves for 200 pieces of eight to James Booth:

Saint Croix

To all to whom these presents shall or may concern know ye that I Jemima Gurley of the island aforesaid Widow, for and in consideration of the sum of two hundred pieces of eight say 200 ps in gold & silver money, to me in hand paid by James Booth of the island aforesaid and merchant the receipt whereof I do hereby acknowledge, have bargained & sold and by these presents do hereby bargain & sell a certain negroe woman named Leth, and her child named Teresa, to have and to hold the said negroe woman Leah her child Teresa unto him the said James Booth his heirs and assigns forever more the said negroe woman Leah & her child unto him the said James Booth and against all other person or persons what or wheresoever do by these presents warrant & forever defend, in witness whereof I have hereunto sett my hand & seal this 19th October 1761.

Jemima Gurley

Witness
Joseph Friderick
Charles Pemberton[65]

Despite being on St. Croix in 1761, Jemima does not appear in any matrikels after 1759. Perhaps she was no longer a resident of the island. Alternatively, she evidently owned no taxable property, i.e., land or slaves, and therefore was not counted or was counted as a member of another household.

Elizabeth Gurley Dies on St. Croix

On September 14, 1762, an Elizabeth Gurley, "aged 17," was buried in the churchyard of Christiansted's St. John's Anglican Church.[66] It will be recalled that this may have been a daughter of Richard and Jemima Gurley.[67]

However, just seventeen months later, on February 14, 1764, another Elizabeth Gurley was also buried.[68] It is not known how this Elizabeth Gurley was related to the others, especially since no age was given.

Charles Iles Dies in 1759

It will be recalled that Charles Iles was listed in St. Croix's 1758 matrikel along with his wife and two children. The 1759 matrikel, compiled on December 10, 1759, states that "Charles Iles is dead and left nothing behind except his widow and 1 child."[69] It thus appears that one of Charles Iles's children also died. Charles's widow and remaining child stayed in Queen's Quarter and they perhaps lived with William Iles at No. 20 Queen's Quarter.

Charles Iles's widow and child are not listed in the matrikel for 1760. Perhaps they left the island. Or possibly they were counted among someone else's family. Or perhaps Charles Iles's widow remarried and thus was counted with her new husband. Alternatively, perhaps they owned no land or slaves and simply were not counted in the matrikel, which was really a tax list.

William Iles Jr.: 1758–1762

It will be recalled that William Iles, presumably the son of Jemima and William Iles Sr., was listed in the 1758 matrikel with a woman, probably a wife, living on land he leased in Queen's Quarter from the heirs of Henry Hodge. William Iles stayed on the lease for the next three years, but after 1758 he is no longer listed in the matrikels as living on that property or anywhere else on St. Croix.[70]

Later documents show that it was Edward Daniel, as one of Henry Hodge's heirs or as an executor, who had rented the St. Croix estate to William Iles. According to a financial account, Iles had rented the land from Daniel for £500 per annum.[71]

Even though he leased an estate on St. Croix, William Iles Jr. apparently wanted more. On January 3, 1759, on St. Thomas, another Danish island not far from St. Croix, Iles took out a mortgage of 40,000 rigsdalers from Johann Adolph Gravenhorst and provided as collateral a plantation in St. Thomas's North Quarter, which he presumably purchased at that time.[72]

According to St. Thomas's matrikel for 1759, William Iles Jr. owned the sugar plantation in North Side Quarter "formerly belonging to Johan Horn's heirs." The matrikel shows one man living on the plantation, presumably William Iles himself, but no wife or children with him. Iles also owned 54 slaves, who worked the plantation for him. This plantation and the slaves were probably what Iles acquired with his 40,000 rigsdaler loan.[73]

Thus, William Iles Jr. owned a plantation on St. Thomas, leased another on St. Croix, and owned slaves on both islands. He obviously was a man of considerable holdings.

Back on St. Croix, 53 slaves continued to work the combined Queen's Quarter plantation leased by Iles, William Hartman, and Francis Pearce,[74] the same as the previous year. Although counted in the aggregate, each slave was apparently owned by one of the lessees rather than in partnership. In December 1759, a group of slaves allegedly planned to rebel against their masters and take over the island of St. Croix. According to an account of the planned slave insurrection, a slave named Cudio owned by William Iles was accused but acquitted of any involvement in the scheme.[75]

Apparently, the 40,000 rigsdaler debt William Iles took on to acquire his St. Thomas plantation along with the cost of leasing the plantation from Henry Hodge's heirs, i.e., Edward Daniel, and perhaps other debts as well were too much for him to handle. Iles evidently defaulted on his mortgage and in 1760 his St. Thomas plantation was taken over by Johann Adolph Gravenhorst. St. Thomas's matrikels show that Gravenhorst had 46 slaves on the plantation in 1760 versus the 54 Iles had there in 1759, suggesting that Gravenhorst also acquired most if not all of Iles's slaves.[76]

With this setback, William Iles returned to St. Croix in early 1760.[77] But on September 19, 1760, "William Iles of the Island of St. Croix but now in the Island of Montserrat" appointed two attorneys to represent him on St. Croix in his absence. One of the two witnesses to this power of attorney was Thomas Iles,[78] perhaps the son of Thomas Iles and Sarah Lytton, who at last account lived on Nevis. Either way, this document shows that William Iles had moved to Montserrat, probably to escape his debts.

William Iles's financial troubles followed him from St. Thomas to St. Croix and then to Montserrat. Continuing to lease No. 20 Queen's Quarter on St. Croix and having his slaves work it, William Iles fell behind on his payments to Edward Daniel. A financial account from May 1761 shows that Iles had rented the land from Edward Daniel for the period August 1758 to March 1761 at a rate of £500 per annum. In 1759, Iles paid most of what he owed for the first year's rent, but he then fell behind and by the end of March 1761 he owed Daniel £795 4s.[79]

Edward Daniel entered into a legal "action" against William Iles in May 1761, but it was difficult for Daniel to collect since Iles was now living on the British island of Montserrat. The authorities on St. Croix looked into the matter and questioned people familiar with it, including Abraham Harris, Thomas Stevens, William Daniel, and Alexander Moir. The records that have been found show that no resolution to this "action" had been reached by January 1762. It is not known whether Edward Daniel ever recovered the £795 4s that William Iles Jr. owed him.[80]

Nothing has been found regarding William Iles Jr. after this date. Relying on scattered records from multiple islands provides a partial but incomplete picture of this first cousin of Alexander Hamilton. A more thorough search of the records of St. Thomas and Montserrat may yield additional details.

Richard Gurley Jr. on Nevis in 1764

On February 1, 1764, a Richard Gurley started working in a boiling house and as an overseer at the Mountravers sugar plantation on Nevis. According to an in-depth work about that estate:

For about a year and a half from 1 February 1764, Richard Gurley was employed in the boiling house and as an overseer. He may have been a young man in his early twenties (born on 12 February 1743 and baptised six months later) but, equally, the man working on Mountravers could have been his father of the same name. Married in 1740, Richard Gurley senior would perhaps have been in his forties or early fifties. His wife, Gemima Isles, came from a large, established Nevis family while his appears to have been a small one: the only reference to another Gurley found so far is to a William Gurley, whose 'base son' was baptised in 1751. Like William Vaughan, the overseer before him, Richard Gurley also lived in St George's Gingerland. Eight months after he started work, Coker increased his salary from N£48 a year to N£50. JPP [John Pretor Pinney] arrived in December 1764 and Richard Gurley left his employment in June the following year.[81]

As has already been seen, Richard Gurley Sr., the husband of Jemima, had died by 1747. Accordingly, this Richard Gurley who worked on Nevis's Montravers plantation probably was Jemima's son Richard Gurley Jr.

What happened to Richard Gurley Jr. after June 1765 is not known. A Richard Gurley is found on St. Eustatius in 1782,[82] but whether this was the same person is not known.

Lillingston Iles in 1769

In January 1769, Lillingston Iles submitted his account to the estate of Christian Leonard regarding work he had done in 1758, as mentioned earlier. This financial account included the following note:

Sir,
Please to pay or cause to be paid unto Mrs. Mary Iles the above balance and her quittance[?] shall be a sufficient discharge from your very humble servant

his
Lillingston ⊗ Iles
Mark

A few things are worthy of notice here. Lillingston Iles requested that the money owed to him be given to Mary Iles. One assumes that this was his wife. Also noteworthy is that Lillingston Iles left his mark rather than sign his name, just as he had done eleven years earlier.[83]

Jemima Moves to St. Vincent, Dies

Jemima Faucett Iles Gurley Peters, who was last seen on St. Croix in 1761, had apparently moved to St. Vincent by 1771. A financial account for Peter Gurley on St. Vincent, but found in the records of St. Croix, shows a transaction for "our sister Mrs. Peters" on August 16, 1771.[84] It will be recalled that Peter Gurley probably was the brother of Jemima's husband Richard Gurley and that Jemima had subsequently married a John Peters. Thus, Peter Gurley's "sister Mrs. Peters" probably was Jemima Faucett Iles Gurley Peters. Another transaction on December 18, 1771, also involved "Sister Peters."[85]

On May 29, 1772, Peter Gurley was charged 20 pieces of eight and 7 reals for "Mrs. Peters Coffin."[86] Thus, Jemima Faucett Iles Gurley Peters passed away in May 1772. She was about sixty years old. Despite facing many struggles, she had been blessed with many children and an interesting life.

Jemima Faucett's Family Tree

Jemima Faucett (ca. 1710 – May 1772)
+ William Iles (married April 19, 1730; died ca. 1737)
   1. William Iles (baptized April 15, 1731)
   2. Jemima Iles (baptized September 16, 1733)
   3. Lillingston Iles (baptized April 9, 1735)
   4. Charles Iles (born ca. 1737; died 1759)
+ Richard Gurley (married May 23, 1740; deceased by 1747)
   1. John Gurley (baptized March 2, 1741; buried March 2, 1741)
   2. Richard Gurley (born February 12, 1743)
   3. Elizabeth Gurley? (born ca. 1745; buried September 14, 1762)
+ John Peters (married ca. 1747)
   1. Richard Peters (born December 1748; baptized December 18, 1748)
   2. Catharina Peters (born March 3, 1753; baptized March 18, 1753)
   3. Sarah Peters (born March 5, 1755; baptized March 22, 1755)

Did Alexander Hamilton Know Jemima or Her Children?

According to Jemima's testimony, she met and talked to her sister Rachel on St. Eustatius in 1757. The "about" three-year-old Alexander Hamilton may have met his aunt at this time. After moving to St. Croix, Jemima visited St. Eustatius again in November 1759. Perhaps she met her sister and nephews then as well. In addition to these two instances, it is likely that Jemima and Alexander Hamilton had at other times also been on the same island at the same time.

If Rachel, James Hamilton, and their children moved to Nevis or visited the island between 1759 and 1765, they may have met Richard Gurley Jr., who lived there. Other Gurleys and Iles also lived on Nevis and they may have treated James Hamilton, Rachel, and their children like the family they were, for Jemima's children were first cousins to Alexander Hamilton and Rachel was their aunt.

When Rachel and her family moved to St. Croix in 1765, Lillingston Iles was living there. Lillingston had known Rachel on Nevis back in the 1730s and 1740s. Other Iles and Gurleys not found in the records could have also been living on St. Croix. One assumes that young Alexander Hamilton knew Lillingston Iles and any other first cousins named Iles, Gurley, or Peters who lived on St. Croix, but whether any kinship developed between them is not answered by the evidence.

Notes

1. For a discussion of the possibility that John Faucett had more than one wife and thus that the Faucett children may have had different mothers, see Newton, *Alexander Hamilton: The Formative Years* 9.
2. Newton, "The Story of Jemima Faucett."
3. See page 78; Divorce proceedings of John Michael Lavien v. Rachel Faucett Lavien, 14r–16r, in *Christiansted Retsdokumenter 1740-1759.*
4. *Caribbeana* 3:179.
5. Newton, *Alexander Hamilton: The Formative Years* 9 and 513.
6. *Caribbeana* 2:266–272.
7. For a discussion of the possibility that John Faucett had married two women by the name of Mary and thus the Faucett children may have had different mothers, see Newton, *Alexander Hamilton: The Formative Years* 9.
8. *Caribbeana* 3:218.
9. *Caribbeana* 3:72, 75, 77.
10. *Caribbeana* 3:177.
11. Index of losses claimed and debentures issued, in CO 243/9, page 15, debenture #479; Debentures issued by the Board of Trade, in CO 243/8, folio 126r, #479.
12. On January 5, 1720, Sarah Lytton, James Lytton's sister (see page 31; Copy of the

Will of John Lytton of Nevis, May 1, 1709, in CO 243/5, Item 400), married Thomas Iles, probably a relative of William Iles and perhaps his brother (*Caribbeana* 2:269). They had a son together, Thomas Iles Jr., in 1721 (*Caribbeana* 2:268) and another son, named Joseph, in 1723 (*Caribbeana* 2:269). Sarah Lytton Iles may have died in the mid- to late-1720s, during a gap in the parish records, because no further trace of her has been found and a Thomas Iles, perhaps Sarah's widower, is married to an Ann in 1733 (*Caribbeana* 3:219).

13. *Caribbeana* 2:267, 268, 269, 3:219, 352.
14. *Caribbeana* 3:219.
15. *Caribbeana* 3:219.
16. *Caribbeana* 3:220.
17. *Caribbeana* 3:219.
18. *Caribbeana* 3:220.
19. *Caribbeana* 3:221.
20. Email from Christine Eickelmann, citing CO 186/2. See also Eickelmann, *The Mountravers Plantation Community* 1045 note 469.
21. Minutes of Council in Assembly of Nevis, 1738–1752, June 21, 1739, in CO 186/3.
22. Extract from the Common Records of Nevis, 1725–1746, in Atherton, *A Few of Hamilton's Letters* 269–272; Newton, *Alexander Hamilton: The Formative Years* 12.
23. *St. Croix Matrikel 1738*.
24. Email from Christine Eickelmann, citing CO 186/3.
25. Minutes of Council in Assembly of Nevis, 1738–1752, June 21, 1739, in CO 186/3.
26. *Caribbeana* 3:352.
27. *Caribbeana* 3:108; Eickelmann, *The Mountravers Plantation Community* 1045 note 470.
28. *Caribbeana* 2:263.
29. *Caribbeana* 3:352.
30. *Caribbeana* 3:354.
31. See page 94; *St. John's Anglican Church, Christiansted, St. Croix, Burial Registry 1761–1787* page 2.
32. *Hollandske Kirke, Sint Eustatius, Kirkebog, Baptisms 1743–1765*, December 18, 1748. No record of the wedding of John Peters and Jemima has been found, probably because the St. Eustatius marriage records between May 1745 and March 1749 are missing.
33. *Hollandske Kirke, Sint Eustatius, Kirkebog, Baptisms 1743–1765*, March 18, 1753, and March 22, 1755.
34. It is unlikely that this person was another woman named Jemima Gurley since no one else by that name from this time has been found, Jemima was an unusual name, and her daughter Jemima was an Iles not a Gurley and she was just fifteen at this time.
35. See page 98.
36. *Hollandske Kirke, Sint Eustatius, Kirkebog, Marriages 1741–1764*, March 20, 1750.
37. *The Tryal of John Barbot, Attorney at Law, for the Murder of Mathew Mills* 48.
38. *The Diary of John Baker* 70.
39. *The London Magazine . . . For the Year 1753* 350; *The Diary of John Baker* 71.

40. *The London Magazine . . . For the Year 1753* 347–350.

41. Chernow, *Alexander Hamilton* 18–19.

42. *The Tryal of John Barbot, Attorney at Law, for the Murder of Mathew Mills* 5.

43. *Caribbeana* 2:267, 268, 269, 271, 3:221.

44. *Hollandske Kirke, Sint Eustatius, Kirkebog, Baptisms 1743–1765*, March 18, 1753. Catharina Peters was given a middle name but damage to the register makes it illegible.

45. *Hollandske Kirke, Sint Eustatius, Kirkebog, Baptisms 1743–1765*, March 22, 1755.

46. Email from Christine Eickelmann, citing Pinney Papers [University of Bristol Special Collections], Dom Box P: General's Tax Notebook 1755.

47. *Caribbeana* 2:268.

48. See page 78; Divorce proceedings of John Michael Lavien v. Rachel Faucett Lavien, 14r–16r, in *Christiansted Retsdokumenter 1740-1759*.

49. See page 78; Divorce proceedings of John Michael Lavien v. Rachel Faucett Lavien, 14r–16r, in *Christiansted Retsdokumenter 1740-1759*.

50. See page 83.

51. *Christiansted Notarialprotokoller 1746–1759* 15r–v.

52. See page 76; *St. Croix Panteprotokoller 1756–1772* 43r–44r; transcribed in Ramsing, "Alexander Hamilton Og Hans Modrene Slaegt" 232–234; translated in Ramsing, *Alexander Hamilton's Birth and Parentage* 8–10.

53. See pages 79–80; Divorce proceedings of John Michael Lavien v. Rachel Faucett Lavien, 21v–27r, in *Christiansted Retsdokumenter 1740-1759*.

54. Deed of Trust, May 5, 1756, in the Common Records of St. Kitts, quoted in Atherton, "The Hunt for Hamilton's Mother" 237–238; Atherton, *The Conqueror* 49 and 538; Ramsing, *Alexander Hamilton's Birth and Parentage* 6; Mitchell, *Alexander Hamilton: Youth to Maturity* 478 note 4.

55. *Hollandske Kirke, Sint Eustatius, Kirkebog, Baptisms 1743–1765*, February 1, 1758.

56. See page 92; *St. Croix Diverse Regnskabssager* 55.13.31 image 375.

57. *St. Croix Matrikel 1758* 12.

58. *Christiansted Bytingsprotokoller 1754–1756* 73r, 120r, 121r, 139r.

59. *Christiansted Skiftesager på Enkeltpersoner* 38.63.42 image 303.

60. *St. Croix Matrikel 1758* 18.

61. *St. Croix Hovedbog 1756–1757* 43.

62. *St. Croix Matrikel 1758* 19.

63. *St. Croix Diverse Regnskabssager* 55.13.31 image 375.

64. *Hollandske Kirke, Sint Eustatius, Kirkebog, Baptisms 1743–1765*, November 18, 1761.

65. *Christiansted Panteprotokoller 1760–1762* 242r.

66. *St. John's Anglican Church, Christiansted, St. Croix, Burial Registry 1761–1787* page 2.

67. See page 86.

68. *St. John's Anglican Church, Christiansted, St. Croix, Burial Registry 1761–1787* page 4.

69. *St. Croix Matrikel 1759* 25.

70. *St. Croix Matrikel 1759* 23; ibid. *1760* 23; ibid. *1761* 25.

71. *St. Croix Diverse Regnskabssager* 55.13.31 image 415.

72. Mortgage between William Iles and Johann Adolph Gravenhorst, January 3, 1759, in *Christiansted Retsdokumenter 1740-1759* images 154b–155b; *Extract from St. Croix*

Pante Boger 37, in *St. Croix Diverse Regnskabssager* 55.13.23 image 21b.
Interestingly, in March 1760, on St. Croix, William Iles served as a witness to a contract between John James and Johann Adolph Gravenhorst (*Christiansted Sager vedr. Arrest- og Eksekutionsforretninger 1758–1776* image 161b).

73. *St. Thomas Matrikel 1759* 30.

74. *St. Croix Matrikel 1759* 23.

75. Hesselberg, "Detailed description of the negro insurrection planned on the island of St. Croix in the year 1759" 61.

76. *St. Thomas Matrikel 1760* 7; ibid. *1761* 7.

77. *Christiansted Sager vedr. Arrest- og Eksekutionsforretninger 1758–1776* image 161b; *St. Croix Landstinget Justitsprotokol 1758–1760* 154v, 164v, 170v, *1760–1761* 9r, 27v; *Christiansted Panteprotokoller 1760–1762* 15r.

78. *Christiansted Panteprotokoller 1760–1762* 115r.

79. *St. Croix Diverse Regnskabssager* 55.13.31 image 415.

80. *St. Croix Bytings- & Ekstraretssager 1761–1850* image 3; *Christiansted Retsdokumenter 1760* image 184–189; ibid. *1762* image 225b–226b.

81. Eickelmann, *The Mountravers Plantation Community* 1045.

82. *Hollandske Kirke, Sint Eustatius, Kirkebog, Marriages 1775–1791*, June 4, 1782.

83. *Christiansted Skiftesager på Enkeltpersoner* 38.63.42 image 303.

84. Unnamed Hovedbog, in *St. Croix Diverse Regnskabsprotokoller* 55.12.131 image 290.

85. Unnamed Hovedbog, in *St. Croix Diverse Regnskabsprotokoller* 55.12.131 image 290.

86. Unnamed Hovedbog, in *St. Croix Diverse Regnskabsprotokoller* 55.12.131 image 290.

James Hamilton Working as a Sailor, Coming to St. Croix, and a Legal Dispute

After trying his hand as a merchant, James Hamilton took a job as a watchman or weighman at the port of Basseterre, St. Kitts, in July 1748.[1] In 1753, he moved from St. Kitts to St. Eustatius "on account of debt." It appears that he spent much of the next twelve years on that island, but may have also spent some time on Nevis and St. Kitts.[2]

What jobs did James Hamilton have on St. Eustatius or on Nevis and St. Kitts from 1753 until he is found again in the records in 1765?

John Davis's Voyages

According to the customs journals of St. Croix, Captain John Davis "of Christiansted" and his brigantine *Jægeren* [*Hunter*] arrived in Frederiksted, St. Croix, from Puerto Rico on February 11, 1765, and was preparing on that same day to depart for St. Thomas.[3]

Seven days later, on February 18, John Davis was outbound for St. Thomas.[4]

Four days after that, February 22, Captain Davis returned from St. Thomas to Frederiksted.[5]

At some point over the next few days, John Davis sailed from Frederiksted to Christiansted. On March 5, 1765, Davis returned to Frederiksted and on that same day was outbound for Puerto Rico.[6]

On April 6, John Davis returned to St. Croix from Puerto Rico.[7]

James Hamilton v. John Davis

One man who sailed with John Davis on all or some of these voyages was James Hamilton. Upon returning to St. Croix on April 6, 1765, John Davis and James Hamilton had a falling out and the matter was taken to the courts. A Hendrich Oved was involved in an identical dispute with Davis.

On April 19, 1765, both James Hamilton and Hendrich Oved sued John Davis, captain of the brigantine *Hunter*, for money owed them for their recent voyage. Oved sought 14 rigsdalers owed to him as his salary for said voyage plus legal expenses while James Hamilton sued for 10 rigsdalers plus legal expenses. The bailiffs summoned John Davis before the court. Davis's lawyer, Christian Anthon Seybeck, argued that Oved and Hamilton had "left the brigantine here at St. Croix without permission or any legal reason before the voyage was ended" and requested a postponement until the next day.[8]

The following day, Davis's lawyer requested another delay, to which Hamilton's lawyer, Christen Lind, asked that this be the last delay unless something truly unexpected comes up.[9]

Gathering again on April 27, the court recorded that Davis was countersuing Hamilton for leaving the ship before the voyage was over without being sick or any other legitimate reason and that Hamilton should be punished in accordance with the law and the contract, and required to pay the costs of the proceeding. Hamilton's lawyer argued that there is no question that the ship arrived on St. Croix and that since the contract stated the voyage ended on St. Croix, Hamilton was in his right to leave. On this date, both lawyers agreed that it was time to bring the case to judgment.[10]

The court met again on May 7, the dispute continued, but nothing was resolved.[11]

Finally, on May 17, the court reconvened and issued its decision. The court record for this date also provides full details of the dispute. According to the record, James Hamilton sued John Davis in Christiansted municipal court for "an outstanding debt of 10 rigsdalers in sailor's wages, for a voyage the plaintiff made in a brigantine commanded by the defendant." The facts of the case were that the "crew was to go with the brigantine from St. Thomas here to St. Croix and from here to Portorico where they if possible were to take in a cargo and thereafter come here to St. Croix or St. Christopher whereupon the voyage should end." When the ship came to St. Croix from Puerto Rico, Hamilton believed the voyage had ended. Davis's attorney argued that Hamilton "without permission or a valid reason left the ship before the voyage was completed and its cargo unloaded." The court agreed with Hamilton and ordered that "Captain John Davis should pay the plaintiff James Hamilton the 10 rigsdalers in question, as well as 26 rigsdalers cash towards the costs of this proceeding, to be paid within a certain time after the issuing of this judgment, under penalty of law." As for Hendrich Oved, the court also ruled in his favor and ordered Davis to pay him the 14 rigsdalers in question plus the same 26 rigsdalers in legal expenses.[12]

On May 23, John Davis appealed the rulings against him in both the Hamilton and Oved cases.[13] That very same day, Davis was outbound for Tortola, an island less than fifty miles north of St. Croix.[14] Apparently, Davis's lawyer would handle the case in his absence.

On May 29, St. Croix's appeals court took up the case of "John Davis Contra Matros James Hamilthon [John Davis against sailor James Hamilton]," but immediately postponed the case until June 5.[15]

On June 8, the appeals court postponed the case again until June 15.[16]

John Davis, who had sailed for Tortola on May 23, returned on his 25-ton barque "of Jamaica" from the Spanish coast to Frederiksted on June 11 and was outbound for New York on June 17.[17] Apparently, his lawyer was handling the appeal in his absence.

On June 17, the appeals court again postponed the case to June 19.[18]

Finally, on June 19, 1765, the appeals court took up the matter of "John Davis Contra James Hamilthon." According to the appeals court record, John Davis's lawyer claimed that James Hamilton had been contracted for a voyage from St. Thomas to St. Croix, then to Puerto Rico, and finally back to St. Croix or St. Kitts. Hamilton left the ship without the captain's permission after it returned from Puerto Rico to St. Croix and refused to continue with the ship to St. Kitts. Davis's lawyer argued that the ship stopped at St. Croix not to unload cargo but for other reasons and therefore Hamilton was still under contract to sail to St. Kitts with the ship and its cargo. Davis's lawyer further argued that the lower court had improperly interpreted the contract between him and Hamilton.

In rebuttal, Hamilton's lawyer argued that he had served on the ship and performed his duties from St. Thomas to St. Croix, from St. Croix to Puerto Rico, and then back again to St. Croix, where the voyage according to the contract was to end, and that he had remained in service aboard the ship for several days after its return to St. Croix. Moreover, Hamilton's lawyer argued that Davis refused to increase the wages of his crew for the additional stop and had not paid them at all for their service. [19]

Ten days later, on June 29, 1765, reviewing the details of the case again, the appeals court decided that "Davis had been free, under the contract, to go to St. Christopher and not here [St. Croix], and Hamilton would have been obliged to accompany him there, but now [Davis] first called here, and the court cannot see otherwise than that the voyage, according to the agreed-upon articles, is in fact ended." The appeals court ruled that the decision by the lower court was "in all ways well grounded" and that "the costs of the appeal to this court is to be paid by skipper John Davis to Matros James Hamilthon with fifty-two rigsdaler in cash money, which is to be laid out and paid within three full days after this judgment's lawful issue."[20] The same judgement was made in the case of Hendrich Oved v. John Davis.[21]

Identifying James Hamilton

James Hamilton and Alexander Hamilton were then and still are relatively common names. In fact, there were multiple people with those names on St. Croix around this time. On July 13, 1769, a James Hamilton, aged 37, was buried in the churchyard of Christiansted's St. John's Anglican Church.[22] Less than two months later, on September 1, 1769, an Alexander Hamilton who "had come from Scotland, but most recently from St. Christopher," died with an estate valued at just 27 rigsdalers, which went entirely to cover the costs of his "final illness and his burial" and to "the officers of the court as compensation for their trouble in this matter."[23] Accordingly, whenever people with common names are found, one must be careful not to assume that such an individual is the person one is searching for.

In the case of the above sailor James Hamilton, there is nothing to identify this man as the father of Alexander Hamilton. However, it has long been known that James Hamilton, Rachel, and the children came to St. Croix in the spring of 1765.[24] The arrival of this sailor James Hamilton in April 1765, exactly when James, Rachel and the children came to the island, is too perfect to be a coincidence. Accordingly, the above James Hamilton who sailed with John Davis and entered into a legal dispute against him almost certainly was the father of Alexander Hamilton.

Rewriting the Biography of James Hamilton

With the discovery of these records, a number of details regarding James Hamilton's life have to be questioned or altered.

James Hamilton gained employment as a watchman or weighman at the port of Basseterre, St. Kitts, in July 1748,[25] but he must have left that job by 1753 when he abandoned St. Kitts for St. Eustatius.[26] It is not known what he did next, but at some point James Hamilton became a sailor and he was working at this job in 1765. It is likely that his sailing with John Davis was not the only time he was employed in this position. It seems likely that James Hamilton took whatever jobs he could get because he is later found working as an "attorney" collecting debts for others.[27] Going from a merchant to a watchman or weighman to a sailor and debt collector shows how James Hamilton struggled in business ever since this son of a Laird left Scotland.

Until now, historians believed that James Hamilton was sent to St. Croix in 1765 to collect a debt,[28] but that information is not found anywhere in the records regarding that business.[29] This had merely been assumed, which given the available information at the time was a logical deduction. It is now clear that James Hamilton came to St. Croix on April 6, 1765, on board John Davis's brigantine *Hunter*, or *Jægeren* in Danish, and that Hamilton had joined Davis's crew on St. Thomas around February 20, 1765. This does not imply that Hamilton had been living on St. Thomas. More likely, he had been on another sailing voyage, perhaps with the same John Davis, which completed its journey on St. Thomas and there he got another job as a sailor on another voyage.

With James working as a sailor, Rachel would have been left to fend for herself and her children for weeks or months at a time. She presumably rented out her slaves and perhaps worked, possibly in a store, giving her the experience she needed later to keep her own store on St. Croix. Of course, she was also busy raising two young children.

James Hamilton's arrival with John Davis on April 6, 1765, also raises the question of when Rachel and the children came to St. Croix. Clearly they would not have come with James Hamilton since he came as a sailor working on board a merchant vessel. Likely, James Hamilton sent for Rachel and his children after he arrived on St. Croix and decided to stay, first to collect the money owed to him by John Davis but then to collect a debt for another.[30]

James Hamilton's employment as a sailor on board merchant vessels could also explain why he does not appear in St. Croix's matrikels even though Rachel is listed with her two children.[31] As a sailor who constantly came and went and owning no taxable property on the island, there was no reason for

James Hamilton to appear in the census and tax lists.

At some point in 1766 or 1767, James Hamilton left St. Croix and his family forever.[32] Perhaps this occurred when James Hamilton was on a lengthy voyage and was detained elsewhere, possibly by injury, illness, debt, or legal disputes, and then was unable to return due to a lack of money and perhaps some embarrassment regarding his financial situation. Alexander Hamilton did not blame his father for the "separation between him and me,"[33] so perhaps something happened to James Hamilton on one of his voyages and he never intended to abandon his family.

Notes

1. Chernow, *Alexander Hamilton* 15.
2. See chapter "John Michael Lavien v. Rachel Faucett: The 1759 Divorce Court Proceedings."
3. *Frederiksted Toldregnskaber for 1765*, in *St. Croix Regnskabsvæsen Sager* image 17a, and in *Intraderne for Frederiksted Toldbog, January–April 1765*, in Vestindisk-Guineisk Generaltoldkammeret, *Indkomne Vestindiske Breve 1760–1767* B550 image 18b.
4. *Frederiksted Toldregnskaber for 1765*, in *St. Croix Regnskabsvæsen Sager* image 19b.
5. *Frederiksted Toldregnskaber for 1765*, in *St. Croix Regnskabsvæsen Sager* image 21a, and in *Intraderne for Frederiksted Toldbog, January–April 1765*, in Vestindisk-Guineisk Generaltoldkammeret, *Indkomne Vestindiske Breve 1760–1767* B550 image 20b.
6. *Frederiksted Toldregnskaber for 1765*, in *St. Croix Regnskabsvæsen Sager* image 26a, and in *Intraderne for Frederiksted Toldbog, January–April 1765*, in Vestindisk-Guineisk Generaltoldkammeret, *Indkomne Vestindiske Breve 1760–1767* B550 image 25b.
7. *Customs Journal (Toldbog), Christiansted, St. Croix, May–December 1765* page 28b.
8. *Christiansted Gæsteretsprotokoller 1765* 306r–308r, 310v.
9. *Christiansted Gæsteretsprotokoller 1765* 313r–v.
10. *Christiansted Gæsteretsprotokoller 1765* 316r–318v.
11. *Christiansted Gæsteretsprotokoller 1765* 327v.
12. *Christiansted Domprotokoller 1764–1766* 128r–v.
13. *St. Croix Landstinget Justitsprotokol 1764–1765* 151r.
14. *Customs Journal (Toldbog), Christiansted, St. Croix, May–December 1765* page 28b.
15. *St. Croix Landstinget Justitsprotokol 1764–1765* 151r.
16. *St. Croix Landstinget Justitsprotokol 1764–1765* 163r.
17. *Intraderne for Frederiksted Toldbog, May–August 1765*, in Vestindisk-Guineisk Generaltoldkammeret, *Indkomne Vestindiske Breve 1760–1767* B640 image 484a.
18. *St. Croix Landstinget Justitsprotokol 1764–1765* 170v–171r.
19. *St. Croix Landstinget Justitsprotokol 1764–1765* 171r–173v.
20. *St. Croix Landstinget Justitsprotokol 1764–1765* 174r; *St. Croix Landstinget Domprotokoller 1760–1766* 283–285.
21. *St. Croix Landstinget Domprotokoller 1760–1766* 285–287.

22. *St. John's Anglican Church, Christiansted, St. Croix, Burial Registry 1761–1787* page 12.

23. *Christiansted Registrerings og Vurderingsprotokoller for Borgere og Plantere 1768–1773* 133–134.

24. Ramsing, "Alexander Hamilton Og Hans Modrene Slaegt" 237–238; Ramsing, *Alexander Hamilton's Birth and Parentage* 15–16; Mitchell, *Alexander Hamilton: Youth to Maturity* 13; Chernow, *Alexander Hamilton* 21; Newton, *Alexander Hamilton: The Formative Years* 36.

25. Chernow, *Alexander Hamilton* 15.

26. See pages 19 and 79.

27. See chapter "James Hamilton Working as a Debt Collector."

28. Ramsing, "Alexander Hamilton Og Hans Modrene Slaegt" 237; Ramsing, *Alexander Hamilton's Birth and Parentage* 15; Mitchell, *Alexander Hamilton: Youth to Maturity* 13; Flexner, *The Young Hamilton* 24; Chernow, *Alexander Hamilton* 21; Newton, *Alexander Hamilton: The Formative Years* 36.

29. See chapter "James Hamilton Working as a Debt Collector."

30. See chapter "James Hamilton Working as a Debt Collector."

31. *St. Croix Matrikel 1765* 8; ibid. *1766* 5; ibid. *1767* 6.

32. See pages 121–122.

33. Alexander Hamilton to William Hamilton, May 2, 1797, in *The Papers of Alexander Hamilton* 21:77.

James Hamilton Working as a Debt Collector

On April 1, 1765, Alexander Moir of St. Croix announced his intention to leave for Europe during the month of May and asked his creditors to submit their claims against him.[1] Alexander Moir had partnered with Alexander Gordon on commercial ventures. Moir and Gordon were now dissolving their partnership and were in the midst of arbitration.[2]

Previously it was thought that James Hamilton had worked for Archibald Ingram on St. Kitts and that Ingram sent Hamilton to St. Croix to collect a debt from Moir & Gordon. Some historians even write that James Hamilton had been Ingram's "head clerk," which was based entirely on a mistranslation.[3] It is now clear that Hamilton arrived on St. Croix on April 6, 1765,[4] and that his arrival had nothing to do with Ingram or Moir & Gordon. In fact, there is no evidence that Hamilton had worked for Ingram on St. Kitts, though they presumably knew each other there. Nor is it known how Archibald Ingram came to hire James Hamilton to collect some debts from Moir & Gordon. Perhaps James Hamilton learned of Moir's announcement and wrote to Ingram offering his services. Or perhaps Ingram learned of Moir's announcement and knew James Hamilton was on St. Croix so he immediately contacted him to act as his representative. Either way, Archibald Ingram of St. Kitts hired James Hamilton on St. Croix to act as his representative and attorney to collect some debts from Moir & Gordon.

Moir & Gordon refused to pay Archibald Ingram's claims against them. On July 13, 1765, James Hamilton, on behalf of Archibald Ingram of St. Kitts, filed a legal "protest" against Moir & Gordon to collect a "bill" of £400 sterling due to Ingram.[5]

Knowing that such legal matters take time, perhaps it was at this point that James Hamilton sent for Rachel and their two children to join him on St. Croix. Or perhaps they had already moved to St. Croix since he had come to the island three months earlier and had been involved in another legal dispute during the interim.[6]

On November 23, 1765, the court noted that the bill of exchange of £400 sterling issued by Gordon and Moir on June 22 the previous year had been refused in both Amsterdam and London and that Archibald Ingram had given a power of attorney to James Hamilton on August 10 to recover the debt. Alexander Gordon's lawyer protested the case going forward because Moir had already charged Gordon for the £400 sterling and therefore it was Moir alone, not Gordon, who was responsible. Moir was not present so Augustinus Kummel, a lawyer representing Ingram and Hamilton, requested the case be postponed. The court also took up a second case for another bill of £75 9s 10½d owed by Gordon and Moir to Ingram with James Hamilton again acting as Ingram's power of attorney, but this time the question was raised as to whether the plaintiff, either Ingram or Hamilton, as a foreigner had a right to sue.[7]

A week later, on November 30, Kummel argued that it was well known that Moir and Gordon had been partners for more than ten years and were now arguing, but that the obligation or bill of exchange in question had been issued by Alexander Gordon & Company and that this was therefore a matter of "one for both and both for one" and that the difficulties between Moir and Gordon had nothing to do with Archibald Ingram.[8]

Two weeks later, on December 14, the court rendered its judgment in favor of "James Hamilton, as representative of Archibald Ingram on Saint Christophers according to the power of attorney issued last August," and ruled "that Alexander Gordon and Alexander Moir one for both and both for one must pay to James Hamilton, as representative for Archibald Ingram, four hundred pounds sterling" plus "interest of one percent per month from the date of the protest" and court costs.[9] In the second case, the court noted that the debt of £75 9s 10½d had been issued by "Alexander Gordon & Company, which according to the admission of both defendants is the name under which the former but now dissolved partnership between them went" and therefore both Moir and Gordon were responsible.[10]

On January 2, 1766, Alexander Moir "quit all claim, title, & pretensions to" eight slaves "now in the possession of Alexander Gordon and under mortgage to me" because "a judgement has been lately obtained in court against Alexander Gordon & Company for a Sett of Bills of Exchange of £400 sterling drawn on Mr Abram Terborch of Amsterdam in favour of Mr Archibald Ingram of St. Christophers." Two days later, Alexander Gordon made out a mortgage to these slaves to three individuals for "£807 11s 11¼d currency."[11]

On January 8, James Hamilton finally collected the money owed to Archibald Ingram in the first case from "Alexander Gordon and Company / or Alexander Moir and Alexander Gordon as Co-partners." The original debt of £400 sterling had accrued interest of £22 5s 4d over the past five and a half months. An additional £2 2s 3d was tacked on for "½ percent on the whole according to law." This sum was then converted from pounds sterling to "windward currency" and then to "St. Croix currency" and an additional £24 6s in court charges were added, bringing the total to £807 11s 11¼d "Currency St. Croix." Upon collecting the money, Hamilton signed "James Hamilton, atty for Archibald Ingram."[12]

On February 3, the court also ordered "Alexander Moir & Gordon in Company" to pay "James Hammilthon's court claim, as representative for Archibald Ingram," of £75 9s 10½d "with interest of 6 per cent per year from the 20th November 1765" plus "costs for this process" of 18 rigsdalers and 2 reals.[13] No record of James Hamilton collecting this debt or of the final sum after adding interest and expenses has been found.

On February 22, 1766, Alexander Moir was buried "at his own plantation."[14] His death surely complicated matters as Alexander Gordon now had to deal with Moir's estate and Ingram still had other debts to collect from Moir & Gordon.

For example, on March 24, 1766, the court discussed the matter of Moir and Gordon and noted three outstanding claims, one of which was a bill of £436 sterling that "Alexander Gordon, under the name of Gordon & Company, drew on Abraham Terborth in Amsterdam in favor of Archibald Ingram on St. Christophers, which with a protest was returned and payment sought by Ingram, through a representative," i.e., James Hamilton.[15] Nothing has been found about whether this bill was ever paid.

Notes

1. *St. Croix Panteprotokoller 1756–1772* 116r.
2. *Christiansted Panteprotokoller 1765–1767* 105v–109r; *Christiansted Byfogedens Sager 1764–1766* images 158b–159b, 164b–166a; *St. Croix Notarialsager 1763–1776* images 246b–247a.

James Hamilton, attorney for Archibald Ingram, collects a debt from Moir & Gordon, in *Christiansted Panteprotokoller 1765–1767* 118v–119r.

3. Ramsing, "Alexander Hamilton Og Hans Modrene Slaegt" 237; Ramsing, *Alexander Hamilton's Birth and Parentage* 15; Mitchell, *Alexander Hamilton: Youth to Maturity* 13; Flexner, *The Young Hamilton* 24; Chernow, *Alexander Hamilton* 21; Newton, *Alexander Hamilton: The Formative Years* 36.

   The idea that James Hamilton had been Archibald Ingram's "head clerk" on St. Kitts comes from a mistranslation. H. U. Ramsing wrote in his essay on Alexander Hamilton's birth and parentage that James Hamilton was "som Fuldmægtig for Archibald Ingram" (Ramsing, "Alexander Hamilton Og Hans Modrene Slaegt" 237). In a translation of this essay by Solvejg Vahl, which English-speaking historians have largely relied upon, this phrase was translated to "as head clerk for Archibald Ingram" (Ramsing, *Alexander Hamilton's Birth and Parentage* 15). But the term "Fuldmægtig" or "Fuldmagt" means, according to every Danish-English dictionary this author could find, "full powers; power of attorney." Thus, James Hamilton was not the head clerk of Archibald Ingram, but he had power of attorney for him. There is no evidence that James Hamilton was head clerk or even an employee of Archibald Ingram on St. Kitts.

4. See chapter "James Hamilton Working as a Sailor, Coming to St. Croix, and a Legal Dispute."

5. *Christiansted Panteprotokoller 1765–1767* 118v–119r.

6. See chapter "James Hamilton Working as a Sailor, Coming to St. Croix, and a Legal Dispute."

7. *Christiansted Gæsteretsprotokoller 1765–1766* 119v–120v.

8. *Christiansted Gæsteretsprotokoller 1765–1766* 133v–135r.

9. *Christiansted Domprotokoller 1764–1766* 257v–258v.

10. *Christiansted Domprotokoller 1764–1766* 259r–260v.

11. *Christiansted Panteprotokoller 1765–1767* 123r–v.

12. *Christiansted Panteprotokoller 1765–1767* 118v–119r. This, of course, is a copy and not an original signature.

13. *Christiansted Domprotokoller 1764–1766* 297r.

14. *St. John's Anglican Church, Christiansted, St. Croix, Burial Registry 1761–1787* page 7.

15. *Christiansted Domprotokoller 1764–1766* 330v.

Rachel Fatzieth on St. Croix

As noted earlier, the name Faucett has been spelled and misspelled many different ways. No fewer than twenty-four different spellings have been found in the available records.[1] It would seem that court clerks, census takers, bookkeepers, and just about everyone else spelled this name their own way.

Rachel Fatzieth in the St. Croix Matrikel

Perhaps the oddest spelling of the Faucett name appears when Rachel Faucett is listed in various records on St. Croix after her return in 1765.

In the matrikels of St. Croix for 1765 and 1766, she is listed as "Rachel Fatzieth."[2]

This unusual spelling is no new discovery. Having already seen these records, or relying on those who had already written about them, Hamilton biographers assumed that Fatzieth was a simple misspelling of Faucett, albeit a bizarre one. For example, H. U. Ramsing wrote that "she appears on the list . . . at first in 1765 and '66 under her maiden name Rachael Fatzieth (!)."[3] Broadus Mitchell remarked in an endnote, "She and her sons appear in tax lists; in 1765 and 1766 she is called Rachael Fatzieth."[4] James T. Flexner noted that "the poll tax reveals she lives there . . . under her maiden name of Faucett (spelled by the tax collector with fine abandon as Fatzieth)."[5] Even this author reported in *Alexander Hamilton: The Formative Years* that "poll-tax lists from 1765 and 1766 spelled it Fatzieth,"[6] as if this was just a normal misspelling of Faucett.

As these matrikels were the only known records in which Rachel appeared as Fatzieth, it was logical to assume that this was a mere misspelling and not the result of some purposeful act by Rachel or by the authorities.

Rachel Fatzieth in the St. Croix Account Books

However, another set of records, St. Croix's hovedboger (account books) for 1758–1766 and 1766–1770, also lists Rachel's name as Fatzieth.[7]

Yet another set of records, a list of debtors "to 30 Sep. 1766" but apparently compiled years later, listed her as "Rachel Falziet."[8] The information in this volume clearly was taken from the 1758–1766 hovedbog and the name then further misspelled.

Rachel Faucett Hiding Her Identity?

Rather than having just one set of documents listing Rachel with the last name of Fatzieth, there are now two independent sets of records showing this, for one assumes that the accountants or clerks who maintained the account books were not the same people who took and recorded the matrikels. Moreover, it is clear that the information in one set of books was not copied from the other because the numbers do not match.

Is it plausible that two independent sets of people misspelled the name Faucett in the same bizarre fashion? A slight and common misspelling would not be unusual but for two different people to independently spell Faucett as Fatzieth must be more than a mere accident.

Moreover, Fatzieth does not look or sound like Faucett. It hardly seems like it could be a simple misspelling.

According to Danish Law, "No adultress shall . . . be permitted to marry, or settle in the same parish, tribe, village, or city, where her former husband dwells."[9] If this law was upheld in the colonies, not only was Rachel not allowed to be with James Hamilton, but she was also not even allowed to live in the same city as John Michael Lavien. Fortunately for Rachel, John Michael Lavien had moved to Frederiksted, so she was safe in Christiansted. But did she know that when she came to St. Croix?

According to the divorce proceedings, Rachel reportedly went by the name Rachel Lavien on both St. Kitts and St. Eustatius,[10] so why does she appear under the name Fatzieth rather than Lavien?

Perhaps when Rachel Faucett came to St. Croix in 1765 after a fifteen-year absence, she adopted a false name that was neither Lavien nor Faucett to try to hide her true identity, both to avoid the social humiliation that may result from knowledge of her past and also to keep such information from the authorities, out of fear she would be "further punished (if seized) according to law and ordinances."[11] It will be recalled that Rachel was imprisoned in 1749–1750 for "fornication" with Johan Cronenberg.[12] Perhaps she would now be imprisoned for "fornication" with James Hamilton. Moreover, Rachel may not have been aware of the details of the ruling against her and may have feared that the court had indeed sentenced her to further punishment if she returned to St. Croix, regardless of whether she now had a relationship with James Hamilton or not.

Rachel Faucett had good reason to fear punishment from the authorities if they or John Michael Lavien learned of her arrival. Perhaps the adoption of the Fatzieth name was designed to help hide her identity.

Rachel Faucett's Age

When Rachel Faucett died in February 1768, it was recorded in the burial register that she was "aged 32."[13] It has long been known that her age was recorded incorrectly in this document. If Rachel was thirty-two when she died in February 1768, it would indicate a birth in 1735 or 1736. But it is known that she married around 1745 and gave birth to a son, Peter Lavien, in 1745 or early 1746. As this author concluded in *Alexander Hamilton: The Formative Years*, based on a gap in the baptismal records from her family's church on Nevis, Rachel must have been born "sometime between the spring of 1725 and the end of 1729."[14] Whereas many biographers, including this one, argued that "a recording or transcription error is the most likely cause of Rachael's mistaken age"[15] and others contended that Rachel "exercised the feminine prerogative of forgetting a few of her years,"[16] perhaps the change in Rachel's age was not the result of a clerical error or an attempt to merely appear younger, but was instead an effort to hide her true identity. Rather than being Rachel Faucett Lavien born in 1725–1729, she was Rachel Fatzieth born in 1735–1736. It may be that Rachel changed not just her last name to try to hide her identity but also her age.

Did Rachel Faucett Try to Hide Her Identity?

The major flaw in the above theory is that the name Fatzieth is remarkably similar to Faucett. If Rachel wanted to hide her identity, she could have chosen a completely different name not in any way resembling her real name.

Why would Rachel choose such an unusual name (no other instance of the Fatzieth name has been found) and yet one so similar to her real name? Would not a more common name, like Jones or Smith or anything else, been a better way to hide one's identity? Perhaps Rachel reasoned that choosing a more common name would have led to questions she could not answer. People would have asked her if she was related to this Smith or that Jones. By choosing a unique name, she could possibly avoid those questions, though it might instead prompt questions about the name itself, i.e., the origin of the name and the identity of Rachel's parents, but one could easily plead ignorance or invent an answer that would avoid further inquiry.

Moreover, Rachel may have chosen a unique but similar last name to provide cover for herself if someone discovered the truth. If she had chosen a totally different last name and someone revealed her true identity, it would prove her to be a liar. By choosing a similar name, she could claim that the clerk had recorded it incorrectly and she either was not aware of the error or had not bothered to correct the insignificant mistake.

Why didn't Rachel avoid the Faucett name entirely and just call herself Hamilton? Again, if her goal was to avoid punishment, using the Hamilton name would not only have put herself at risk but also James Hamilton. Of course, her children were named Hamilton, but it was common with deaths and remarriages for parents and children to have different last names.

It would seem then that Rachel's goal was not to fully hide her identity, but rather to hide it enough so as to avoid punishment. Whispers about her true identity and her past, which had clearly circulated on St. Kitts and St. Eustatius, would be acceptable. The goal was to avoid legal prosecution.

Using a false name but one close enough to her real one so as to appear to be a misspelling and providing an incorrect age perhaps with the pretense of exercising "the feminine prerogative of forgetting a few of her years" might be enough to delay wider knowledge of her true identity while those more closely connected to her would of course know the truth from the start.

Why Return to St. Croix?

If Rachel feared discovery of her identity and possible prosecution, why would she come to St. Croix at all, even with a false identity? Why not just stay on Nevis, St. Kitts, or St. Eustatius, her previous places of residence, where according to the scant evidence that is available,[17] it appears that she and James Hamilton lived together happily as a married couple?

James Hamilton came to St. Croix in April 1765 and had to stay on the island for some time.[18] Joining her partner would, of course, be one strong motivation for Rachel to come as well. On top of this, Rachel had family, most notably the Lyttons, on St. Croix, who not only would provide her with friends on the island but could also give her financial assistance if needed, which indeed they did.[19] And probably even more important, Rachel might have thought that St. Croix, an island more prosperous at this time than Nevis or St. Kitts and with wealthy relatives living there, would be a better environment for her two sons, James Hamilton Jr. and Alexander Hamilton. It is not difficult to imagine that Rachel was willing to risk her own reputation and even possible legal punishment to benefit her children.

Additionally, perhaps Rachel did not plan to stay on St. Croix for long, just until James collected the debt, and thought her secret would be safe for a short time. When she ended up staying longer than expected, she probably suspected that her secret would eventually be discovered.

Rachel Fatzieth Discovered?

After appearing as Rachel Fatzieth in the 1765 and 1766 matrikels, she is listed in 1767 as Rachel Lewin, a common misspelling of Lavien. The following year, in the 1768 matrikel, which was compiled after Rachel's death, her slaves are listed as the possessions of the estate of Rachel Lewin.[20]

The change from Fatzieth to Lewin suggests that Rachel no longer feared persecution and gave up the ruse, perhaps because James Hamilton had already left St. Croix.

Alternatively, perhaps the authorities discovered Rachel's true identity and she was forced to abandon her alias and use her legal name. If so, this discovery may have also forced James and Rachel to separate rather than risk legal prosecution and James may have been forced to leave St. Croix permanently to avoid punishment, which he did sometime between June 1766 and February 1768,[21] whereas Rachel was safe as long as James stayed away from the island.

All this, of course, is speculation until additional evidence is found.

Notes

1. See page 28.
2. *St. Croix Matrikel 1765* 8; ibid. *1766* 5.
3. Ramsing, "Alexander Hamilton Og Hans Modrene Slaegt" 238; Ramsing, *Alexander Hamilton's Birth and Parentage* 15–16.
4. Mitchell, *Alexander Hamilton: Youth to Maturity* 477 note 3.
5. Flexner, *The Young Hamilton* 25.
6. Newton, *Alexander Hamilton: The Formative Years* 10.
7. *St. Croix Hovedbog 1758–1766* 894; ibid. *1766–1770* 331; ibid. *1766–1770* index 8v.
8. *Debitor list to September 1766,* page 13, in *St. Croix Diverse Regnskabsprotokoller* 55.12.80 image 236b.
9. *The Danish Laws* 175–176.
10. See page 79.
11. *St. Croix Panteprotokoller 1756–1772* 43r–44r; transcribed in Ramsing, "Alexander Hamilton Og Hans Modrene Slaegt" 232–234; translated in Ramsing, *Alexander Hamilton's Birth and Parentage* 8–10.
12. See chapter "The Extramarital Affair of Rachel Faucett."
13. *St. John's Anglican Church, Christiansted, St. Croix, Burial Registry 1761–1787* page 10.
14. Newton, *Alexander Hamilton: The Formative Years* 12.
15. Newton, *Alexander Hamilton: The Formative Years* 11.
16. Ramsing, "Alexander Hamilton Og Hans Modrene Slaegt" 248; Ramsing, *Alexander Hamilton's Birth and Parentage* 27–28; Larson, "Alexander Hamilton: The Fact and Fiction of His Early Years" 141.
17. See pages 6 and 17; *Hollandske Kirke, Sint Eustatius, Kirkebog, Baptisms 1743–1765,* October 1, 1758.
18. See chapters "James Hamilton Working as a Sailor, Coming to St. Croix, and a Legal Dispute" and "James Hamilton Working as a Debt Collector."
19. *Christiansted Skiftebrevsprotokoller for Borgere og Plantere* 20:392r; Ramsing, "Alexander Hamilton Og Hans Modrene Slaegt" 238; Ramsing, *Alexander Hamilton's Birth and Parentage* 16; Alexander Hamilton to William Hamilton, May 2, 1797, in *The Papers of Alexander Hamilton* 21:77.
20. *St. Croix Matrikel 1767* 6; ibid. *1768* 6.
21. See page 122.

The Story of James Hamilton from 1766–1799

As mentioned earlier, James Hamilton arrived on St. Croix on April 6, 1765, and he stayed on the island for more than a year. Yet, while "Rachel Fatzieth" was listed with her two sons and one capable slave in the 1765 matrikel,[1] James Hamilton does not appear with her or anywhere else on St. Croix.

There are a number of possible reasons for James Hamilton not appearing in St. Croix's matrikels. For starters, James could not be listed with Rachel because a marriage and even a relationship between them on St. Croix was forbidden by previous court rulings. Still, he is not listed on his own either. Although these matrikels are often called censuses, they are in fact tax lists. If James Hamilton owned no taxable property, he need not have been listed separately and could have been listed as a member of another household. More likely, if he continued to work as a sailor who constantly came and went from the island, he would have had no official residence and therefore would not have been listed.

James Hamilton Acting as a Witness, June 1766

James Hamilton was on St. Croix on June 25, 1766, when he served as a witness to a mortgage for Nathaniel Little to Alexander Anderson and affixed his signature to this legal document.[2]

Was this James Hamilton the father of Alexander Hamilton or another person with the same name? Perhaps it was James Hamilton Jr., Alexander Hamilton's about 14-year-old brother. Although a bit young to be acting as a witness, Alexander Hamilton would do so at an even earlier age.[3] Or perhaps it was the James Hamilton who on July 13, 1769, was buried in the churchyard of St. John's Anglican Church of Christiansted.[4] Or perhaps it was an entirely different James Hamilton.

Since the above is a copy of the mortgage whose original has been lost, this is not an original James Hamilton signature and it cannot be compared to known James Hamilton Sr. signatures.[5]

However, a legal document from 1769 shows that an Alexander Anderson took over for James Hamilton as Archibald Ingram's St. Croix attorney.[6] With James Hamilton acting here as a witness on a mortgage to Alexander Anderson, it is clear that this was indeed the father of Alexander Hamilton.

James Hamilton Leaves St. Croix

After this, James Hamilton disappears from the known extant records of St. Croix. The date of his departure from the island is not known, but he must have left sometime prior to February 1768 when Rachel Faucett died because their children—James Jr. and Alexander Hamilton—did not go to him but instead were taken in by the Lyttons.[7]

It has long been assumed that James Hamilton returned to St. Kitts after his departure from St. Croix. Perhaps this is true. Or perhaps James Hamilton returned to St. Eustatius. It is now known that James Hamilton spent considerable time on St. Eustatius and perhaps he had lived there immediately before coming to St. Croix.[8] Alternatively, perhaps he went southward to the Grenadine Islands, where he would later be found.

Why did James Hamilton leave St. Croix and abandon his wife and children? The old story that James left St. Croix after learning the truth about his wife's background has proven to be untrue.[9]

Alexander Hamilton wrote that his "father's affairs at a very early day went to wreck, so as to have rendered his situation during the greatest part of his life far from eligible. This state of things occasioned a separation between him and me."[10] In other words, it was James Hamilton's financial situation, perhaps unpaid debts, that forced him to leave St. Croix. Thus, just as James "absented" himself from St. Kitts to St. Eustatius "on account of debt" back in 1753,[11] he may have left St. Croix for the very same reason. However, no records of any unpaid debts have been found in St. Croix's account books or legal papers, but a lack of evidence is not proof.

Unlike in 1753, Rachel did not follow James this time, perhaps because the children had already found their places on St. Croix. Or perhaps Rachel meant to follow but before she had the chance she died, in February 1768.

James Hamilton on Tobago?

On January 23, 1771, *The Royal Danish American Gazette* on St. Croix reported that on the island of Tobago, more than five hundred miles to the south, "the slaves of the Coramantie nation, about 30 in number, . . . attacked Mr. Hamilton's house" and "wounded three white men desperately, two of whom are since dead. Mr. Hamilton was shot through the thigh, but is recovering."[12]

It has been said that this "Mr. Hamilton" may have been Alexander Hamilton's father,[13] whose whereabouts at this time are not known.

A thorough investigation shows that the injured "Mr. Hamilton" was not James Hamilton, but instead was John Hamilton, the owner of an estate in Riseland, Tobago. Although no first name is given for the injured "Mr. Hamilton" in the available records of this affair, that is because John Hamilton was a prominent person on Tobago, a member of the Assembly and Council, and everyone knew that "Mr. Hamilton" referred to John Hamilton. Moreover, John Hamilton is the only Hamilton known to have owned an estate in Riseland, where the incident took place. Furthermore, there is no evidence that James Hamilton ever set foot on Tobago.[14]

Alexander Hamilton's Hurricane Account to his Father

Alexander Hamilton's famous hurricane account of September 6, 1772, published on October 3 in *The Royal Danish American Gazette*, was preceded in the newspaper by a note stating that "the following letter was written . . . by a youth of this island to his father."[15] Although James Hamilton's location is not mentioned, it is clear that Alexander knew where his father was living and probably maintained regular correspondence with him.

James Hamilton on Bequia

By 1774, James Hamilton had moved to British-controlled Bequia, the northernmost and second largest of the Grenadine Islands. Just seven square miles in size, Bequia sits about 400 miles south-southeast of St. Croix. It was described at the time as "a beautiful and most healthy island" but "deficient in rivers essential to the comfort and satisfaction" of its inhabitants.[16]

On March 1, 1774, James Hamilton acquired Lot No. 18 on Bequia, a 25-acre parcel of land that had been "reserved for poor settlers" on the north shore of Admiralty or North Bay.[17] One can see on the 1776 map of the island that there were three buildings on James Hamilton's property.

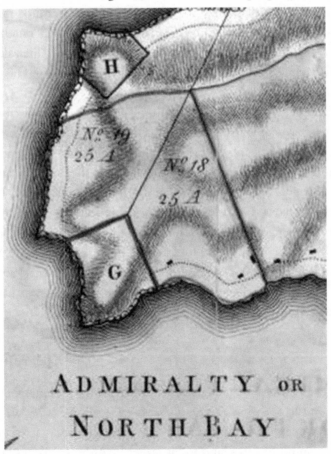

James Hamilton's Lot No. 18 on Bequia, in Byres, *Plan of the Island of Bequia* 1776.

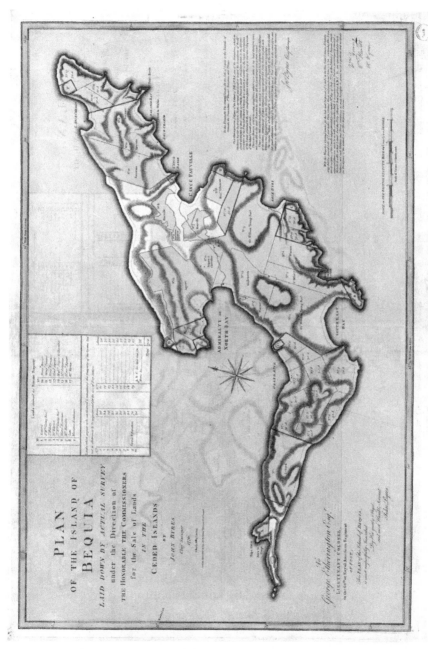

Byres, *Plan of the Island of Bequia* 1776.

According to a map of Bequia from 1763, this property already had at least two buildings on it.[18]

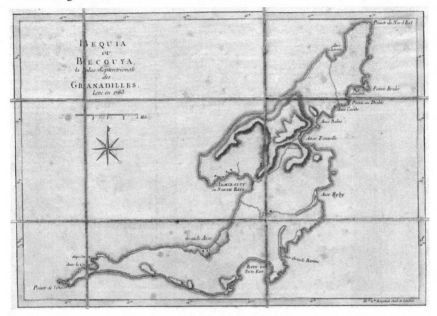

Bequia ou Becouya . . . 1763.

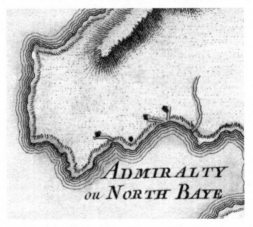

Lot later acquired by James Hamilton,
in *Bequia ou Becouya . . . 1763.*

A plot of land with two or three pre-existing structures seems like a fairly good deal for a "poor settler." Perhaps Hamilton had some influential friends on St. Vincent and the Grenadines. Indeed, an Archibald Ingram, possibly the same one from St. Kitts for whom Hamilton had worked, had moved to St. Vincent by 1768,[19] owned two lots of 183 acres combined,[20] and in 1771 was appointed to the island's privy council[21] and as the island's receiver of quit rents, taxes, etc.[22] Also, Peter Gurley, Jemima's relative and friend from St. Eustatius,[23] had moved to St. Vincent by 1771[24] and owned one lot of 83 acres and co-owned with two others another 198 acres.[25] Perhaps these influential friends helped James Hamilton acquire this choice property.

While James Hamilton acquired Lot No. 18 on Bequia on March 1, 1774, the 1776 map of the island does not show him owning that property but instead indicates that he co-owned or owned part of the 70-acre Lot No. 9 on the west shore of the Southeast Bay, which had also been set aside "for the use of poor settlers."[26]

N.º		Acres	N.º		Acres
1	....	36	11	....	30
2	....	33	12	....	30
3	....	36	13	....	30
4	....	32	14	....	50
5	....	35	15	....	40
6	....	30	16	....	32
7	....	30	17	....	34
8		34	18	....	25
9	Simple & Hamilton	70	19	....	25
10	....	30	A.B.C. &c. laid out for Forts &c.		38
			Total		700

Lands which appear to be unclaimed & remaining the Property of the Crown laid out in allotments to be appropriated for the use of Poor Settlers

Table from Byres, *Plan of the Island of Bequia* 1776.

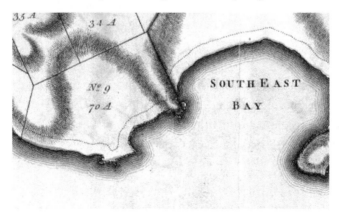

Lot No. 9 on Bequia, in
Byres, *Plan of the Island of Bequia* 1776.

But the map's legend is incorrect. As already noted, the map fails to list James Hamilton's ownership of Lot No. 18. Moreover, thirty of Lot No. 9's seventy acres were granted to James Sempill in March 1774 and another thirty acres were granted to Robert Sempill in April 1775 with the remainder belonging to the King for public use.[27] Clearly, whoever recorded Lot No. 9 as belonging to "Simple & Hamilton" made a mistake. Lot No. 9 should belong to "Sempill & Sempill" and Lot No. 18 to "Hamilton."

An "account of the islands of Grenada and Tobago" from 1776 shows that Hamilton had six slaves and produced 347 pounds of cotton.[28] Thus, just two years after being granted land as a "poor settler," James Hamilton was making productive use of his property and owned or leased slaves to work it.

Alexander Hamilton about James Hamilton in 1780

Sometime in 1780, after getting engaged to Elizabeth Schuyler but prior to the wedding, Alexander Hamilton informed his fiancée:

I wrote you, my dear, in one of my letters that I had written to our father, but had not heard of him since, that the operations in the islands hitherto cannot affect him, that I had pressed him to come to America after the peace. A gentleman going to the island where he is, will in a few days afford me a safe opportunity to write again. I shall again present him with his black-eyed daughter, and tell him how much her attention deserves his affection and will make the blessing of his gray hairs.[29]

Although James Hamilton's location is not given in this letter, it is clear that Alexander Hamilton knew which island his father lived on, that he had written to him recently and planned to do so again soon, and that he hoped his father would "come to America after the peace."

Alexander Hamilton about James Hamilton, June 1785

Alexander Hamilton wrote about his father again in June 1785, this time in a letter to his brother James Hamilton Jr.:

But what has become of our dear father? It is an age since I have heared from him or of him, though I have written him several letters. Perhaps, alas! he is no more, and I shall not have the pleasing opportunity of contributing to render the close of his life more happy than the progress of it. My heart bleeds at the recollection of his misfortunes and embarrassments. Sometimes I flatter myself his brothers have extended their support to him, and that he now enjoys tranquillity and ease. At other times I fear he is suffering in indigence. I entreat you, if you can, to relieve me from my doubts, and let me know how or where he is, if alive, if dead, how and where he died. Should he be alive inform him of my inquiries, beg him to write to me, and tell him how ready I shall be to devote myself and all I have to his accommodation and happiness.[30]

Yet again, this letter reveals nothing about James Hamilton Sr.'s location, though the extant autograph fragment indicates that it was sent to James Hamilton Jr. on St. Thomas. It also shows, yet again, that Alexander Hamilton had written his father "several letters." Not having heard back, Alexander Hamilton was worried his father had moved or died.

This letter also reveals that despite making a fresh start on Bequia and acquiring land there, James Hamilton had yet again fallen on hard times.

James Hamilton Witnesses a Deed, May 1786

In May 1786, James Sempill sold his 30 acres of land known as Black Bird point on Southeast Bay, i.e., his share of Lot No. 9. James Hamilton signed the deed as a witness. No location was given, but one assumes the deed was made out and witnessed on Bequia.[31]

James Hamilton Sells His Property on Bequia, May 1790

In May 1790, James Hamilton "of the Island of Bequia" sold his 25-acre lot, i.e., Lot No. 18, for £500 current money, or about £270 sterling, and signed the deed transferring ownership.[32] This was a decent sum of money for a "poor settler," but it is not known what corresponding debts James Hamilton had to cover.

James Hamilton on St. Vincent

James Hamilton at this time took his money, if any remained after paying his debts, and apparently moved about ten miles north from Bequia to the larger island of St. Vincent.

On August 17, 1792, Alexander Hamilton wrote to William Seton, cashier at the Bank of New York:

> Inclosed, my dear sir, is a letter to Mr. Donald of St. Vincents, which I beg your most particular care in forwarding. I presume he is a merchant there; but a gentleman lately mentioned to me, that he thought the name of the governor of St. Vincents was Donald. If so, he is probably the person intended. I received a letter from him, giving me some information of my father. The letter to Mr. Donald covers one to my father, who, from a series of misfortunes, was reduced to great distress. You will perceive from this, that I must be anxious for the safe conveyance of my letter.[33]

It would seem that James Hamilton was on St. Vincent by this time, but given that the two islands were so close to each other, it is possible James Hamilton was still on Bequia. Alexander Hamilton indicated that he had received "information" about his father and now, more so than in 1785, he was very concerned about his father's "misfortunes" and "great distress." Hamilton was writing to his father, presumably to offer him financial support and to again invite him to America.

Ten months later, on June 12, 1793, in his only known extant letter, James Hamilton Sr. wrote from St. Vincent to Alexander Hamilton:

> I wrote you a letter in June 1792 inclosed in one to Mr. Donald of Virginia since which I have had no further accounts from you. My bad state of health has prevented my going to sea at this time being afflicted with a complication of disorders.
>
> The war which has lately broke out between France & England makes it very dengerous going to sea at this time, however we daily expect news of a peace & when that takes place provided it is not too late in the season I will embark in the first vessel that sails for Philadelphia.

I have now settled all my business in this part of the world, with the assistance of my good freind Mr. Donald who has been of every service to me that lay in his power in contributing to make my life easy, at this advanced period of life. The bearer of this, Capt. Sherref of the Brig, Dispatch sails direct for Philadelphia & has promised to deliver you this letter with his own hands, & as he returns to this Island from Philadelphia I beg you will drop me a few lines letting me know how you & your family keeps your health as I am uneasy at not having heard from you for some time past.[34]

It thus appears that many of the letters Alexander and James Hamilton wrote to each other never reached their destinations. James Hamilton, having sold his property on Bequia, now hoped to join his son on the mainland, but explained that "my bad state of health has prevented my going to sea at this time being afflicted with a complication of disorders." On top of this, "the war which has lately broke out between France & England makes it very dengerous going to sea at this time." Still, James hoped that peace would soon arrive and "provided it is not too late in the season I will embark in the first vessel that sails for Philadelphia."

Alexander Hamilton Supports His Father

With his father unable to come to North America due to ill health and the war between France and England, Alexander Hamilton did all he could to support James Hamilton Sr. on St. Vincent.

In July 1795, Alexander Hamilton told Robert Troup about "two drafts drawn upon me by my father, one for five hundred the other for two hundred dollars." Hamilton considered a possible payment of these drafts as "a merely voluntary engagement." He therefore "doubted the justice of the measure and I have done nothing. I regret it lest they should return upon him and increase his distress. Though as I am informed a man of respectable connections in Scotland he became bankrupt as a merchant at an early day in the West Indies and is now in indigence. I have pressed him to come to me but his great age & infirmity have deterred him from the change of climate."[35]

Alexander Hamilton's cash book shows that he paid drafts for his father totaling at least $1,141.25 between August 1795 and December 1798.[36]

In May 1797, Alexander Hamilton explained to his uncle in Scotland:

It is now several months since I have heared from my father who continued at the island of St Vincents. My anxiety at this silence would be
greater than it is, were it not for the considerable interruption and pre-
cariousness of intercourse, which is produced by the war.
I have strongly pressed the old gentleman to come to reside with me,
which would afford him every enjoyment of which his advanced age is
capable. But he has declined it on the ground that the advice of his
physicians leads him to fear that the change of climate would be fatal
to him. The next thing for me is, in proportion to my means to endeavour to increase his comforts where he is.[37]

Alexander Hamilton later clarified that his father "for some time . . . was
supported by his friends in Scotland, and for several years before his death by
me."[38]

The Death of James Hamilton, June 1799

James Hamilton, the father of Alexander Hamilton, passed away in 1799
on St. Vincent and was buried on June 3, 1799, evidently in the churchyard
of St. George's Cathedral in Kingstown, St. Vincent.[39]

Notes

1. *St. Croix Matrikel 1765* 8.
2. *Christiansted Panteprotokoller 1765–1767* 238r–v.
3. See chapter "The Oldest Known Alexander Hamilton Documents."
4. See page 106; *St. John's Anglican Church, Christiansted, St. Croix, Burial Registry 1761–
   1787* page 12.
5. James Hamilton to Alexander Hamilton, June 12, 1793, in *Alexander Hamilton Papers*; *The Papers of Alexander Hamilton* 14:536–537.
6. *Christiansted Fogedprotokoller 1767 06 20 – 1770 11 08* 270r–274r. For James Hamilton acting as Ingram's attorney, see chapter "James Hamilton Working as a Debt
   Collector."
7. *Christiansted Registrerings og Vurderingsprotokoller for Borgere og Plantere 1761–68*
   360r; *Christiansted Skiftebrevsprotokoller for Borgere og Plantere* 20:386v; Ramsing,
   "Alexander Hamilton Og Hans Modrene Slaegt" 245; Ramsing, *Alexander*

Hamilton's Birth and Parentage 24.

8. See page 19.
9. See pages 15–16.
10. Alexander Hamilton to William Hamilton, May 2, 1797, in *The Papers of Alexander Hamilton* 21:77.
11. See pages 19 and 79.
12. *The Royal Danish American Gazette*, January 23, 1771, p2 c3. The Coromantee Africans originated on the Gold Coast in modern-day Ghana. They were considered "the best and most faithful" of the slaves, but were also known to rebel when mistreated. (Merrill, *The Historical Geography of St. Kitts and Nevis* 72.)
13. For instance, see Ramsing, "Alexander Hamilton Og Hans Modrene Slaegt" 238; Ramsing, *Alexander Hamilton's Birth and Parentage* 16; Mitchell, *Alexander Hamilton: Youth to Maturity* 13–14.; Randall, *Alexander Hamilton: A Life* 20.
14. Council Meeting, Scarborough, Tobago, November 27, 1770, in CO 288/2 folios 75–80; Robert Stewart to Robert Melvill, November 29, 1770, in The Historical Society of Trinidad and Tobago, *Publications* No. 348; An Extract from the State of Tobago, June 25, 1771, in ibid. No. 350; Ottley, *The Story of Tobago* 30–32; *The Edinburgh Magazine, or Literary Miscellany* 17:251; Oliver, *The History of the Island of Antigua* 3:427; George Hamilton, *A History of the House of Hamilton* 723.
15. Alexander Hamilton to James Hamilton Sr., September 6, 1772, in *The Royal Danish American Gazette*, October 3, 1772, p2 c2–3; reprinted in *The Papers of Alexander Hamilton* 1:34 note 1.
16. Young, *An Account of the Black Charaibs* 29.
17. *St. Vincent Deed Book, 1784–1787* 347–352; Byres, *Plan of the Island of Bequia*. Ron Chernow mistakenly wrote that James Hamilton purchased "woodland property along the shore of Southeast Bay." As seen in the main text, Chernow mixed up this property with another that was erroneously attributed to James Hamilton. Chernow also mistakenly gave the date of the deed as March 14, 1774. (Chernow, *Alexander Hamilton* 40.)
18. *Bequia ou Becouya . . . 1763*; Byres, *Plan of the Island of Bequia*.
19. *St. Vincent Deed Book, 1771–1772* 211–212.
20. Byres, *References to the Plan of the Island of St. Vincent* 1, 3.
21. May 25, 1771, "St Vincent, Windward Islands, West Indies: Board of Trade representation recommending Archibald Ingram to be appointed to the council; 7 June read and approved," in PC 1/60/9; *Journal of the Commissioners for Trade and Plantations, 1768–1775* 252.
22. *The Gentleman's Magazine and Historical Chronicle* 41:143. See also "St. Vincent: Archibald Ingram, Receiver of Quit Rents: he has been attacked by a mob. The Council is trying to appropriate the quit rent revenue for their expenses. Related memorials and correspondence relating to previous disputes," in T 1/486/284-301.
23. See page 87.
24. Unnamed Hovedbog, in *St. Croix Diverse Regnskabsprotokoller* 55.12.131 images 290–291, 293; *St. Vincent Deed Book, 1771–1772* 55–61.
25. Byres, *References to the Plan of the Island of St. Vincent* 2.
26. Byres, *Plan of the Island of Bequia*.

27. *St. Vincent Deed Book, 1784–1787* 311–321.

Ron Chernow, who first wrote about James Hamilton on Bequia, did not notice this error and wrote that James Hamilton shared "seventy acres with a man named Simple" (Chernow, *Alexander Hamilton* 40 and 734).

28. "State of Carriacou and the other Grenadine Island," in *Account of the Islands of Grenada & Tobago* 6–7.

29. Alexander Hamilton to Elizabeth Schuyler, 1780, in Allan McLane Hamilton, *The Intimate Life of Alexander Hamilton* 7; *The Papers of Alexander Hamilton* 2:350.

30. Alexander Hamilton to James Hamilton, June 22, 1785, in *Daily National Intelligencer*, February 17, 1859, p3 c3; autograph fragment, New York Public Library; *The Papers of Alexander Hamilton* 3:617–618.

31. *St. Vincent Deed Book, 1786–1787* 489–496.

32. *St. Vincent Deed Book, 1790* 135–138.

33. Alexander Hamilton to William Seton, August 17, 1792, in *The Papers of Alexander Hamilton* 12:222–223.

34. James Hamilton to Alexander Hamilton, June 12, 1793, in *The Papers of Alexander Hamilton* 14:536–537.

35. Alexander Hamilton to Robert Troup, July 25, 1795, in *The Papers of Alexander Hamilton* 18:503–504.

36. *The Law Practice of Alexander Hamilton* 5:381, 459, 548, 557, 564; Newton, *Alexander Hamilton: The Formative Years* 529 note 131.

37. Alexander Hamilton to William Hamilton, May 2, 1797, in *The Papers of Alexander Hamilton* 21:79.

38. Alexander Hamilton, addressed to William Jackson but sent to James McHenry, August 26, 1800, in *The Papers of Alexander Hamilton* 25:89.

39. John C. Hamilton, *The Life of Alexander Hamilton* 1:2; Atherton, *The Conqueror* 544.

New James Lytton Discoveries, 1743–1757

James Lytton is well known to any student of Alexander Hamilton. James Lytton married Alexander Hamilton's aunt Anne Faucett. He supported Hamilton's mother when she returned to St. Croix in 1765 and then supported young Alexander and James Jr. when their mother died. Hamilton's mother was buried in the Lytton family graveyard.

While a complete biography of James Lytton's life would be a welcome addition to the Hamilton literature, such an essay would include much that is already known and therefore is not fit for this volume. So instead, the focus here will be on some interesting and important new James Lytton discoveries.

James Lytton Switches from Cotton to Sugar

On May 24, 1738, James Lytton purchased the 150-acre cotton plantation at No. 9 Company's Quarter.[1]

For the first several years, it appears that James Lytton produced only cotton on his plantation. By 1743, he was also producing sugar.[2] According to the matrikels, Lytton's plantation switched officially from cotton to sugar in 1747.[3]

This shift from cotton to sugar was quite common. While sugar plantations were more profitable than cotton, they also required more capital because sugar plantations were more expensive to purchase, taxes were higher, more time was needed for the produce to grow, more slaves were needed to plant and harvest, a costly mill and boiling house needed to be built, and expensive equipment purchased. As one resident explained, "Land purchased for a sugar plantation costs 500 rigsdalers, whereas a large piece of land for cotton cultivation, on the other hand, costs only 150 rigsdalers. . . . Considerable profit can be made from a cotton plantation, with few expenses. Indeed, at times such a plantation produces more than a sugar plantation. A man does not run nearly the risk with illness among his slaves as he does operating a sugar factory inasmuch as night work is not at all necessary on a cotton plantation. Yes, a sugar works is of greater importance and value when well managed and free of unfortunate, unforeseen circumstances. Nevertheless, there are citizens on St. Croix who own considerable capital but who have nothing more than a cotton plantation, with which they are contented. With two slaves, such a man can produce 2000 to 3000 pounds of cotton per year, making a considerable sum of money when the price per pound is eight or nine stivers. There are those citizens on the island who make 700, 800 to 1000 pounds of cotton and are satisfied with it and, in fact, do not fret about not owning a sugar plantation."[4] Accordingly, many planters started by producing cotton, which yielded crops quickly at relatively low cost, and would then switch to sugar as they accumulated capital.

James Lytton Hires a Schoolteacher

In 1744, James Lytton hired a white man, one Richard Yates, to come live and "work on [his] plantation" and to "also hold school." Along came Yates's wife, their slaves, and probably any children they may have had.[5] This Richard Yates must have taught the Lytton children as well as the Evans children, whose parents recently passed away with James Lytton becoming their guardian.[6] Perhaps other children from the area also attended this "school."

Yates passed away in 1746. His widow apparently stayed with the Lyttons because she lived two more years in Company's Quarter. After disappearing from the matrikels, Yates's widow again lived with the Lyttons in 1752. Perhaps she had been with the Lyttons the whole time or perhaps she left and then returned. After 1752, she is no longer listed as living with the Lyttons.[7]

There is no record of whether Yates had been preceded by another teacher or was replaced after his death and if so by whom.

James Lytton Lives a Year in "North America"

In early 1749,[8] James Lytton traveled to "North America," i.e., the mainland, where he, according to St. Croix's matrikel, "this year and for more has been a resident." Lytton took four of his slaves with him.[9] Lytton and the four slaves returned to St. Croix in early 1750.[10]

In October and November 1749, a James Lytton in Philadelphia advertised in *The Pennsylvania Gazette*, "To be sold by James Lytton, Next door to the Royal Oak, in Lombard-street, near the New-market, Exceeding good melasses, by the single cask, or larger quantity, Muscovado sugar, by the cask, barrel, or smaller quantity, and one cask of very good West-India rum."[11] As later evidence connects James Lytton to Philadelphia,[12] this clearly was the James Lytton from St. Croix. It is not known whether Anne Lytton or any of their children traveled with him to North America.

To be fold by
JAMES LYTTON,
Nxxt door to the Royal Oak, in Lombard-ftreet, near the New-market,

EXceeding good melaffes, by the fingle cafk, or larger quantity, Mufcovado fugar, by the cafk, barrel, or fmaller quantity, and one cafk of very good Weft-India rum.

The Pennsylvania Gazette, October 19, 1749.

The Lyttons at this time had children between the ages of two and about nineteen.[13] In addition, the Evans children were between perhaps eleven and twenty-two years old,[14] and James Lytton was their guardian, except for the oldest who was already an adult and married.[15] Perhaps James Lytton took some of these children with him to Philadelphia and enrolled them in school there, as it was common practice for the wealthier planters to send their children to England, Scotland, or North America for an education.

One of the more interesting implications of this trip to the Hamilton story is that James and perhaps Anne Lytton were away from St. Croix when Rachel was arrested and sat in prison for many months for "fornication." Had James Lytton been on St. Croix to pay legal expenses and wield his influence, perhaps Rachel would have suffered less at the hands of John Michael Lavien and the legal system.

James Lytton Hires An Overseer

In addition to his ownership of the 150-acre plantation at No. 9 Company's Quarter, which he purchased in 1738,[16] James Lytton acquired another

150 acres in Queen's Quarter in 1752.[17] He had come to St. Croix with just nine slaves in 1738 but by the end of 1752 he owned forty-one.[18] Also by this time, as seen in his trip to Philadelphia, James Lytton was acting in some respects as a merchant. And with a large family of his own and the Evans children as well, James Lytton must have been a very busy man.

At some point, James Lytton hired a Mr. Frissard to work as an overseer. The only record found regarding this person is Dr. Lawrence Grundel's account with "Mr. Frissard Overseer at Mr. Lyttons" with entries from September to December 1753.[19] This Mr. Frissard has not been found in any other record. He is not included in the matrikels, whose purpose at this time was merely to collect tax information regarding land and slave ownership, which means Frissard owned neither. Nor is he found in the Danish West India Company's account books.

Accordingly, it is not known when James Lytton hired this man. One would assume that Lytton had hired him or another individual to oversee his estate prior to his departure to North America in early 1749. It is also not known how long this man stayed in Lytton's employ. When St. Croix's matrikels started counting whites in 1755, Lytton employed one white servant,[20] who could have been an overseer, perhaps Mr. Frissard, or possibly it was just a house servant or a field hand.

So while it is clear that Lytton employed an overseer for more than just the four months of September to December 1753 and it makes sense that one worked for him when he was in North America in 1749–1750, it is impossible to know exactly how long he employed one, whether it was always Mr. Frissard or different people over the course of the years, and what tasks they performed.

James Lytton: Top Planter

Having a good piece of land and hiring good overseers certainly helped, but James Lytton was not some absentee owner. Observers specifically attributed Lytton's success to his own hard work. One resident, Reimert Haagensen, in 1757 singled out James Lytton as one of "the best planters on the island" and explained that Lytton did "the work of four slaves" and "can make 40 to 50 oxheads" of sugar "with 12 to 13 slaves," whereas many others required double the number of slaves or more to produce the same quantity.[21]

Notes

1. *St. Croix Matrikel 1738* Mandtalsliste #61; ibid. Forteignelse #82; ibid. *1739* #9; *1740* #9; ibid. *1741-42*, folio 8; Missive from St. Thomas, May 15, 1739, in Vestindisk-Guineisk Kompagni, *Breve og Dokumenter fra Vestindien 1739*; Vestindisk-Guineisk Kompagni, *Breve og Dokumenter fra Vestindien 1742–1743* image 101a; Vestindisk-Guineisk Kompagni, *Hovedbog paa St. Croix 1741* 122; *Christiansted Registrerings og Vurderingsprotokoller for Borgere og Plantere 1773–1777* image 187b #1651; *Christiansted Skiftebrevsprotokoller for Borgere og Plantere* 32:333v #1651.

2. Vestindisk-Guineisk Kompagni, *Hovedbog paa St. Croix 1743* 129.

3. *St. Croix Matrikel 1746* 9; ibid. *1747* 10.

4. Haagensen, *Description of the Island of St. Croix in America in the West Indies* 37, 40.

5. *St. Croix Matrikel 1744* 21; ibid. *1745* 26. For Richard Yates being married, see ibid. *1746* 13. Yates can also be found in the island's account books for the first time in 1744 (Vestindisk-Guineisk Kompagni, *Hovedbog paa St. Croix 1744* 155).

6. *Christiansted Skiftebrevsprotokoller for Borgere og Plantere* 2:88r–v, 3:260v–262r, 271r; Ramsing, *Alexander Hamilton's Birth and Parentage* 2–3.

7. *St. Croix Matrikel 1746* 13; ibid. *1747* 14; ibid. *1752* 13.

8. James Lytton was on St. Croix throughout 1748 (Vestindisk-Guineisk Kompagni, *Hovedbog paa St. Croix 1748* 182) and his last transaction with the Danish West India Company before leaving the island was on January 17, 1749 (Vestindisk-Guineisk Kompagni, *Hovedbog paa St. Croix 1749* 168).

9. *St. Croix Matrikel 1749* 10. James Lytton had 24 slaves [16 capable] on St. Croix in 1748 (ibid. *1748* 8), then 20 [10 capable] in 1749 (ibid. *1749* 10), but was back up to 24 [16 capable] in 1750 (ibid. *1750* 15). Normally one would attribute these changes to deaths, sales, purchases, and births, but they match perfectly with Lytton's taking four slaves with him to North America.

10. James Lytton had no transactions with the company on St. Croix between January 17, 1749, (Vestindisk-Guineisk Kompagni, *Hovedbog paa St. Croix 1749* 168) and February 28, 1750 (Vestindisk-Guineisk Kompagni, *Hovedbog paa St. Croix 1750* 170).

11. *The Pennsylvania Gazette*, 1749 10 19 p3 c1, 1749 10 26 p5 c1, 1749 11 09 p5 c3.

12. Later evidence shows James Lytton was connected to Philadelphia: Anne Lytton was buried in Philadelphia in 1765 (*The Inscriptions in St. Peter's Church Yard, Philadelphia* 162) and James Lytton's grandson John Hallwood went to school in Philadelphia (*University of Pennsylvania Biographical Catalogue of the Matriculates of the College* xxxiii). Also, Anne Lytton Venton lived in Philadelphia from about 1776 to 1779 (*Christiansted Skiftebrevsprotokoller for Borgere og Plantere* 33:656v, 667r; *The Papers of Alexander Hamilton* 2:4–5; Ramsing, *Alexander Hamilton's Birth and Parentage* 33; Newton, *Alexander Hamilton: The Formative Years* 525 note 59).

13. *Caribbeana* 3:219, 221; *Danske Folkekirke, St. Croix, Kirkebog 1740–1753* page 30 and transcript 35b–36a; ibid. page 32 and transcript 38b; ibid. page 34 and transcript 41b; ibid. page 36 and transcript 45a.

14. The age of one of the Evans children has not been determined. The ones that have

been ascertained were in 1749 between the ages of about thirteen and twenty-two (*Christiansted Skiftebrevsprotokoller for Borgere og Plantere* 3:261r; *Caribbeana* 3:220). The other child, listed last in Edward Evans's will, must have been under thirteen in 1749, but she married in 1751 (*Christiansted Panteprotokoller 1749–1752* 139r–v, 146v–147r), so she must have been about eleven or perhaps twelve years old in 1749.

15. *Danske Folkekirke, St. Croix, Kirkebog 1740–1753* pages 25–26 and transcript 31a.
16. See page 135.
17. *St. Croix Matrikel 1752* 17.
18. *St. Croix Matrikel 1752* 10.
19. *Christiansted Skiftesager på Enkeltpersoner* 38.61.233 image 438.
20. *St. Croix Matrikel 1755* 41.
21. Haagensen, *Beskrivelse over Eylandet St. Croix i America i Vest-Indien* 34; Haagensen, *Description of the Island of St. Croix in America in the West Indies* 30.

Naming the Grange Plantation of St. Croix

Reading biographies of Alexander Hamilton, one learns that Hamilton's uncle and aunt, James and Anne Lytton, built "a substantial estate" on St. Croix "called the Grange," that the wedding of Rachel Faucett and John Michael Lavien "took place at the Grange," that the Lyttons "sold the Grange," and that Hamilton's mother, Rachel Faucett, "was laid to rest" in February 1768 in "a graveside ceremony at the Grange."[1]

Ignoring the fact that the location of the wedding of Rachel Faucett and John Lavien is not known, the question remains as to when James and Anne Lytton's estate was given the name of Grange. Was it known as the Grange when the Lyttons lived there? Was it known by that name when Rachel Faucett, Alexander Hamilton's mother, was buried there? Or was it given this name sometime later?

No. 9 Company's Quarter

For the first sixty-plus years that St. Croix's matrikels were compiled, the plantations were listed by quarter and number, although in a few volumes, especially the earliest, no numbers were included. With just a few exceptions, the names of the plantations, if they had any, were not given. It was not until 1803 that the matrikels included the names of the various plantations.

Thus, in the matrikels up until 1803, James Lytton's estate appears merely as No. 9 Company's Quarter.

So when was No. 9 Company's Quarter named the Grange? Was it in 1803? Or was it at some earlier date?

Records of James Lytton's Plantation

An extensive search through St. Croix's records has yielded no mention of the Grange during James Lytton's ownership of No. 9 Company's Quarter.

When James Lytton sold the plantation in December 1764 to John Denn, several months before the Hamiltons arrived on St. Croix, the "indenture" between them described the plantation's boundaries but did not call the estate the Grange.[2]

Of course, it is possible that the Lytton plantation was known as the Grange, officially or unofficially, even though the name has not been found in any record of the plantation during Lytton's ownership of it. But the timing of the first mention of the Grange suggests otherwise.

Earliest Records of "the Plantation Grange"

In June 1766, just eighteen months after James Lytton sold No. 9 Company's Quarter to John Denn, the estate appears in a mortgage record as "the Plantation Grange."[3] This is the earliest known record of the plantation being called the Grange.

Six months later, in December 1766, the estate in a registration and appraisement again appears as "Plantation Grange."[4]

Thus, after never appearing in the records as the Grange during Lytton's ownership of No. 9 Company's Quarter, it is called the "Plantation Grange" just eighteen months after Lytton sold it and again just six months after that. This probably was no coincidence. It is likely that it was John Denn who gave the plantation the name of Grange after he purchased it in December 1764.

Inconsistent Naming in Subsequent Records

In the records going forward, this plantation is sometimes referred to as the Grange, other times as No. 9 Company's Quarter, and other times by the name of the owner.

For example, in February 1767, when the plantation was put up for auction, it was repeatedly referred to as "John Denn's Plantation" but never as the Grange.[5]

Likewise, in February 1768, when "Rachael Levine," i.e., Alexander Hamilton's mother Rachel Faucett, was buried in the Lytton family graveyard, the property was described in the church burial record as "Mr. Tuite's Plantation," for the man who owned it at the time, without calling it the Grange.[6]

In contrast, in August 1769, when James Lytton was buried in the family plot, the church burial record described the location as "Mr. Tuite's Grange Plantation."[7]

The above are just a few examples. There are many more instances from the years 1767 and onwards in which this plantation is sometimes referred to as the Grange, other times as No. 9 Company's Quarter, and other times by the name of the owner.

When Did the Grange Plantation Acquire Its Name?

The inconsistency of the records regarding the name of this plantation and plantations in general makes it impossible to determine precisely when this estate first received the name of "Grange." But there is sufficient evidence to draw a reasonable conclusion.

The lack of any records calling it the Grange during Lytton's ownership of the property and the multiplicity of records of it with that name shortly after James Lytton's sale of it to John Denn suggests that John Denn named the estate the Grange after he bought it from James Lytton in December 1764. It is possible, however, though unlikely, that the plantation was known as the Grange during Lytton's ownership of it, but that this name was never recorded due to the inconsistency of record keeping.

Without any evidence that the plantation was known as the Grange while owned by the Lyttons, it would be incorrect to state that James Lytton built "a substantial estate" on St. Croix "called the Grange," that the wedding of Rachel Faucett and John Lavien "took place at the Grange," or that Lytton "sold the Grange," without clarifying that it probably was not known by that name during any of those events.

On the other hand, this plantation was definitely called the Grange by June 1766. Thus, it certainly was known as the Grange when young Alexander Hamilton buried his mother Rachel Faucett in the Lytton family graveyard at No. 9 Company's Quarter.

Hamilton Grange in Harlem, New York

Three decades later, when Alexander Hamilton built his home in Harlem, he named it the Grange, as his son later wrote, "in commemoration of his family residence in Ayrshire [Scotland]."[8] Undoubtedly, Alexander Hamilton had another reason to call it the Grange: as a recollection of the final resting place of his beloved mother.

Hamilton Grange thus stands not just as a monument to the "most remarkable Founding Father"[9] and as a testament to Alexander Hamilton's prestigious Scottish ancestry, but also as a tribute to his mother, to whom "he was indebted for his genius" and who he "recollected . . . with inexpressible fondness, and often spoke of . . . as a woman of superior intellect, highly cultivated, of elevated and generous sentiments, and of unusual elegance of person and manner."[10]

Notes

1. Chernow, *Alexander Hamilton* 10, 11, 22, and 25.
2. *Christiansted Panteprotokoller 1765–1767* 71v–72v.
3. *Christiansted Panteprotokoller 1765–1767* 284v.
4. *Christiansted Registrerings og Vurderingsprotokoller for Borgere og Plantere 1761–68* 269r–272r.
5. *Christiansted Auktionsprotokol 1767* 16r–v, 20v–21r, 22r–v.
6. *St. John's Anglican Church, Christiansted, St. Croix, Burial Registry 1761–1787* page 10.
7. *St. John's Anglican Church, Christiansted, St. Croix, Burial Registry 1761–1787* page 12.
8. John C. Hamilton, *History of the Republic* 7:487.
9. Newton, *Alexander Hamilton: The Formative Years* 1 and 505.
10. John C. Hamilton, *The Life of Alexander Hamilton* 1:2–3; John C. Hamilton, *History of the Republic* 1:42.

Contemporary Descriptions of the Grange Plantation

D espite the repeated appearance of No. 9 Company's Quarter, the Grange Plantation, in the Hamilton story, few biographers give any description of the plantation and those who do describe how it looked at the time they wrote or speculate about how it must have looked in the eighteenth century. The reason for this omission was not necessarily a lack of interest but rather a lack of any known contemporary descriptions.[1]

In fact, three contemporary descriptions of No. 9 Company's Quarter, the Grange Plantation, have been found.

December 1764 Description of No. 9 Company's Quarter

A description of No. 9 Company's Quarter was included in the "indenture" or sales contract between James Lytton and John Denn in December 1764.[2]

The "indenture" states that the plantation featured the following buildings and equipment:

- "A dwelling house & offices"
- "A wind mill"
- A "boyling house"
- A "curing house"
- A "stillhouse"
- "Stills"
- "Coppers"
- "All or every their appurtenances [accessories]"

The "indenture" also mentions "the burying place of the said Lytton's family" as an exception to the sale, which the Lyttons were "at all times to have free ingress and egress to & fro."

It is noteworthy that in addition to the mill, boiling house, and curing house, the plantation also had a stillhouse and stills. This shows that James Lytton produced rum in addition to sugar.

In addition to the land, buildings, and equipment, the sale of the plantation included:

- Sixteen "men" slaves
- One "manboy" slave
- Nine "women" slaves
- Four "children" slaves
- "Two horses"
- "Five cows"
- "Two mules"
- "Five draft cattle"
- "Sixteen sheep"

James Lytton sold all this to John Denn for "the sum of sixty thousand pieces of eight," about ninety-six hundred pounds sterling, equivalent to perhaps $25 million in current money.[3] It should also be noted that only the thirty plantation slaves noted in the indenture were sold to Denn. James Lytton also owned house slaves, over whom he retained ownership.[4]

Although this accurately describes James Lytton's No. 9 Company's Quarter plantation when he sold it in December 1764, it is a bit light on details. There is no information about the layout of the plantation, the size of the dwelling house, the number or sizes of the offices, or the sizes of the windmill, boiling house, curing house, still house, stills, or coppers.

June 1766 Description of "the Plantation Grange"

In June 1766, an "inventory and appraisement" of "the Plantation Grange" was conducted. The plantation was the same as before and the buildings little changed, but the description is more detailed.[5]

This description notes that the plantation was laid out as follows:

- 110 acres of sugar cane
- 10 acres of "yams, potatoes, &c."

- 30 acres of "pasturage ranges about the works, negro houses, house, garden, &c."

One assumes that the distribution of land under John Denn was the same as it had been under James Lytton just eighteen months earlier.

According to this "inventory and appraisement," the "Plantation Grange" had the following buildings and equipment:

- "A boyling house with 4 coppers & a furnace with all utensils"
- "A curing house for 30 hogsheads"
- "A still house with liquor casks and a good cellar underneath with 5 iron bound butts to contain about 1400 gallons"
- "2 stills one of 200 gallons & 1 ditto 120 gallons new"
- "A windmill compleat, wooden"
- "Materials for a cattle mill"
- "A good lofted dwelling house"
- "Out houses"
- "Negro houses"

One notices that the 120-gallon still is listed as "new" and presumably this was added by John Denn after he purchased the estate from James Lytton in December 1764. One also notes the "materials for a cattle mill." John Denn evidently was building a cattle mill to complement the windmill that James Lytton had built there years earlier. The only other notable difference is that "negroe houses" appear in the June 1766 list but not in the 1764 description. But James Lytton had slaves working his plantation in 1764 and therefore must have had "negroe houses" even though they did not appear in the description of the estate. Additionally, the "dwelling house" of December 1764 is described in June 1766 as a "good lofted dwelling house." Clearly, it was the same house, but this provides a more detailed description than before.

According to this inventory, John Denn owned sixty-one slaves. Based on the names in this list and the previous one, many of these slaves were the same as those James Lytton sold to him in December 1764.

Also listed in the inventory of John Denn's estate are:

- "2 mules"

- "2 horses"
- "2 mares"
- "9 bulls"
- "1 cow"
- "1 bull calf & yearling"

Many of these animals were probably the same as those James Lytton sold Denn just eighteen months earlier.

The estate at this time was appraised at 67,670 pieces of eight, an increase of 7,670 pesos or about thirteen percent, largely due to the additional thirty-one slaves.

Thus, this June 1766 "inventory and appraisement" of "the Plantation Grange" describes, for the most part, the plantation as it existed under James Lytton's ownership, but with some additional details.

December 1766 Description of the "Plantation Grange"

John Denn passed away in December 1766 and his estate was appraised by the probate court. This provides yet another description of the "Plantation Grange," the third in just two years. This description, for the most part, is the same as the previous two, but does provide some additional information.[6]

The plantation is again described as having:

- "110 acres cane"
- "10 acres in yams & potatoes"
- "30 acres in pasture ranges"

The buildings and equipment are listed as:

- "A boiling house with 4 coppers & a furnace with utensils"
- "Curing house for 30 hogsheads"
- "Still house with a cellar and 5 iron bound butts"
- "2 stills & worms, one of 200 gallons & one of 120 gallons"
- "A wooden wind mill complete"
- "A new cattle mill"
- "A large lofted dwelling house"

- "Out houses"
- "Negroe houses"

This description is nearly identical to that of June 1766 and little changed from December 1764. One notices that the cattle mill that had been under construction six months earlier was now complete. The residence described in December 1764 as a "dwelling house" and in June 1766 as "a good lofted dwelling house" is now called "a large lofted dwelling house."

There were now seventy-seven slaves, an increase of sixteen from the previous inventory.

As for animals, there were now:

- "2 mules"
- "2 horses"
- "1 mare"
- "9 bulls"
- "1 cow"
- "1 calf"
- "One yearling"

Again, this is little changed from the previous inventories.

There are some other items listed here that were not listed six months earlier. The most significant was "110 acres in cains, we value now at ps 66.5.2 pr acre" coming to a total value of 7,333 pieces of eight. There also were "20 hogsheads of rum" and "10 hogsheads of sugar" along with some potatoes and other crops. Another addition was "one cart & one wagon," but one assumes that these existed beforehand and were included in December 1764's "all or every their appurtenances." With these additions, the estate was appraised at 79,743 pieces of eight, nearly 20,000 pesos more than James Lytton had sold it for two years earlier, the increase largely accounted for by the additional slaves and sugar cane in the field.

Alexander Hamilton's Memory of the Grange Plantation

When James Lytton purchased No. 9 Company's Quarter in 1738, the property was uncultivated and undeveloped. Over the next twenty-six years,

Lytton cleared and planted 110 acres of sugar, built a "good" and "large lofted dwelling house," "negroe houses," "out houses," "a boiling house with 4 coppers & a furnace with all utensils," "a curing house for 30 hogsheads," a "still house with liquor casks and a good cellar underneath with 5 iron bound butts to contain about 1400 gallons," at least one still of 200 gallons, and "a wooden wind mill." He sold the plantation along with thirty of his slaves for a hefty sum, sixty thousand rigsdalers, in December 1764, a few months before the Hamiltons arrived on St. Croix. Although Alexander Hamilton would not have stayed in this house, he buried his mother there in "the burying place of the said Lytton's family" and probably attended the funeral of others there, including his uncle James Lytton in August 1769.

As the site of his mother's grave, Alexander Hamilton must have frequently visited "the burying place of the said Lytton's family" at the Grange Plantation prior to leaving St. Croix in 1772. The windmill, dwelling house, negro houses, boiling house, curing house, still house, other buildings, and fields of sugar cane surely formed a vivid impression on Alexander Hamilton's mind. Just as Hamilton "recollected" his mother "with inexpressible fondness,"[7] he surely carried a vision of her burial site and the surrounding landscape with him to mainland North America.

Notes

1. Actually, H. U. Ramsing must have seen at least one of the contemporary descriptions shared here because he cited the same record in which it appears (Ramsing, "Alexander Hamilton og hans Mødrene Slaegt" 243 note 75; Ramsing, *Alexander Hamilton's Birth and Parentage* 58 note 75). But Ramsing did not describe the Lytton plantation in his essay and the Hamilton biographers who relied upon his work did not check the original sources and therefore did not know about this description.
2. *Christiansted Panteprotokoller 1765–1767* 71v–72v.
3. There are numerous ways to estimate the present value of this sum. In pure commodity inflation or purchasing power terms, sixty thousand pieces of eight or about ninety-six hundred pounds sterling would be equal to about $1.7 million today. In income or labor earnings terms, it would be about $25 million. ("Five Ways to Compute the Relative Value of a UK Pound Amount, 1270 to Present.") As a 150-acre productive plantation with a mansion, other buildings, slaves, etc., $1.7 million definitely underestimates the value of the estate. Looking at how much such a business along with land and buildings would be worth today, $25 million may be close to the mark.
4. The 1763 matrikel shows that James Lytton owned 56 slaves (*St. Croix Matrikel 1763*

18) and in 1764 after selling his plantation Lytton had 21 slaves with him in Christiansted (*St. Croix Matrikel 1764* 16).

5. *Christiansted Panteprotokoller 1765–1767* 284v–285v.
6. *Christiansted Registrerings og Vurderingsprotokoller for Borgere og Plantere 1761–68* 270r–271v.
7. John C. Hamilton, *The Life of Alexander Hamilton* 1:2.

Population Growth and Demographics
of Eighteenth Century St. Croix

Because St. Croix played such a central role in Hamilton's biography, a better comprehension of life on the island is necessary to more fully understand Hamilton's youth and origins. While there are a number of good books about eighteenth century St. Croix and even some contemporary accounts,[1] a more objective look at the population trends and demographics of the colony from its earliest days through the end of Hamilton's stay on the island and beyond can provide additional insights into the nature of life on St. Croix and the changes it saw during the eighteenth century.

Unfortunately, St. Croix's census and tax lists were inconsistently maintained in both their timing and contents, especially in the early years of Danish rule over the island. In fact, although historians refer to these volumes generically as matrikels or censuses, they are for the most part tax lists and therefore track what was being taxed, i.e., land and slave ownership. Only later did the authorities start to include counts of white people and later still of free blacks. On top of these inconsistencies, a number of volumes have been lost or have suffered heavy damage.

Despite the gaps and inconsistencies, the so-called matrikels provide a wealth of objective information regarding St. Croix's development during the eighteenth century.

1733–1742

In 1733, Denmark purchased St. Croix from France for 750,000 livres, equal to 141,926 rigsdalers and 52 styvers, or about £33,000 sterling.[2] Except for "a few English settlers" who expressed a desire to stay, the island at this time was virtually uninhabited.[3]

Largely undeveloped when they purchased the island, the Danish government and Danish West India Company encouraged settlement by selling land cheaply. Sugar plantations were initially sold for just a thousand rigsdalers, about £160 sterling, and cotton plantations for half that amount. Each purchaser also received a seven-year exemption from the land tax, a benefit of forty rigsdalers per year for sugar plantations and half that for cotton plantations. To further entice settlement, the Danish authorities in 1736 cut the price of plantations by up to fifty percent and offered a six-year payment plan, but at the same time reduced the land-tax exemption from seven years to three. They also set the duty on the importation of slaves to St. Croix at the low rate of four rigsdalers per head, half of what was charged to import slaves to the more established Danish island of St. Thomas.[4]

The earliest matrikels give counts of slaves but not of whites. However, some of these matrikels provide the number of "inhabitants and their families," which are counts not of total individuals but of families. In the earliest matrikel that has been found, and possibly the first to be recorded, dated March 28, 1736, and titled "Lands Liste," 42 families and 137 slaves lived on St. Croix. Just over a year later, on May 21, 1737, the number of white families had nearly doubled to 75 while the number of slaves more than doubled to 284. Another year later, on May 12, 1738, the number of families had risen only slightly to 85 but the number of slaves had nearly doubled again to 558. By May 18, 1742, there were 125 families on St. Croix and 1,749 slaves. Thus, between March 1736 and May 1742, a period of just six years, the number of white families tripled while the number of slaves increased thirteenfold.

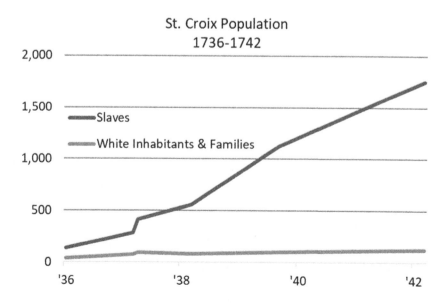

1742–1757

After 1742, the matrikels stop providing counts of white families. In theory, one could go through the matrikels and count up the number of families listed, but this would require significant effort because these are lists of properties and a person could own more than one property.

For the next fifteen years, only the number of slaves was tabulated. The island saw a steady increase in the number of slaves, to the tune of just over twelve percent per annum. Although this does not sound very large, it resulted in a near sextupling over the fifteen year period, from 1,749 slaves in May 1742 to 9,956 in April 1757.

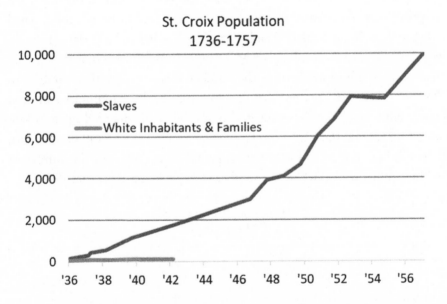

The matrikels starting in 1746 also begin to differentiate between slaves living on the plantations and those living in cities, first Christiansted and later Frederiksted as well. While the number of slaves on the plantations vastly outnumbered those in the cities and always would during the eighteenth century, St. Croix saw significant urbanization as successful planters built town houses while the merchants, who imported foodstuffs and other goods for the planters while exporting their cotton, sugar, and rum, developed the cities' ports. As a result, although the number of slaves living on plantations more than tripled from 2,940 in 1746 to 9,091 in 1757, the number living in cities rose eighteenfold from 47 to 865. As result, the percentage of St. Croix's slaves living in cities rose from 1.6 percent in 1746 to 8.7 percent in 1757 and in fact had been as high as 12.6 percent in 1754.

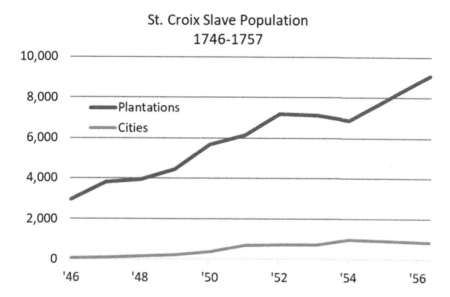

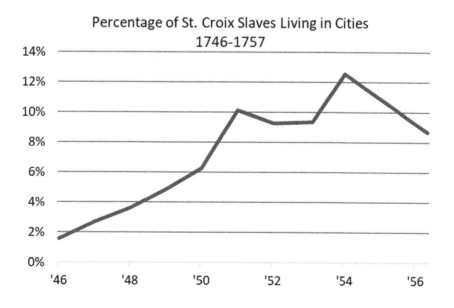

1757–1773

Starting in 1757, most matrikels included counts of whites in addition to slaves. The number of whites over the next sixteen years rose 70 percent from 1,260 in 1757 to 2,145 in January 1773, but the number of slaves increased an even larger 123 percent from 9,956 to 22,251. As a result, the white proportion of the island's population fell from 11.2 percent to 8.7 percent.

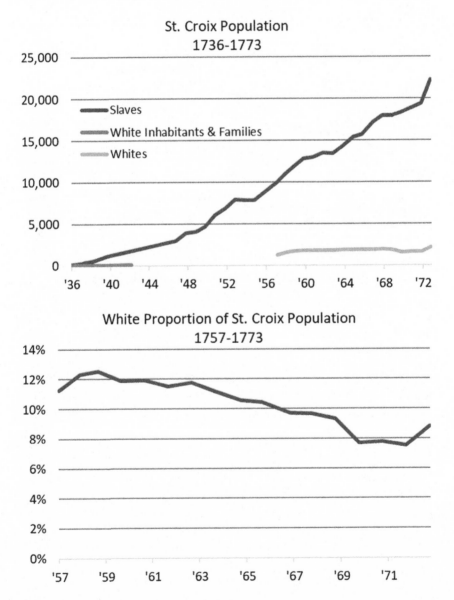

During this period of 1757 to 1773, the number of slaves on the plantations and in the cities increased at approximately the same rates, albeit with great inconsistency. Much of this volatility, however, was due to variability in reporting rather than actual changes in residence. People with homes both in town and on the plantations could have some or all of their slaves reported in either location, regardless where the slave actually lived and worked.

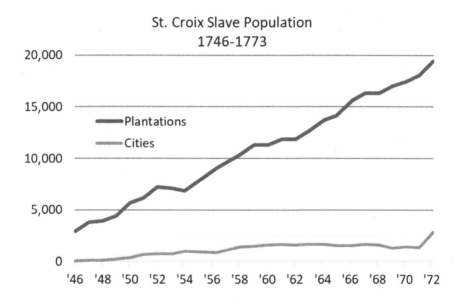

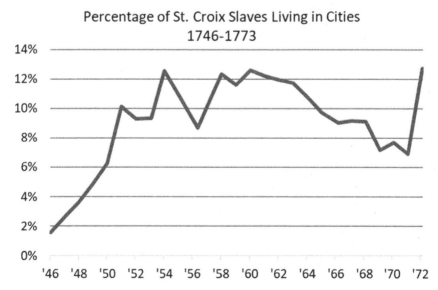

The residence of whites provides a better look at the continued urbaniza-tion of St. Croix. While the number of whites living on plantations stayed in a relatively narrow range of 733 to 927 and increased just 7.4 percent over the sixteen-year period, the number living in the cities tripled from 399 to 1,220. As a result, the proportion of whites living in cities rose from 31.7 per-cent of the population in April 1757 to 56.9 percent in January 1773.

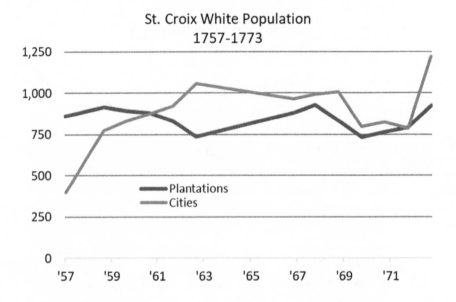

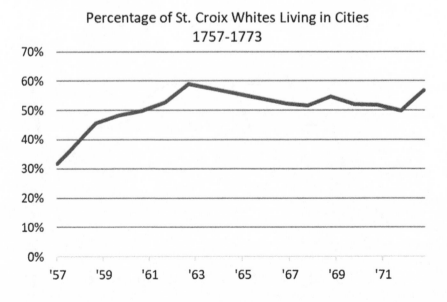

1773–1799

Starting around 1773, the growth of St. Croix's population, both white and black, slowed considerably in one case and stopped entirely in the other. The matrikels also start reporting the number of free blacks in 1773 and their numbers increase considerably throughout the survey period and beyond.

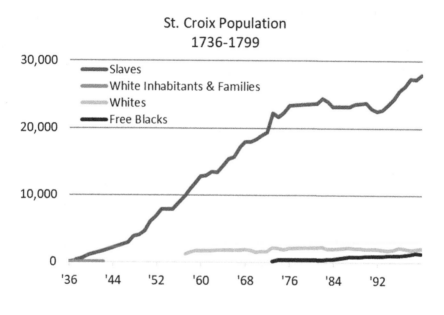

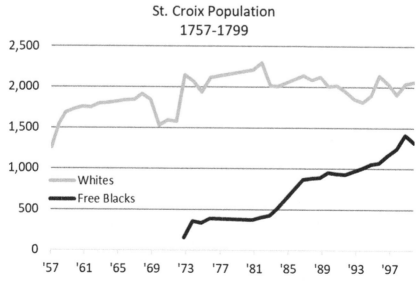

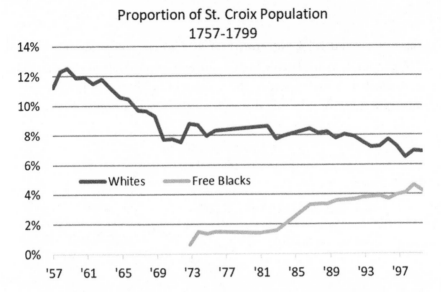

The urbanization of St. Croix, especially of the white population but also to a lesser degree of slaves, continued during this period, albeit at a slower pace. Whites living in the cities rose from 56.9 percent in January 1773 to 66.0 percent in December 1799 while the proportion of slaves in the cities rose from 12.7 percent to 14.3 percent. Adding in the free blacks, 18.2 percent of all St. Croix's blacks lived in the cities.

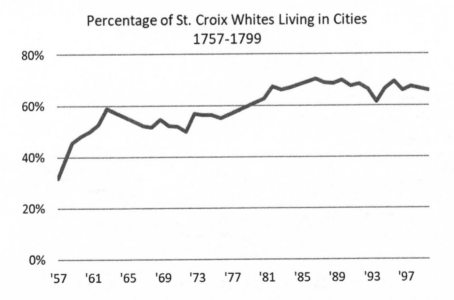

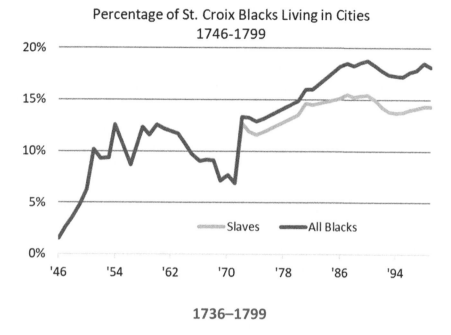

1736–1799

Looking at the population growth and demographics of St. Croix from 1736 to 1799 as a whole, a few key features and trends become apparent.

The most obvious and significant trend on eighteenth-century St. Croix was the overall growth of the population. The white population grew steadily from the earliest records until about 1773 and then leveled off for the remainder of the century. In contrast, the black population continued to grow. As a result, an island that was basically uninhabited in 1733 supported more than ten thousand people within less than twenty-five years and over twenty-five thousand by the outbreak of the American Revolution.

Meanwhile, the key demographic feature of eighteenth century St. Croix was the ratio of black slaves to whites. From the very earliest records, there were more black slaves on St. Croix than white people. And this ratio increased over time, from perhaps two black slaves for each white in 1736 to a ratio of about eight-to-one in the 1750s and up to about sixteen-to-one in the 1790s.

Another demographic change that took place on St. Croix during this period was the urbanization of the island, especially of the white population. The accumulated wealth of the planters enabled many of them to leave their plantations and move to the city or even overseas. Adding to the growth of the cities was the arrival of the merchants, who were increasingly necessary to export the plantation's goods and provide planters and their slaves with food-stuffs as the plantations focused on cash crops like cotton and sugar, thereby producing few or no provisions of their own. As a result, whereas only one in three whites lived in the cities in 1757, by the early 1760s there were more whites living in the cities than on the plantations and by the 1780s two-thirds of whites were in the cities. As whites moved to the cities, they brought some of their slaves with them, further boosting the urban population. Add to that the free blacks, nearly all of whom lived in the cities, and the urbanization trend gained further momentum. As a result, the percentage of blacks living in the cities rose from under two percent in 1746 to over fifteen percent by the 1780s. But this still means that more than eighty percent of all slaves lived and worked on the plantations.

These statistics confirm what was already well known: that St. Croix's economy depended entirely on the use of slavery and that the white population grew rich on the backs of these black slaves. Of course this statement is a broad generalization. It ignores the many whites who were either outright poor or struggling to make ends meet. It also ignores the growing class of free blacks, many of whom owned slaves and perhaps more than a few would have been considered middle class if they were white. But these remain exceptions to the rule. Over ninety percent of blacks were slaves and most of the whites were relatively well off, as long as there was a ready market for their sugar.

Comments regarding the data:

Many of the matrikels were compiled over a period of time, usually a couple of weeks. The dates given for those in the following table are estimated mid-points. A few matrikels give only the year, so their dates were estimated based on the dates of previous and subsequent matrikels.

The 1757 matrikel (3/31/58) suffered damage, and the breakdown by cities and quarters is difficult to read. That data is therefore not included in the tables and graphs, whereas island-wide data for that year is still included.

An error was made in the 1762 matrikel (12/10/62) on folio 14 whereby the count of slaves was reduced by 200. This has been corrected.

	St. Croix			Cities			Plantations		
	White Inhabit- ants & Families	Whites	Slaves	Free Blacks	Whites	Slaves	Free Blacks	Whites	Slaves	Free Blacks
3/28/36	42		137							
5/21/37	75		284							
6/30/37	95		415							
5/12/38	85		558							
11/2/39			1,127							
5/18/42	125		1,749							
12/31/46			2,987			47			2,940	
12/31/47			3,926			105			3,821	
12/31/48			4,085			148			3,937	
12/31/49			4,648			226			4,422	
12/31/50			6,040			377			5,663	
12/31/51			6,838			693			6,145	
12/31/52			7,929			736			7,193	
1/20/54			7,857			735			7,122	
12/31/54			7,841			985			6,856	
4/16/57		1,260	9,956		399	865		861	9,091	
3/31/58		1,548	11,031							
12/30/58		1,690	11,807		773	1,454		917	10,353	
12/14/59		1,728	12,792		834	1,484		894	11,308	
12/10/60		1,755	12,956		876	1,633		879	11,323	
12/10/61		1,753	13,489		923	1,648		830	11,841	
12/10/62		1,796	13,447		1,059	1,605		737	11,842	
12/10/63			14,360			1,682			12,678	
1/20/65			15,390			1,642			13,748	
12/20/65			15,699			1,529			14,170	
2/10/67		1,846	17,197		964	1,556		882	15,641	
1/15/68		1,918	17,967		991	1,645		927	16,322	
1/10/69		1,843	17,952		1,007	1,636		836	16,316	
1/15/70		1,529	18,332		796	1,311		733	17,021	
1/10/71		1,590	18,884		824	1,454		766	17,430	
1/10/72		1,577	19,401		786	1,338		791	18,063	
1/10/73		2,145	22,251	157	1,220	2,832	147	925	19,419	10
1/15/74		2,067	21,698	361	1,165	2,580	346	902	19,118	15
1/15/75		1,937	22,350	336	1,091	2,588	330	846	19,762	6
1/15/76		2,121	23,384	389	1,170	2,769	361	951	20,615	28
1/10/81		2,213	23,662	374	1,386	3,196	374	827	20,466	0
1/15/82		2,297	24,426	408	1,548	3,570	408	749	20,856	0
1/15/83		2,019	23,973	425	1,335	3,471	425	684	20,502	0
12/10/83		2,006	23,175	513	1,340	3,392	513	666	19,783	0
12/10/86		2,144	23,197	863	1,509	3,514	863	635	19,683	0
12/10/87		2,083	23,552	884	1,432	3,651	884	651	19,901	0
12/10/88		2,123	23,627	889	1,457	3,597	889	666	20,030	0
12/10/89		2,007	23,748	953	1,402	3,643	953	605	20,105	0
12/10/90		2,012	22,944	936	1,361	3,542	936	651	19,402	0
12/10/91		1,946	22,568	926	1,330	3,374	926	616	19,194	0
12/10/92		1,852	22,689	971	1,231	3,238	971	621	19,451	0
12/10/93		1,816	23,487	1,010	1,115	3,250	1,010	701	20,237	0
12/10/94		1,898	24,353	1,053	1,262	3,333	1,053	636	21,020	0
12/10/95		2,138	25,591	1,070	1,481	3,523	1,070	657	22,068	0
12/10/96		2,043	26,200	1,164	1,346	3,665	1,164	697	22,535	0
12/10/97		1,907	27,359	1,243	1,284	3,870	1,243	623	23,489	0
12/10/98		2,038	27,324	1,413	1,359	3,919	1,413	679	23,405	0
12/10/99		2,060	27,903	1,320	1,359	3,988	1,320	701	23,915	0

Notes

1. A couple of good eighteenth century descriptions of St. Croix are Haagensen, *Description of the Island of St. Croix in America in the West Indies*; Schmidt, *Various Remarks Collected on and about the Island of St. Croix in America*. A good and popular modern book about eighteenth-century St. Croix is Dookhan, *A History of the Virgin Islands of the United States*. An older but essential work that covers St. Croix's early years through 1754 is Westergaard, *The Danish West Indies under Company Rule*.
2. *Vestindisk-Guineisk Kompagni Direktionen Protokoller 1697–1734* 140r–144v; Westergaard, *The Danish West Indies under Company Rule* 206. The transaction in other places is recorded as "750,000 livres or 150,000 rigsdalers."
3. Westergaard, *The Danish West Indies under Company Rule* 215.
4. Westergaard, *The Danish West Indies under Company Rule* 155 and 217; Lewisohn, *Divers Information on the Romantic History of St. Croix* 24; Lewisohn, *St. Croix Under Seven Flags* 90.

The Birthdate of Edward Stevens

Alexander Hamilton's earliest extant letter was written in November 1769 to his good friend Edward Stevens. Addressed to "Dear Edward," Hamilton in this letter referred to Stevens as "Ned" and "Neddy."[1] Alexander Hamilton later called Stevens his "particular friend"[2] and explained that their "intimate acquaintance" had "begun in early youth."[3] Hamilton and Stevens remained lifelong friends and Dr. Edward Stevens even helped save Hamilton's life when he was struck with yellow fever in 1793.[4] Thus, Edward Stevens appears in nearly every Hamilton biography.

Edward Stevens's Birthdate?

Just as there has been much debate regarding Alexander Hamilton's birthdate, the same was true regarding Edward Stevens's date of birth.

According to the 1909 *Den Danske Lægestand* [*The Danish Medical Condition*] by Kristian Carøe, Edward Stevens was born on the West Indian island of Antigua on February 28, 1752.[5] Unfortunately, Carøe provided no source for this information.

In his 1939 essay on Alexander Hamilton's birth and parentage, H. U. Ramsing revealed that Edward Stevens was baptized on Antigua in November 1754. Ramsing concluded, "It is therefore an error when K. Carøe gives his birthday as Feb. 28, 1752."[6] It is of course possible for someone to be baptized two years and nine months after his birth, but it is unlikely.

Lacking any contemporary record of his birth, it was not clear whether Edward Stevens had been born on February 28, 1752, or in 1754.

Contemporary Record of Edward Stevens's Birthdate

In a collection of "letters received and drafts for letters sent" by Denmark's "West Indian medical administration," a "List of practising Physicians in the danish Westindia Islands" compiled in early 1816 gives ages, birthdates, locations of birth, places of education, and years of practice for each licensed doctor. At the top of the list is Edward Stevens. He is listed as 61 years old, born February 21, 1754, on Antigua.[7]

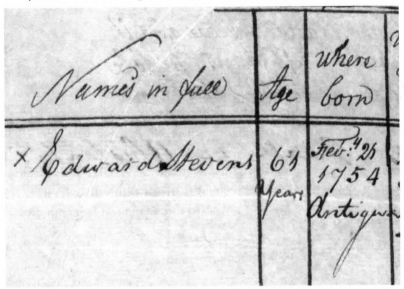

"List of practising Physicians in the Danish Westindia Islands," 1816, in *Medicinalvæsenet på de vestindiske, Indkomne breve og koncepter til udgåede skrivelser 1753–1852* image 51.

With this newly discovered contemporary record, February 21, 1754, must be considered the most reliable date of birth for Edward Stevens. This date also makes sense given Stevens's baptism in November 1754.

This new birthdate also puts Edward Stevens closer in age to Alexander Hamilton. It will be recalled that Hamilton was evidently born between February 23 and August 5, 1754.[8] This means that Edward Stevens was just days, weeks, or a few months older than Hamilton.

Notes

1. Alexander Hamilton to Edward Stevens, November 11, 1769, in *The Papers of Alexander Hamilton* 1:4–5.
2. Alexander Hamilton to John Langdon, September 6, 1794, in *The Papers of Alexander Hamilton* 17:200.
3. Alexander Hamilton to the College of Physicians, September 11, 1793, in *The Papers*

of Alexander Hamilton 15:331–332.

4. Alexander Hamilton to the College of Physicians, September 11, 1793, in *The Papers of Alexander Hamilton* 15:331–332.

5. Carøe, *Den Danske Lægestand* 1:120.

6. Ramsing, "Alexander Hamilton Og Hans Modrene Slaegt" 260; Ramsing, *Alexander Hamilton's Birth and Parentage* 41. The record of Edward Stevens's baptism has not been located by this author.

7. "List of practising Physicians in the Danish Westindia Islands," ca. 1815, in Medicinalvæsenet på de vestindiske, *Indkomne breve og koncepter til udgåede skrivelser 1753–1852* image 51.

8. See pages 7–9.

Edward Stevens: President of St. Croix

In the records of Christiansted's sheriff's archives, there sits a letter regarding the collection of taxes that was written from St. Croix's "Government House" by "Edward Stevens, Pres^t" on January 2, 1810, to St. Croix's Burgher Council.[1] A note on the back of the letter written by a member of the Burgher Council reads: "Letter of 2^d January 1810 from the President approving of our proposal relative to the Taxes."[2]

Why did St. Croix have a president in 1810? As a Danish colony, St. Croix had a governor general, not a president. So where did this president come from? And how did Edward Stevens become president?

A search through books mentioning Edward Stevens, including a short biography published in 1969,[3] yielded nothing. Apparently, no one writing about Stevens knew that he had been president of St. Croix.

The British Occupation of St. Croix

In the midst of the Napoleonic Wars, the United Kingdom and Denmark went to war with each other. In August and September 1807, Britain bombarded Denmark's capital city, killing about two hundred civilians and wounding hundreds more, as it tried to capture or destroy the Danish fleet in a battle known as the Bombardment of Copenhagen or the Second Battle of Copenhagen. When news of the war and battle reached the West Indies in December 1807, a British fleet sailed from Barbados to the Danish West Indies. St. Thomas surrendered on December 22; St. Croix on December 25.

Edward Stevens Under the British Occupation

As a former U.S. ambassador to Haiti in the early 1800s and a leading citizen of St. Croix after his return from the United States, Edward Stevens was appointed to a series of increasingly prominent positions by the British.

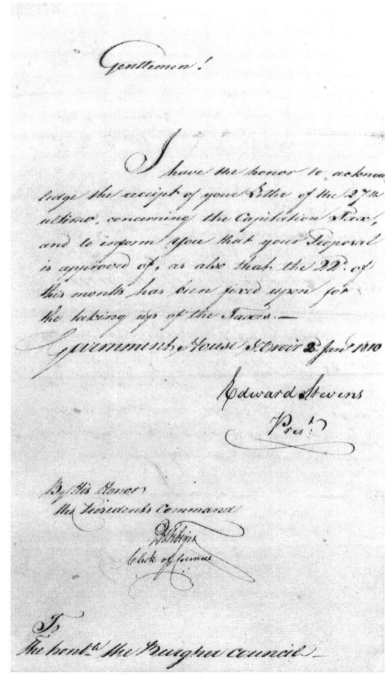

Edward Stevens to St. Croix's Burgher Council, January 2, 1810, in *Christiansted Embedsarkiver for Byfogeden 1772–1828* image 264b.

On May 26, 1808, Edward Stevens was named Second Commissioner for the Dutch and Danish Loans.[4]

On September 29, 1808, Stevens was appointed a Member of His Majesty's Honorable Council for St. Croix.[5]

On December 19, 1809, Major General George Harcourt, Lieutenant Governor and Commander in Chief of St. Croix, announced that "circumstances may occasion and require . . . temporary absences" by him. Accordingly, Harcourt proclaimed that Edward Stevens, the "Senior Member of His Majesty's Council for this Island," would serve in the "Capacity of President of this Island and it's Dependencies" during his "aforesaid eventual absence."[6]

On December 27, 1809, St. Croix's burgher council wrote to Edward Stevens concerning a proposed "capitation tax." President Stevens "approved" the tax on January 2, 1810, and "fixed upon" January 22 as the date "for the taking up of the taxes."[7] (See image on previous page.)

In another prominent act as president, Stevens on January 9, 1810, issued a proclamation permitting the importation of certain scarce goods.[8]

The presidency of St. Croix was a temporary position which Stevens filled until Lieutenant Governor George Harcourt returned on March 3, 1810, after an absence of about 2½ months. In a letter to the Burgher Council, Harcourt praised Stevens's short term as president:

In the arrangements adopted for the administration of the Civil Department during my Absence, my boundless Duty was to provide for the preservation of His Majesty's right, and for the happiness, welfare, and prosperity of His Subjects in this Island.

These great and important Trusts could not be reposed in the hands of any Man, more fully qualified in every possible respect to hold them, than the Honorable Councellor STEVENS, That he has fulfilled them to your Advantage, and his own Honor,—that he has maintained unimpaired that confidence which you are pleased to record, and that to the general respect and regard he so justly experiences in private life, he has now to add this your Testimony,—will be as lasting a Source of gratification to him henceforward, as it is of real joy to me, in finding his measures and Conduct to have so fully justified and confirmed the high opinions I entertain of him.[9]

Control of St. Croix Returns to Denmark

With the end of the Napoleonic Wars, the United Kingdom returned control of St. Croix to Denmark in April 1815.[10]

St. Croix Under the United States

St. Croix remained a Danish possession until the United States acquired it along with the other Danish West Indian colonies in 1917.

As U.S. citizens, Cruzans (or Crucians) now have a president, i.e., the President of the United States. More than two hundred years ago, they also had a president for a brief period of time, namely Dr. Edward Stevens, who served as president of St. Croix for about 2½ months in 1809–10.

Notes

1. *Christiansted Embedsarkiver for Byfogeden 1772–1828* image 264b.
2. *Christiansted Embedsarkiver for Byfogeden 1772–1828* image 265a.
3. Day, *Edward Stevens.*
4. *The St. Croix Gazette,* May 26, 1808, p1 c1.
5. *The St. Croix Gazette,* October 17, 1808, p1 c1.
6. *The St. Croix Gazette,* December 19, 1809, p1 c1.
7. *Christiansted Embedsarkiver for Byfogeden 1772–1828* image 264b.
8. *The St. Croix Gazette,* January 12, 1810, p1 c1.
9. *The St. Croix Gazette,* March 6, 1810, p1 c2 – p2 c1.
10. *Dansk Vestindisk Regierings Avis,* April 1, 1815, p1 c1.

The Arrival of
David Beekman and Nicholas Cruger
on St. Croix

When Alexander Hamilton started working for the mercantile oper-ation of Beekman & Cruger in 1766 or early 1767,[1] David Beek-man and Nicholas Cruger were relative newcomers to St. Croix. Until now, it was not known exactly when these two New Yorkers arrived.

The Oldest Known Beekman & Cruger Bill

Previously, the earliest known record of Beekman and Cruger on St. Croix was a bill dated April 2, 1766. This record was found by H. U. Ramsing and shared in his groundbreaking 1939 essay on Alexander Hamilton's birth, par-entage, and life in the West Indies.[2]

Beekman & Cruger in St. Croix's Matrikels

Ramsing also noted that Beekman & Cruger were "first noticed on the poll-tax list from 1766," which for King's Street, where they lived and worked, was compiled on January 5, 1767. They owned two slaves.[3]

Neither David Beekman nor Nicholas Cruger was found on King's Street in the 1765 matrikel, which was compiled for that street on January 13, 1766, nor were they found anywhere else in that matrikel. Accordingly, they must have taken up residence and opened their store after January 13, 1766.

Thus, it would appear that Beekman and Cruger arrived on St. Croix and started selling goods sometime between January 13 and April 2, 1766.

Beekman & Cruger's First Imports

In the waste [account] book for the partnership of brothers Henry and John Cruger of New York City, the father and uncle of Nicholas Cruger, there appears a record on January 16, 1766:

Voyage to St. Croix D^r to Cash for our 1/6 part of sundries shipt on Snow Min^a [Minerva] Jno Clark Maj^r Consign'd Beekman & Cruger / in C^o with ye Owners as pr Invoice . . . £129.16.10.[4]

Clearly, David Beekman and Nicholas Cruger had formed their partnership by this date, i.e. January 16, 1766, but this transaction was recorded in New York, not in St. Croix. Were Beekman and Cruger still in New York at this time? Or were they already on St. Croix?

On January 18, 1766, "John Clarck af Nye Ork [of New York]," the same John Clark mentioned in Henry and John Cruger's waste book, was entered into Christiansted's customs journal as having arrived in port. The customs journal states that Clark imported 8,475 rigsdalers of goods "for Beckmann & Cruger." John Clark also imported two adult male slaves, presumably for Beekman & Cruger and possibly the two capable slaves they owned in January 1767 as recorded in the 1766 matrikel.[5]

Based on these records, it appears that Beekman & Cruger were on St. Croix and had begun operations by January 18, 1766. But it will be recalled that they were not listed in the matrikel that was recorded just days before this. It is possible, perhaps likely, that David Beekman or Nicholas Cruger, maybe both, arrived on St. Croix on January 18, 1766, on board John Clark's snow *Minerva*. One assumes that Beekman & Cruger, around this time, opened their store on King's Street, for they needed a place to sell the goods they had just imported and were found at this location the following year.

Confirmation of David Beekman's Arrival on St. Croix

On March 8, 1766, David Beekman's brother Gerard G. Beekman, a New York merchant, wrote "to David Beekman, St. Croix," and mentioned that "this day vya Philadelphia we had the Pleasure to hear of Your safe Arrival."[6]

Since it must have taken at least three weeks for David Beekman's letter to travel from St. Croix to Philadelphia and then to New York, Beekman must have arrived on St. Croix by the middle of February 1766. This confirms that David Beekman, and possibly Nicholas Cruger as well, arrived on St. Croix in January or early February 1766. This also supports the theory that Beekman and Cruger arrived on board John Clark's snow *Minerva* on January 18, 1766.

Updated Timeline

David Beekman and Nicholas Cruger were apparently not on St. Croix as of January 13, 1766, or at least had not yet taken up residence or opened their store, because they are not listed in the 1765 matrikel. The earliest record of their partnership, known as Beekman & Cruger, appears in the waste [account] book of John and Henry Cruger on January 16, 1766. Beekman & Cruger received 8,475 rigsdalers of goods on St. Croix on January 18, 1766, which they imported from New York on John Clark's *Minerva*. Perhaps they came to St. Croix aboard this ship. By the middle of February, David Beekman was writing to his brother from St. Croix and one assumes that Nicholas Cruger was on the island as well. By January 1767, they were operating a store on King's Street, but one assumes that they had opened this store shortly after their arrival on St. Croix in January or early February 1766.

Notes

1. See page 179.
2. *Christiansted Skiftebrevsprotokoller for Borgere og Plantere* 14:186r; Ramsing, "Alexander Hamilton Og Hans Modrene Slaegt" 265–266; Ramsing, *Alexander Hamilton's Birth and Parentage* 48.
3. *St. Croix Matrikel 1766* 1; Ramsing, "Alexander Hamilton Og Hans Modrene Slaegt" 265; Ramsing, *Alexander Hamilton's Birth and Parentage* 47.
4. Henry and John Cruger, *Waste Book*, January 16, 1766.
5. *Customs Journal (Toldbog), Christiansted, St. Croix, 1766* 20a, 21a.
6. Gerard G. Beekman to David Beekman, March 8, 1766, in *The Beekman Mercantile Papers* 1:495.

The Oldest Known Alexander Hamilton Documents

On page 1 of volume 1 of *The Papers of Alexander Hamilton* there appears the "Probate Court Transaction on Estate of Rachel Lavien [St. Croix, February 19, 1768]." This document, which was discovered by H. U. Ramsing and first shared in his groundbreaking essay published in 1939, mentions in a section dated February 22, 1768, that Alexander Hamilton was one of the sons of the recently deceased Rachel Lavien. The editors of *The Papers of Alexander Hamilton* noted, "Although this is not strictly an H document, it is printed here because it is the first extant document in which H is mentioned."[1]

In fact, this section of the "probate court transaction" about Alexander Hamilton had been recorded in a volume of registrations and appraisements on February 22, 1768, and only later copied into the probate record.[2] Either way, this record was "the first extant document in which H is mentioned."

As the editors of *The Papers of Alexander Hamilton* noted, the above record of February 1768 is "not strictly an H document." A stricter definition of a Hamilton document would include only those written, drafted, or signed by Hamilton, or accurate copies of such documents if the originals have been lost, precise contemporary records of his verbal statements such as legal testimony, and letters written to him. According to this definition, the oldest Hamilton document in *The Papers of Alexander Hamilton* or anywhere else is a letter he wrote to his friend Edward Stevens on November 11, 1769.[3]

One other "document" must be added to the list of oldest "known" Hamilton documents. Back in 1858, George Bancroft claimed, "The first written trace of his existence is in 1766, when his name appears as witness to a legal paper executed in the Danish island of Santa Cruz [St. Croix]."[4] In 1899, Henry Cabot Lodge added, "The character of his signature is of more importance than the fact of his affixing it to a deed. I have carefully examined an exact tracing of this signature. The handwriting is obviously Hamilton's."[5] However, this document and even Lodge's "exact tracing" have been lost.

Accordingly, one cannot be certain that this "legal paper" was in fact from 1766 or that it was Alexander Hamilton who signed it. Accordingly, this missing "legal paper" cannot be considered a Hamilton document.

In sum, there have been three different documents that could be considered the oldest known Alexander Hamilton document. The oldest is from 1766, but that document has apparently not been seen for well over a century and one cannot be certain it is a Hamilton document or that the date given is correct. The second is from February 22, 1768, but this is not strictly a Hamilton document because it merely mentions Hamilton in passing and he had nothing to do with writing it. The third is Hamilton's letter to Edward Stevens of November 11, 1769.

Witnessing an Appraisal, April 22, 1767

On April 22, 1767, "an appraisal of the effects belonging to Master William Pond Deceased, late of Munserate [Monserrat]," was conducted "at the request of the honourable Dealing Court" of Christiansted, St. Croix. The original document has not been found, but on that same day the text of the appraisal was transcribed into the official records of Christiansted.

Two men conducted the appraisal while two other men acted as witnesses. All four signed the original document, and their signatures were copied into the official record. One of the two witnesses is recorded as "Allexander Hamilthon." The other was David Beekman.[6]

Christiansted Registrerings og Vurderingsprotokoller for Borgere og Plantere 1761–1768 300v.

By himself, one could not be certain that this was Alexander Hamilton the Founding Father because there were other people with that name who could have been on St. Croix at this time.[7] But appearing alongside his employer, there can be little doubt that this was the correct Alexander Hamilton.

That makes this appraisal of April 22, 1767, the oldest known Alexander Hamilton document. It is older than the letter Hamilton wrote to Edward Stevens in November 1769 and older than the mere mention of Alexander Hamilton in February 1768, as found in the probate record. It is not as old as the supposed 1766 document, but that record has been lost and cannot be considered a Hamilton document without further evidence that it was signed by Alexander Hamilton and that the date is correct.

So again, this appraisal of April 22, 1767, witnessed and signed by Alexander Hamilton and David Beekman, is now the oldest known Alexander Hamilton document.

Witnessing a Mortgage, August 10, 1767

Less than four months later, on August 10, 1767, "John Cebra of this island [St. Croix] merchant" assumed a debt that his "brother-in-law Joseph Robinson Esqr of the Province of New York" owed to "David Beekman of said island merchant" for the "sum of sixteen hundred pounds New York currency." Acting "by virtue of" Robinson's "power of attorney," John Cebra "mortgage[d] unto the said David Beekman . . . a plantation belonging to the said Joseph Robinson Esqr & lying here in this island and situate[d] in the Kings Quarter No. 36."

The original mortgage, which has not been located, was signed by "John Cebra, Attorney to Mr. Joseph Robinson." It was also "Signd Seald and Deliverd in the Presence" of two men: "Nich^{ls} Cruger" and "Allex^r Hamilton." The text of the mortgage document along with the accompanying signatures were all copied into the official record of Christiansted, St. Croix, on August 17, 1767, and subsequently published on August 20, 1767.[8]

Christiansted Panteprotokoller 1767–1769 51r.

Here is an Alexander Hamilton acting as a witness alongside Nicholas Cruger for a mortgage benefiting David Beekman, with the original mortgage document being "delivered" to Beekman "in the presence of" Cruger and

Hamilton, who then signed the document. To see an Alexander Hamilton together with both Beekman and Cruger at this time is clear evidence that this was the famed Alexander Hamilton and not someone else with the same name. It also supports the conclusion that the Alexander Hamilton who acted as a witness and signed the appraisal alongside David Beekman on April 22, 1767, was also the future Founding Father.

That makes this mortgage record of August 10, 1767, the second oldest known Alexander Hamilton document, behind only the appraisal record of April 22, 1767.

Implications

In addition to being noteworthy as the oldest known Alexander Hamilton documents, these recently discovered records provide numerous insights into Hamilton's childhood on St. Croix.

Perhaps the most remarkable implication relates to Alexander Hamilton's youth and maturity. These documents show Alexander Hamilton serving as a legal witness and signing legal papers as a mere twelve- or thirteen-year-old boy. For Hamilton to have acted as a witness, both the parties to the transactions and the courts must have thought Hamilton mature enough to perform this duty. It was already known from later evidence, e.g., Hamilton's November 1769 letter to Edward Stevens and Hamilton's management of Nicholas Cruger's company in 1771–72, that Hamilton was a child prodigy and more mature than his years would suggest, but these documents show a mature and responsible Hamilton years earlier than previously known. They also show that others had noticed Hamilton's precocity even at this early date.

These documents also provide strong evidence regarding the commencement of Hamilton's employment with Beekman & Cruger. Prior to the discovery of these documents, the question of when Hamilton started working had been the subject of much speculation with a wide range of conjectures. Some believed that Hamilton started working for Beekman & Cruger shortly after the partners opened their St. Croix mercantile operation in early 1766. Others supposed that Hamilton worked in his mother's store and perhaps went to school until his mother died in February 1768, at which point he needed a job and was at that time hired by Beekman & Cruger. Others speculated that since his wealthy uncle and cousin, James and Peter Lytton, took him in after his mother died, Hamilton did not start working for Beekman & Cruger until after his guardians passed away in the summer of 1769, just prior to his November 1769 letter to Edward Stevens, in which he mentioned his employment as a clerk.[9] But these possibilities were mere speculation. There was no evidence for any of these conjectures over the others.

With the discovery of these new documents, in which Hamilton is found with Beekman in April 1767 and with both Beekman and Cruger in August 1767, it is clear that Alexander Hamilton was already working for Beekman & Cruger by this time. When David Beekman or Nicholas Cruger needed someone to act as a witness, they simply enlisted the services of their trusted clerk, Alexander Hamilton. Not only does this show Hamilton working for Beekman & Cruger in April 1767, but it also shows that he was a trusted member of the organization and must have been working there for some time. It is impossible to determine with certainty based on these newly discovered documents when Hamilton started working for Beekman & Cruger, but it is apparent that it was in 1766 or early 1767.

With this clearer idea of when Hamilton began working for Beekman & Cruger, another remarkable fact emerges. Knowing that Hamilton worked for Nicholas Cruger until September 1772, if he started working for Beekman & Cruger in April 1767, it would mean that Hamilton was employed by Beekman & Cruger and then by Cruger alone for five years and six months. And it is quite possible that Hamilton worked at this job for six years or more since it is clear that by April 1767 he had already been employed by Beekman & Cruger for some time. In contrast, Hamilton worked as an aide to George Washington during the American Revolution for four years and two months and was Secretary of the Treasury for five years, four months, and twenty days. He worked many years as an attorney, but never more than a few continuously because public service repeatedly interrupted his private practice. Accordingly, what previously had only been conjectured[10] is now clear: Alexander Hamilton's employment with Beekman & Cruger and then with Cruger alone was his longest continuous full-time job.

These new facts also call into question a popular myth often told about Alexander Hamilton. If Hamilton started working for Beekman & Cruger in 1766 or early 1767, when exactly was Alexander Hamilton "impoverished" and living in "squalor," as some have asserted?[11] When Hamilton's mother was alive, he did not live in squalor. Hamilton's mother ran a business, turned a profit, owned leather chairs, silverware, slaves, etc. She may not have been among the upper class, but she was far from impoverished. Moreover, Hamilton's uncle and cousin, who served as his guardians after his mother's death, were quite wealthy; indeed they were among the wealthiest people on St. Croix. It is now known that Alexander Hamilton was already employed as a clerk for Beekman & Cruger and therefore making a decent salary long before his mother, cousin, and uncle died. Although far from wealthy, there is no record of Alexander Hamilton being "impoverished" or living in "squalor."

The discovery of these records also enables a further analysis of George Bancroft's claim in 1858 to have seen a 1766 "legal paper" signed by Hamilton. In *Alexander Hamilton: The Formative Years*, this author speculated that "Alexander Hamilton's signature on a 1766 legal document, which has been lost since its discovery, could have been related to his work for Beekman and Cruger."[12] With the discovery of these 1767 legal documents, it seems even more plausible that this 1766 "legal paper" was indeed signed by Alexander Hamilton, that the 1766 date is correct, and that it probably was related to Hamilton's work for Beekman & Cruger.

Notes

1. Probate Court Transaction on Estate of Rachel Lavien, February 19, 1768, in *The Papers of Alexander Hamilton* 1:1–3; Ramsing, "Alexander Hamilton Og Hans Modrene Slaegt" 245; Ramsing, *Alexander Hamilton's Birth and Parentage* 24.

2. *Christiansted Registrerings og Vurderingsprotokoller for Borgere og Plantere 1761–68* 359v; *Christiansted Skiftebrevsprotokoller for Borgere og Plantere* 20:386v.

3. Alexander Hamilton to Edward Stevens, November 11, 1769, in *The Papers of Alexander Hamilton* 1:4–5.

4. Bancroft, *A History of the United States* 7:790.

5. Lodge, *Alexander Hamilton* 283–285.

6. *Christiansted Registrerings og Vurderingsprotokoller for Borgere og Plantere 1761–1768* 300r–v.

7. See page 106; *Christiansted Registrerings og Vurderingsprotokoller for Borgere og Plantere 1768–1773* 133–134.

8. *Christiansted Panteprotokoller 1767–1769* 50v–51r.

9. Alexander Hamilton to Edward Stevens, November 11, 1769, in *The Papers of Alexander Hamilton* 1:4–5.

10. Newton, *Alexander Hamilton: The Formative Years* 48.

11. Chernow, *Alexander Hamilton* 2, 5, 362; Miranda, "Alexander Hamilton."

12. Newton, *Alexander Hamilton: The Formative Years* 45.

Nicholas Cruger's Supposed Duel

Just days after appearing as a witness alongside Nicholas Cruger on a mortgage for David Beekman, Alexander Hamilton had a front-row seat to a sensation involving one of his employers that created much "disorder . . . in town."

On the morning of August 24, 1767, Nicholas Cruger rode out to the East End of the island. A John Heyliger had also gone out in the same direction.

A William Davis "informed" the governor general that someone "had seen [John] Heyliger and [Nicholas] Cruger ride out to the East End" and that it was said they had gone to duel "because they were rivals."[1]

The governor and the privy council "ordered" that the "2 young men" be "taken into custody because of a supposed duel" and instructed the sheriff's office to immediately "arrest" said persons and their movable and real possessions, in accordance with Danish law.[2]

Sheriff Peder Willumsen "immediately made ready with two men to set out after these duelers" but then "Merrich Turnbull came riding up" and said that "Cruger and Heyliger had stood with pistols facing one another but he prevented it coming to anything."[3]

Sheriff Willumsen along with witnesses then went to Peter Heyliger Sr.'s house to arrest John Heyliger and his effects. John Heyliger was not found at home, nor did they find any effects belonging to him there. The court's agent proclaimed that Heyliger should be arrested and brought to the fort when he is found. The agents of the court then went to Mr. Cruger's lodging to arrest him and his effects. The agent searched his house but could not find him and declared him to be under arrest and to be brought to the fort when he is found. The court took possession of Cruger's effects, which David Beekman had turned over to them, including some linen shirts and stockings, three coats, a bed, bedding, and a mosquito net, which was all there was belonging to him in the house. While the agents were in Cruger's house, David Beekman showed them the account books of their partnership and declared himself responsible for Cruger's portion of the goods belonging to them in partnership.[4]

It was still morning when William Davis, the man who had "informed" on Cruger and Heyliger, sent a letter of retraction to the governor:

> I this morning told your Excellency that I had heard of a Duell between Mr. John Heyliger and Mr. Cruger to be att the East End, But upon enquiring find that there was no Just Foundation for such a Report, and that the Surmize arose from those Gentl & some others being seen going out towards the East End, and that as these Gentn were spoke of as paying their addresses to one Lady, the Publick Idly Imagined their Business was a Duell.
>
> I hope your Excellency will Pardon my Mistake in the Report as I had a great Regard for the Partis & woud take the Earliest Opportunity by mentioning the same to Your Excellency, thereby to prevent mischeif had there been any such Duell.
>
> I am with great Respect
> Your Excellency's Most obed[t] hum[e] Servant
> William Davis[5]

When John Heyliger and Nicholas Cruger returned to town that afternoon and "learned that the arrest of their persons and goods had been ordered solely on account of a groundless rumor,"[6] they wrote to the governor explaining what had taken place:

> To his Excellency Peter Clausen Esq[r]. Major General of Infantry and Commander in Chief over all his Majestys Islands in the West Indies. We this Morning had Information that your Excellency had Entered Judge Williamsen to make an Arrest on our Bodys and Goods, arriving from a Report that we had gone to the East Ende to duel; which is entirely without Foundation, as we never went there upon any such Matter, but on the Contrary, each going upon his proper Business; but on hearing a Report was spread in Town that we were gone upon such an Assent, occasion'd us to humour the Joke, but to our great Distress, it has prov'd to our Disadvantage & likely to be of Ill Effect. We therefore request that your Excellency would recall the Arrest issued against

To his Excellency Peter Clausen Esq.r Major
General of Infantry and Commander in Chief
over all his Majestys Islands in the West
Indies ⸺

We this Morning had Information that your
Excellency had Order'd Judge Williamsen to
make an Arrest on our Bodys and Goods,
arrising from a Report that we had gone to
the East-End to duel; which is entirely
without Foundation, as we never went there
upon any such Matter, but on the Contrary
each going upon his proper Business; but
on hearing a Report was spread in Town
that we were gone upon such an Afsair,
occasion'd us to humour the Joke, but to
our great Distress, it has prov'd to our
Disadvantage, & likely to be of Ill Effect,
We therefore request that your Excellency
would recall the Arrest issued against
us, so that we may return to our Business
& Friends, and for our Imprudence in
agreeing to humour the Jest of the Report,
are very well satisfied to pay all the Expence
which has been occasion'd in this Affair
thro' such Report, as we are with all Respect imaginable
                        Your Excellencys
Monday Afternoon the   Most Ob.t Serv.ts
24th August 1767   J. Heyliger

                              Nich.s Cruger

John Heyliger and Nicholas Cruger to Governor Peter Clausen,
August 24, 1767, in the afternoon, in *St. Croix Notarialsager
1763–1776* image 250b.

us, so that we may return to our Business & Friends, and for our In-
dependence in agreeing to humour the Jest of the Report, are very well
satisfied to pay all the Expence which has been occasion'd in this Affair,
thro' such Report, as we are with all Respect imaginable
Your Excellencys Most Ob^r Serv^{ts}
J Heyliger
Nich^{ls} Cruger
Monday afternoon the 24th August 1767[7]

Likewise, John Heyliger's father, Peter Heyliger, wrote to the governor and
privy council to explain "that the accusations against my son are altogether
unknown to me, and I am also assured that no duel between him and
Mr. Cruger was ever intended." He added that "it may be possible that they
met one another this morning, since I know that my son took a little tour to
the East End, but with no other intention than solely for the exercise for the
sake of his health, and not to duel with Mr. Cruger." Heyliger senior therefore
asked the governor and privy council "to relax the arrest laid upon" his son.[8]
The privy council met again on August 26. William Davis's retraction
letter was presented, as were the letters written by Peter Heyliger and by John
Heyliger and Nicholas Cruger. After the letters were read, John Heyliger and
Nicholas Cruger appeared "to show that they had not done anything other
than what they had written, and declared that the preceding had happened
thus. And they asked that they as young persons were not to be made unhappy [i.e., ruined] on account of such a jest, which they hoped the Council
would regard as such." The Governor General then said he "would like to see
this [arrest] annulled" because "they are young men and of respectable families here in the country." The governor added, however, that "he does not
think that they ought to be entirely free, but they should be punished in some
measure so that other such jesters might think again." The Council decided
that due to the "disorder" this had created "in town" and how the council
was "inconvenienced" by the ordeal, Cruger and Heyliger were each ordered
to pay "the incurred costs of the arrests" plus another 500 rigsdalers, a considerable sum of money, "which would go to the Church and the Hospital to
share equally." On top of this, the court required each to "submit their written promise . . . that they would not in the future make such jest that causes
discord among the public" and if they did this again or "a dispute come

between them," then the present case "would be accounted as open against them and considered as intended in all seriousness." The Council then ordered the sheriff "to relax the arrest" once Heyliger and Cruger "fulfilled" the abovementioned obligations.[9]

That very day, August 26, 1767, Heyliger and Cruger paid their fines,[10] and must have also submitted "their written promise . . . that they would not in the future make such jest that causes discord among the public." On August 27, Sheriff Willumsen received a written communication of the same date from the privy council informing him of their decision and ordering him to relax the arrests on Heyliger's and Cruger's persons and effects, which he did.[11]

Alexander Hamilton

As an employee of Beekman & Cruger and friend to Nicholas Cruger, Alexander Hamilton surely stayed apprised of this affair as it proceeded. For three days, Hamilton must have been on edge wondering what would happen to his employer and his job.

Perhaps Hamilton had heard about duels before,[12] but this is the earliest known case in which he had a personal interest in the outcome of what everyone believed to be an affair of honor. Of course, no duel took place nor was one ever contemplated according to the parties involved, but the rapidity in which the privy council took up this issue and the steep fines assessed against the jesters showed Hamilton that affairs of honor were no joking matter.

Notes

1. *St. Croix Secrete Råd Forhandlingsprotokoller 1765–1771* 104; Peder Willumsen's report, August 24, 1767, in *St. Croix Notarialsager 1763–1776* images 256–259.
2. *St. Croix Secrete Råd Forhandlingsprotokoller 1765–1771* 104; Peder Willumsen's report, August 24, 1767, in *St. Croix Notarialsager 1763–1776* images 256–259. Danish law clearly stated that anyone challenging or accepting a duel "shall forfeit all their posts, places, and all their goods moveable and immoveable, and even suffer death, according to the circumstances of the offence" (*The Danish Laws* 409).
3. Peder Willumsen to Governor Peter Clausen, August 24, 1767, in *St. Croix Notarialsager 1763–1776* images 254b–255a.
4. *St. Croix Secrete Råd Forhandlingsprotokoller 1765–1771* 104; *Christiansted Fogedprotokoller 1767 06 20 – 1770 11 08* 39r–v; Peder Willumsen to Governor Peter Clausen,

August 24, 1767, in *St. Croix Notarialsager 1763–1776* images 248b; Peder Willum-sen's report, August 24, 1767, in *St. Croix Notarialsager 1763–1776* images 256–259.

5. William Davis to Governor Peter Clausen, August 24, 1767, in the morning, in *St. Croix Notarialsager 1763–1776* image 260b.

6. *St. Croix Secrete Råd Forhandlingsprotokoller 1765–1771* 104.

7. John Heyliger and Nicholas Cruger to Governor Peter Clausen, August 24, 1767, in the afternoon, in *St. Croix Notarialsager 1763–1776* image 250b.

8. Pieter Heyliger to Governor Peter Clausen and the Privy Council, August 24, 1767, in *St. Croix Notarialsager 1763–1776* images 252b–253a; *St. Croix Secrete Råd Forhandlingsprotokoller 1765–1771* 104.

9. *St. Croix Secrete Råd Forhandlingsprotokoller 1765–1771* 104–105.

10. *St. Croix Cassabog [Cashier Book]*, August 21, 1769, in *St. Croix Diverse Regnskabsprotokoller* 55.12.64 image 6b.

11. *Christiansted Fogedprotokoller 1767 06 20 – 1770 11 08* 42r.

12. See pages 87–88.

Alexander Hamilton Working for Nicholas Cruger on St. Croix: More Newly Discovered Records

D espite spending about six years working for Nicholas Cruger,[1] little is known about what Hamilton did in this job prior to the five-month period when he ran the company in late 1771 and early 1772.[2] There are records showing Hamilton acting as a legal witness alongside his bosses Nicholas Cruger and David Beekman in April and August 1767,[3] but this was not directly related to his work for the company. There is Hamilton's November 1769 letter to Edward Stevens complaining about "the grov'ling and condition of a clerk or the like to which my fortune etc. condemns me,"[4] but he did not describe the responsibilities of his job as a clerk. There are records showing that Hamilton copied letters for Cruger into his letterbook, and perhaps he had drafted some of these letters as well,[5] but Hamilton surely did more than just take dictation and copy letters.

From these sources, one could guess at the tasks Hamilton performed as Cruger's clerk and assistant, but the certainty that comes with distinct records was lacking.

Alexander Hamilton and the Privy Council

Three previously unknown records dated November 6 and December 11, 1770, and February 11, 1771, show Nicholas Cruger selling goods, primarily peas but also bread, to St. Croix's Privy Council. When it came time to pay, the money was "received" by Alexander Hamilton, who then signed the receipts.[6] While the original orders and receipts have not been found and probably no longer exist, the information was dutifully transcribed into St. Croix's account books.

Whether Hamilton went to the Privy Council's treasurer or the money was sent to Cruger's office is not known. Either way, these records show that Hamilton, just sixteen years old at the time, was more than just a clerk sitting at a desk in a back office keeping books and writing letters for his boss.

St. Croix Cassa Regnskab 1770 147r–v, 167v–168r, *1771* 30–31, in *St. Croix Diverse Regnskabsprotokoller* 55.12.17 images 285b–286a, 306a–b, 330a–b.

Acting as a cashier for Nicholas Cruger, Hamilton also collected payments from customers.

One should not, however, read too much into these records. In receiving these payments, Hamilton probably dealt with a clerk or cashier and not with the Privy Council itself.

That said, it is possible, perhaps likely, that the members of the Privy Council knew Hamilton. Even before finding these records, this author speculated that, "through his work for Nicholas Cruger, Alexander Hamilton surely met many of St. Croix's leading citizens."[7] Certainly, Hamilton's management of Nicholas Cruger's company in late 1771 and early 1772 would have attracted attention, but it is likely that the island's "leading citizens," including the members of the Privy Council, who along with the Governor General were the island's foremost government officials, had already noticed the young clerk who worked as Nicholas Cruger's right-hand man.

Just as Nicholas Cruger recognized Hamilton's talents and therefore chose him to manage his company when he left for five months, others on the island, including planters, merchants, ship captains, lawyers, and government officials, must have been similarly impressed by Cruger's young clerk. With these newly discovered records showing some of the tasks Hamilton performed for Nicholas Cruger and establishing a connection between him and the Privy Council, one reckons that the members of the council and perhaps even the Governor General himself noticed the talents and maturity of Nicholas Cruger's clerk and expected great things from Alexander Hamilton.

Alexander Hamilton Delivering Goods, Testifying in Court

On August 5, 1771, Alexander Hamilton, "being in Cruger's employ," testified in a case between his boss and a William Millward. Because of his youth, Alexander Hamilton was first asked for some biographical details to ascertain his suitability to testify in the case. Hamilton was asked "who he was and where he resided, how old he was and of what religion, and if he had received the sacrament of the altar, as well as if he understood the meaning of the oath." Hamilton "answered he was 17 years old, in service to Mr. Nicholas Cruger, and was brought up in the Reformed religion as it was observed in the English Established Church, and that he knew the meaning of the

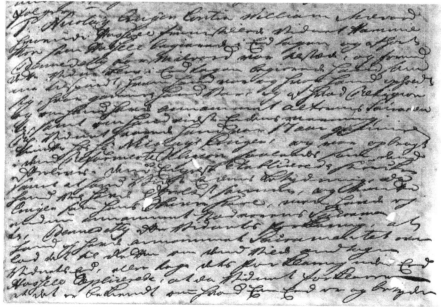

Alexander Hamilton providing biographical information to the court, in *Christiansted Tingsvidneprotokoller 1771–1772* 74v.

oath, . . . but that he had not yet received communion." Millward's lawyer argued that Hamilton should not be sworn in but Cruger's argued that he should.[8]

The significant implications of the above biographical information provided by Hamilton have already been discussed in the chapter "Alexander Hamilton's Birth, Early Biography, and More."

Returning to the case at hand, Hamilton "declared," "tho not upon oath," that he had delivered "to the Negroes of Milward the greatest part" of the goods in question "partly out of Cruger's own store and partly from the wharf but the other goods he says were delivered by Cruger himself." Hamilton also provided a detailed accounting of the dates and quantities of goods delivered to Millward.[9]

Thus Hamilton can be seen delivering goods for his boss, knowing the full details of Cruger's financial accounts, and even testifying in court about both his own actions and his boss's operations.

Notes

1. See page 179.
2. *The Papers of Alexander Hamilton* 1:8–30.
3. See chapter "The Oldest Known Alexander Hamilton Documents."
4. Alexander Hamilton to Edward Stevens, November 11, 1769, in *The Papers of Alexander Hamilton* 1:4–5.
5. *The Papers of Alexander Hamilton* 1:30–34.
6. *St. Croix Cassa Regnskab 1770* 147r–v, 167v–168r, *1771* 30–31, in *St. Croix Diverse Regnskabsprotokoller* 55.12.17 images 285b–286a, 306a–b, 330a–b.
7. Newton, *Alexander Hamilton: The Formative Years* 59.
8. *Christiansted Tingsvidneprotokoller 1771–1772* 74v–75r.
9. *St. Croix Notarialsager 1763–1776* image 264a; *Christiansted Tingsvidneprotokoller 1771–1772* 75r–76v.

The St. Croix Epidemic of 1771–1772

Given the poor understanding of human diseases and the lack of proper medicine, epidemics were common occurrences in the eighteenth century. The hot, humid weather of the West Indies promoted insect-borne diseases and weakened the bodies of men and women alike, thus making epidemics of yellow fever, malaria, and other diseases regular events.

Nicholas Cruger

On October 15, 1771, Nicholas Cruger left St. Croix for New York "by reason of a very ill state of health."[1] Details of Cruger's illness are not given in any known record, but it is possible that his ill health was part of a larger epidemic that struck St. Croix.

Nicholas Cruger put Alexander Hamilton in charge of his mercantile company until he recovered and returned to St. Croix. Thus, if Cruger's illness was part of a larger epidemic, it is due to this outbreak that Hamilton owed a significant share of his meteoric ascent.

Alexander Hamilton

Less than three weeks after Cruger's departure, Alexander Hamilton fell ill. On November 4, 1771, Hamilton wrote to Nicholas Cruger, "I am so unwell that it is with difficulty I make out to write these few lines."[2] Subsequent letters show that Hamilton recovered from this illness within a few days.[3]

Bertrand Pieter De Nully

In the same letter of November 4 to Cruger, Hamilton reported that "the Major," i.e., Town Captain and Major Bertrand Pieter De Nully, the father of Cruger's fiancée, "lies so ill that no one expects he'll live till night."[4]

Indeed, Bertrand Pieter De Nully was so ill that he and his wife made out a new joint will just two days prior to Hamilton's letter.[5]

Within three days of Hamilton's letter, by the seventh of November, Bertrand Pieter De Nully had passed away and the probate court had taken up his estate.[6]

Johannes van Veen

Later that month, in a letter to Nicholas Cruger written on November 27, Alexander Hamilton informed his boss that "Mr. Van Vain is upon the brink of eternity."[7] Johannes van Veen[8] died within a week and was buried on December 5, 1771.[9]

"I have lost 4 percent of my friends"

Nicholas Cruger returned to St. Croix in March 1772. He was instantly struck by the toll the apparent epidemic had taken on the island. "It has been sickly since I left this [place]," Cruger reported to his brother. "I have lost 4 percent of my friends." Cruger concluded that if he had not returned when he did, it would have seemed like he was "an inhabitant of another world." In another letter, Cruger reported that one of his friends, "Poor Peter," was still sick and "can't get rid of his fever." But in general, Cruger found that the epidemic had ended and those friends who survived were "all well."[10]

An Epidemic?

There is no evidence that an epidemic struck St. Croix at this time. It is possible that each person who became ill or died contracted a different illness and it was just happenstance that St. Croix was so "sickly" during Cruger's five-month absence. However, when one considers that Nicholas Cruger was "very ill," Alexander Hamilton was "so unwell," Bertrand Pieter De Nully was "so ill" that he died, Johannes van Veen died after an apparent illness, "poor Peter" caught a "fever" he could not "get rid of," and Nicholas Cruger lost four percent of his friends, it is logical to assume that there was "a widespread occurrence of an infectious disease in a community at a particular time," which is the very definition of an epidemic.

Notes

1. Alexander Hamilton to Tileman Cruger, November 16, 1771 in *The Papers of Alexander Hamilton* 1:12–14.
2. Alexander Hamilton to Nicholas Cruger, November 4, 1771, in *The Papers of Alexander Hamilton* 1:10–11.
3. For instance, see Alexander Hamilton to Nicholas Cruger, November 12, 1771, in *The Papers of Alexander Hamilton* 1:11–12, in which Hamilton made no comment about his health, apparently having fully recovered.
4. Alexander Hamilton to Nicholas Cruger, November 4, 1771, in *The Papers of Alexander Hamilton* 1:10–11. The editors of *The Papers of Alexander Hamilton* mistakenly thought that "this may refer to the Mr. Van Vain, who, H later wrote, was on 'the brink of eternity.'"
5. *St. Croix Genparter af Testamenter 1749–1813* images 56b–58a; *Christiansted Skiftebrevsprotokoller for Kgl. Betjente 1771–1777* 2–3; *Christiansted Registrerings og Vurderingsprotokoller for Borgere og Plantere 1768–73* 289v–292r; *Christiansted Testamentprotokoller 1808–1815* 18–23..
6. *Christiansted Skiftebrevsprotokoller for Kgl. Betjente 1771–1777* 2–3; *Christiansted Registrerings og Vurderingsprotokoller for Borgere og Plantere 1768–73* 289v–292r; *St. Croix Matrikel 1770* 27; ibid. *1771* 29.
   Some have written that Bertrand Pieter De Nully died in the summer of 1772 (Ramsing, "Alexander Hamilton Og Hans Modrene Slaegt" 268; Ramsing, *Alexander Hamilton's Birth and Parentage* 51), but it was Johannes De Nully, Bertrand's younger brother, who died July 15, 1772 (Hoff and Barta, "De Windt Families of the West Indies" [1985] 113).
7. Alexander Hamilton to Nicholas Cruger, November 27, 1771, in *The Papers of Alexander Hamilton* 1:16–17.
8. His name is spelled many different ways in the various records, but his original signature reads Johannes van Veen.
9. *St. John's Anglican Church, Christiansted, St. Croix, Burial Registry 1761–1787* page 15.
10. Nicholas Cruger to John Rengger, March 11, 1772, in Nicholas Cruger's letterbook, in *Alexander Hamilton Papers*; Nicholas Cruger to John Harris Cruger, March 19, 1772, in ibid.

Anne Lytton Venton:
The Woman Who Paid for
Alexander Hamilton's Education

In his groundbreaking 1939 essay, H. U. Ramsing shared his discovery of numerous entries related to the estate of James Lytton, Alexander Hamilton's uncle, found in the probate record of Thomas Lillie of St. Croix. Among the hundreds of entries are dozens pertaining to Anne Lytton Venton, the daughter of James and Anne Lytton and thus Alexander Hamilton's first cousin. Among these entries for Anne Lytton Venton are four quittances [receipts] "with" Alexander Hamilton for 120 rigsdalers, 1 hogshead of sugar, and 1 hogshead of rum. There is also one "order in favor of Alexander Hamilton" for 15 hogsheads of sugar. These entries are dated May 16 and 23, 1772, and May 3, 26, and June 3, 1773.[1]

While H. U. Ramsing found these entries in Thomas Lillie's probate record, which was compiled in 1780, they previously appeared in a volume of registrations and appraisals back in 1776,[2] and were subsequently copied into that probate record.

But the records of the four quittances and one order as found in these two volumes are mere one-line summaries and are missing information vital to understanding the transactions.

Full Transaction Details

Fortunately, these transactions appear in more detail in another location. Overlooked by H. U. Ramsing and others, the probate record of James Lytton contains a list of dozens of debits for "Mrs. Ann Venton, To the Estate of James Lytton Senior."[3]

On May 16, 1772, Anne Lytton Venton debited 45 rigsdalers from her father's estate and also debited one hogshead containing 828 pounds of sugar, valued at 45 rigsdalers, 3 reals, and 2 styvers. Both the money and the sugar were "paid [to] Nicolaus Cruger."[4] These two transactions match precisely Anne Lytton Venton's quittance with Hamilton of the same date.[5] Clearly,

Nicholas Cruger acted as Hamilton's banker in this transaction.

A week later, on May 23, 1772, Anne Lytton Venton debited her father's estate one hogshead containing 118 gallons of rum "delivered [to] A. Hammilton, on your account per receipt," with a value of 55rdl 1r 2st.[6] This transaction matches Anne Lytton Venton's quittance with Hamilton of the same date.[7]

The following year, on May 26, 1773, Anne Lytton Venton debited her father's estate 50 rigsdalers for the "sum paid Alexander Hammelton pr. receipt." A week later, on June 3, Anne Lytton Venton paid Hamilton another 25 rigsdalers.[8] These transactions again match two of Anne Lytton Venton's quittances as found in Thomas Lillie's probate record.[9]

Two more transactions appear, with a record date of November 26, 1773. The first, which is backdated to May 6, 1773, is for "14 hogsheads sugar," totaling 13,347 pounds of sugar, and valued at 913rdl 1r 3st. This is followed by another transaction, backdated to May 12, 1773, for "1 hogshead sugar" with 990 more pounds of sugar valued at 69rdl 1r 1st, with an additional note that "this hogshead with the 14 hogsheads delivered the 6th May make the 15 hogsheads which is agreeable to his order in favor of Alexander Hamelton for 15 hogsheads." The value of these 15 hogsheads of sugar totaled 1,001rdl 2r 4st.[10] These 15 hogsheads of sugar are clearly the same as those mentioned in Anne Lytton Venton's order in favor of Alexander Hamilton dated May 3, 1773.[11]

Alexander Hamilton's generous cousin may have also paid some or all of the costs of sending the May 1773 sugar to him in New York. An undated record in a different volume states that Anne Lytton Venton paid "dutys and permissions" of 48 rigsdalers "on 6 hhds sugar shipped to New York by Captain Lightbourn."[12]

St. Croix's customs journal show that Captain William Lightbourn was outbound from Christiansted sailing for New York on May 25–26, 1773, suggesting that the above six hogsheads of sugar may have been part of the fifteen hogsheads given to Hamilton at this time.[13]

If Anne Lytton Venton did indeed pay the shipping costs on these six hogsheads of sugar, it is likely she paid the costs of the other nine as well and possibly paid for other associated expenses. If so, these additional payments by Anne Lytton Venton were either not recorded or the records of those transactions have not yet been found or no longer exist.

Anne Lytton Venton Pays for Alexander Hamilton's Education

Some historians have argued that in receiving the above money, sugar, and rum, Alexander Hamilton acted as Anne Lytton Venton's "middleman," presumably to prevent her estranged husband from taking her share of the proceeds distributed by the estate of her father James Lytton.[14] But the records clearly show that Anne Lytton Venton regularly debited her father's estate without the need of a "middleman." Thus, it is clear that the above transactions in Alexander Hamilton's favor were gifts to him.

As Hamilton by the time of the May 1772 transactions was employed as Nicholas Cruger's head clerk and had lived for many years without apparent financial support from his cousin, he presumably did not need these funds from Anne Lytton Venton for his everyday living. Based on later events, it is clear that these gifts were to help Alexander Hamilton move to mainland North America and to pay for his education. Accordingly, the funds given to Hamilton by his cousin in May 1772 are the first indications that Hamilton was planning and even preparing to go to the mainland for school, further dispelling the notion that Hamilton was sent to North America for an education as a direct result of the impression left by his account of the great hurricane,[15] which he would not write for several more months and would not be published until after he left the island.[16]

Based on the figures provided in these newly discovered records, it is clear that Anne Lytton Venton was the primary if not sole contributor to Alexander Hamilton's education fund. Her gifts of May 1772 consisted of forty-five rigsdalers, a hogshead of sugar, and a hogshead of rum, valued at precisely 145rdl 4r 4st according to the records of the Lytton estate, or approximately £23 sterling. Anne Lytton Venton's gifts of May and June 1773 provided Hamilton with another fifteen hogsheads of sugar and seventy-five rigsdalers, worth precisely 1,076rdl 2r 4st, or about £172 sterling. This brought the total value of Anne Lytton Venton's gifts to Alexander Hamilton to exactly 1,221rdl 7r 2st, or about £196 sterling, at a time when the average British worker earned just £16 per year.[17]

Anne Lytton Venton's gifts to Alexander Hamilton were expected to cover all or most of his educational expenses. According to a 1767 advertisement, the grammar school in Elizabethtown, New Jersey, which Hamilton would attend, charged twenty shillings for admission, five pounds per annum for tuition, and twenty pounds per year for boarding with a local "reputable" family.[18] The cost of a year at this grammar school thus totaled twenty-six pounds New York money, or about £15 sterling. Hamilton, of course, would have additional expenses, such as travel and clothing. Anne Lytton Venton's gifts of May 1772 totaling about £23 sterling were more than enough to get Alexander Hamilton started and were perhaps sufficient to cover the first year at the grammar school he attended.

As for college, tuition at King's College was six pounds New York currency per annum, rent was four pounds per year, and meals cost eleven shillings per week, or about twenty-five pounds per year.[19] Other expenses would have included tutoring, clothing, books, paper, pencils, firewood, candles, and travel.[20] In total, King's College cost an estimated £50 to £80 New York currency per year, £200 to £320 for a full four years, or about £112 to £180 sterling.[21] Tuition at the College of New Jersey at Princeton was one-third less than at King's College while food and rent were also considerably cheaper.[22] Hamilton hoped to further reduce the cost of his college education by demanding that he be "permitted to advance from class to class with as much rapidity as his exertions would enable him to do." Although the College of New Jersey rejected these terms, King's College accepted Hamilton on the same "terms he had proposed at Princeton."[23]

Thus, the £172 sterling Anne Lytton Venton gave Hamilton in 1773 probably was sufficient to cover any remaining expenses from his year in grammar school plus the cost of four years in college, and she surely offered to provide him with additional funds if these were insufficient. Although others may have contributed to Hamilton's education fund, it is clear from these records that Anne Lytton Venton was Alexander Hamilton's primary if not sole benefactor.

In the end, Alexander Hamilton spent just two and a half years at King's College before "the American Revolution supervened."[24] He used what remained in his education fund, provided to him entirely or mostly by his cousin Anne Lytton Venton, to equip the artillery company he raised in early 1776.[25]

Ever thankful for his cousin's generosity, Alexander Hamilton wrote in his final letter to his wife that Anne Lytton Venton, by this time known as Anne Mitchell, was "the person in the world to whom as a friend I am under the greatest obligations."[26]

Notes

1. *Christiansted Skiftebrevsprotokoller for Borgere og Plantere* 32:324v–325v #965, #994, #1045, #1059, and #1060; Ramsing, "Alexander Hamilton Og Hans Modrene Slaegt" 251–252; Ramsing, *Alexander Hamilton's Birth and Parentage* 32; *The Papers of Alexander Hamilton* 1:32, 33, 40, and 41.
2. *Christiansted Registrerings og Vurderingsprotokoller for Borgere og Plantere 1773–1777* 179r–v #965, #994, #1045, #1059, and #1060.
3. *Christiansted Skiftebrevsprotokoller for Borgere og Plantere* 33:664v.
4. *Christiansted Skiftebrevsprotokoller for Borgere og Plantere* 33:664v.
5. Anne Lytton Venton's Quittance with Alexander Hamilton, May 16, 1772, in *The Papers of Alexander Hamilton* 1:32.
6. *Christiansted Skiftebrevsprotokoller for Borgere og Plantere* 33:664v.
7. Anne Lytton Venton's Quittance with Alexander Hamilton, May 23, 1772, in *The Papers of Alexander Hamilton* 1:33.
8. *Christiansted Skiftebrevsprotokoller for Borgere og Plantere* 33:665r.
9. Anne Lytton Venton's Quittances with Alexander Hamilton, May 26 and June 3, 1773, in *The Papers of Alexander Hamilton* 1:40 and 41.
10. *Christiansted Skiftebrevsprotokoller for Borgere og Plantere* 33:665r.
    The numbers given in these records do not add up. Adding 913rdl 1r 3st and 69rdl 1r 1st totals 982rdl 2r 4st, not 1,001rdl 2r 4st. The 69rdl 1r 1st is probably correct because 990 pounds of sugar at the listed 7 rigsdalers per hundredweight totals 69rdl 2r 2st, nearly the same as the amount recorded. However, 13,347 pounds of sugar at 7 rigsdalers per hundredweight would total 934rdl 2r 2st, well above the 913rdl 1r 3st recorded. The 14,337 pounds of sugar at 7 rigsdalers per hundredweight should total 1,003rdl 4r 4st, close to the 1,001rdl 2r 4st given.
11. Anne Lytton Venton's Quittance with Alexander Hamilton, May 3, 1773, in *The Papers of Alexander Hamilton* 1:40.
12. *Christiansted Skiftebrevsprotokoller for Borgere og Plantere* 32:390v.
13. *Customs Journal (Toldbog), Christiansted, St. Croix, 1773* 89b and 203a.
14. Ramsing, "Alexander Hamilton Og Hans Modrene Slaegt" 251–252; Ramsing, *Alexander Hamilton's Birth and Parentage* 32; Chernow, *Alexander Hamilton* 39.
15. This author asserted in *Alexander Hamilton: The Formative Years* that "the hurricane and Hamilton's account of it may have had nothing to do with his move to the mainland" and that "all that rhetoric about Hamilton riding a whirlwind into history appears to be mistaken" (Newton, *Alexander Hamilton: The Formative Years* 57 and 58).
16. Newton, *Alexander Hamilton: The Formative Years* 57–58 and 59–60.
17. "The Annual RPI and Average Earnings for Britain."
18. *The New-York Mercury*, March 16, 1767, p4 c1.
19. *A History of Columbia University* 27 and 40.
20. Humphrey, *From King's College to Columbia* 252.
21. Humphrey, *From King's College to Columbia* 93–94.
22. Humphrey, *From King's College to Columbia* 91–92.

23. Mulligan, "Narrative."
24. Alexander Hamilton to William Hamilton, May 2, 1797, in *The Papers of Alexander Hamilton* 21:77.
25. John C. Hamilton, *The Life of Alexander Hamilton* 1:52; John C. Hamilton, *History of the Republic* 1:121.
26. Alexander Hamilton to Elizabeth Hamilton, July 10, 1804, in *The Papers of Alexander Hamilton* 26:307.

Anne Lytton Venton Mitchell
Records from 1799–1807

About thirty letters and receipts of Anne Lytton Venton Mitchell from the period of 1799 to 1807 have been found in the records of St. Croix.[1] Their contents primarily concern the collecting of her inheritance from the estate of her father James Lytton, who had passed away in 1769.[2] Some of these letters and receipts also include her daughter, Anne Lytton Venton Widberg, who had married a Philadelphia jeweler named Nicolay Peter Widberg, who himself died in October 1800.[3] Anne Lytton Venton Mitchell and Anne Lytton Venton Widberg were each heirs to one-seventh of the Lytton estate.[4]

These newly discovered records reveal a number of key facts regarding the life of Anne Lytton Venton Mitchell:

- Anne Mitchell signed her name in most of these early records. This indicates she was literate. However, in many of the later records, Anne Mitchell did not sign but instead left her mark. Anne Lytton was born in 1743, so she was about sixty years old at this time.[5] This suggests that age and infirmity may have prevented her from signing.
- Anne Mitchell signed her name "Anne Mitchell." Until now, most people had written her name as "Ann," but it clearly should be "Anne."
- Anne Mitchell's daughter, Anne Lytton Venton Widberg, signed her name "Anne Widberg," and in one record acted as her mother's "curator."
- Since Anne Lytton Venton Mitchell had been named after her mother Anne Faucett Lytton, it is probable that Anne Faucett Lytton's name was also spelled "Anne" rather than "Ann."[6]
- Anne Mitchell purchased a house on St. Croix for 45,000 pieces of eight but had trouble paying her mortgage and sought a loan in September 1799 to help her out.

- When Anne Lytton Venton Widberg's husband passed away in October 1800, Anne Mitchell was "called upon to pay attention to his funeral" but due to her "distressing situation" it was "not in [her] power to do it unless" she was given "money for that purpose."
- In April 1801, Anne Mitchell again complained of her "extreme need" and "want" of money and begged that the "six months' interest" due to her and her daughter, presumably from the Lytton estate, be paid. She accordingly received 120 pieces of eight.
- Six, twelve, and eighteen months later, Anne Mitchell again requested the "six months' interest" owed to her and her daughter. In her requests of April and October 1802, Anne Mitchell again wrote of her "extreme want" of the money owed to them. Clearly, Anne Mitchell and Anne Lytton Widberg struggled to make ends meet and therefore wanted and needed what was owed to them as soon as possible. It is likely that Anne Mitchell and her daughter continued these requests after 1802, but the letters documenting this have been lost.
- In October 1802, Anne Mitchell lived "now next [to] the Dutch Church" in Christiansted, St. Croix. The Dutch Reformed Church was on the corner of King's Street and Queen's Cross Street.[7]
- Dr. Edward Stevens, Alexander Hamilton's close friend, acted as the "curator" for Anne Mitchell and Anne Widberg on St. Croix in 1805.

Thus, Anne Lytton Venton Mitchell, who had been so generous to Alexander Hamilton thirty years earlier, was now struggling to make ends meet. Knowing his cousin's distress, Alexander Hamilton, in his final letter to his wife, encouraged her to help out "the person in the world to whom as a friend I am under the greatest obligations."[8]

Notes

1. *St. Croix Diverse Regnskabssager* 55.13.18 images 248–300.
2. For some details about the continuing operations of James Lytton's estate and disputes concerning it, see Anne Mitchell to Alexander Hamilton, 1796, in *The Papers of Alexander Hamilton* 20:456–460.
3. Ramsing, "Alexander Hamilton Og Hans Modrene Slaegt" 257; Ramsing, *Alexander Hamilton's Birth and Parentage* 38–39.
4. *Christiansted Testamentprotokoller 1764–1772* 128r–129r; *Christiansted Registrerings og*

Vurderingsprotokoller for Borgere og Plantere 1768–1773 124r–v; ibid. *1773–1777* 273r; *Christiansted Skiftebrevsprotokoller for Borgere og Plantere* 33:630r, 664r, 35:695r; Anne Mitchell to Alexander Hamilton, 1796, in *The Papers of Alexander Hamilton* 20:456–457; Ramsing, "Alexander Hamilton Og Hans Modrene Slaegt" 250; Ramsing, *Alexander Hamilton's Birth and Parentage* 30.

5. *Danske Folkekirke, St. Croix, Kirkebog 1740–1753* page 32 and transcript 38b.
6. No original signature for Anne Faucett Lytton has been found, but her name is spelled Ann, Anna, and Anne in the original records.
7. Oxholm, *Map No. 2.*
8. Alexander Hamilton to Elizabeth Hamilton, July 10, 1804, in *The Papers of Alexander Hamilton* 26:307–308.

Discovering Hugh Knox

John C. Hamilton wrote that his father, Alexander Hamilton, "early became a lover of books, and the time which other youth employ in classical learning, was by him devoted to miscellaneous reading, happily directed by the advice of Doctor Knox, a respectable presbyterian divine, who, delighted with the unfolding of his mind, took a deep interest in his welfare."[1]

Accordingly, discovering more about Hugh Knox's life, philosophy, and thoughts on various topics may lead to a better understanding of how he influenced a young Alexander Hamilton.

Hugh Knox Comes to St. Croix

After ministering on the tiny Dutch island of Saba for sixteen years, Hugh Knox "spent the months of September & October [1771] in that fine island" of St. Croix, where he "found a number of Scotch, English, Irish & North American Presbyterians." The island's Presbyterians, and others as well, surely asked Knox to speak in one or more of Christiansted's churches. Hamilton may have been among those who heard the reverend speak. The Presbyterians of St. Croix liked what they heard and extended to Knox "a cordial & unanimous invitation to come among them." St. Croix offered Knox much that Saba lacked. Larger and with more churches and ministers, St. Croix offered greater intellectual and spiritual stimulation. Perhaps more important, Knox earned just "500 pieces of eight per year" on Saba, about £80 sterling a year, "enough for a single man, but it will not support a family," as Knox "found by abundant experience." In contrast, the Presbyterians of Christiansted offered him "a yearly salary of 1,200 pieces of eight subscribed," about £192 per annum,[2] with each member pledging to pay a "subscription for the subsistence of the Reverend Hugh Knox Minister of the Gospel to be paid yearly by us after his entering to the Ministry here in the town of Christiansted."[3]

On October 28, 1771, Hugh Knox petitioned the Privy Council of St. Croix to be appointed "preacher in the Reformed Protestant or Presbyterian Church."[4] The Privy Council granted Knox's request on the condition that they receive positive testimonials of his tenure on Saba.[5]

Knox returned to Saba to gather these testimonials, wrap up his business there, and to collect his family and belongings. With affidavits from the community elders, deacons, town council, governor of Saba, and governor general on St. Eustatius attesting that he had been "diligent . . . in the work of his Ministry" and to his "sober, regular, and every way exemplary and edifying life," Knox in about May 1772 made the move with his wife and three children to Christiansted, St. Croix, and took charge of the city's Presbyterian church.[6]

It appears that the Presbyterians had no physical church building when Hugh Knox arrived since none is listed in the matrikels. However, the church had a building by August 1772 because it is listed as one of the many destroyed in the great hurricane.[7] In 1773, the Presbyterians constructed a new church building at the southwest corner of Prince's Street and Water or North Street.[8]

As of January 1773, Hugh Knox lived along with his wife and three children in a house rented from John Peter Richardsen on Beach Street.[9] If Knox moved into this house when he arrived around May 1772, this is where Hamilton would have visited him at home.

Hugh Knox's oldest child, a daughter, was born in April or May 1758,[10] making her fourteen years old when she arrived on St. Croix, just a few years younger than Alexander Hamilton.

As mentioned above, the members of Christiansted's Presbyterian community formed a "subscription for the subsistence of the Reverend Hugh Knox Minister of the Gospel to be paid yearly by us after his entering to the Ministry here in the town of Christiansted."[11] A few such subscription agreements and payments to Knox have been found.

On June 1, 1779, a Richard O'Cain was debited 10 pieces of eight for "one years' salary subscription." On April 26, 1780, O'Cain "paid Mr Knox balance" of 2 rigsdalers "due him for subscription."[12]

In June 1782, the estate of Alexander Carmichael owed Knox 15 rigsdalers for "one years' church subscription." This was followed by a copy of his subscription agreement:

Subscription for the subsistence of the reverend Mr. Hugh Knox Minister of the Gospel, to be paid yearly by us after his entering to the Ministry here in the town of Christiansted in St. Croix to him or those of the community to be appointed for the collection thereof, to terminate at the death of the subscribers, or at the expiration of three years after our respectively giving proper notice of our declining being longer members of the Presbyterian Congregation of this place.[13]

In June 1789, the estate of John Murray owed an old debt to Hugh Knox of 75 pieces of eight for "5 years salary subscribed from June 1st 1780 to the present date at 15ps per annum" and another 8ps 6r for "7 months ditto from June 1 1785 until this date." This was followed by a copy of his subscription agreement of June 1, 1783:

Subscription for the subsistence of the Revd Hugh Knox Minister of the Gospel to be paid yearly by us after his entering to the Ministerey here in the town of Christiansted to him or those of the community to be appointed for the collection thereof to terminate at the death of the said subscribers or at the expiration of three years after our respectively giving proper notice of our declining being longer members of the Presbyterian Congregation in this place.[14]

On June 1, 1789, Hugh Knox made out a receipt to one subscriber:

St. Croix 1st June 1789
Received in cash from James Towers the sum of fifty pieces of eight for a years' salary or subscription to me as minister of the Presbyterian Church or Congregation this place from 1st June 1788 to this date.
Hugh Knox[15]

Thus, Richard O'Cain paid 10 pieces of eight per year in 1779, Alexander Carmichael in 1782 and John Murray in 1780 to 1785 paid 15ps per annum, and James Towers in 1789 paid 50ps for a years' salary. Even if the rates rose over time, they could not have gone up that much. One can only assume that more prominent people paid higher subscription rates and in exchange received better pews in the church.

Hugh Knox and *The Royal Danish American Gazette*?

In 1939, H. U. Ramsing wrote that Hugh Knox "was a journalist and sometimes, in the absence of the editor, Daniel Thibous, he took over the editing of the official paper, Royal Danish American Gazette."[16] Even though Ramsing presented no evidence or citations to support this claim, it has been repeated by countless biographers, who then further assert that Knox's work at the newspaper helped him get Hamilton's hurricane account published.[17]

No evidence has been found that Knox wrote for, edited, or helped publish *The Royal Danish American Gazette*. Perhaps H. U. Ramsing found evidence that he failed to present. Or perhaps Ramsing saw the abovementioned "subscription" payment to Hugh Knox by Richard O'Cain, one of whose executors was the newspaper's printer Daniel Thibou, and concluded that Knox was involved in the newspaper. Without evidence, Ramsing's assertion and the conclusions being drawn from it must be questioned.

Moreover, even if Hugh Knox at some point wrote for, edited, or helped publish the newspaper, there is no knowing whether he did so in September 1772, just months after arriving on St. Croix. Even if Knox never worked for the paper or did so only at a later date, it is still possible that he encouraged Hamilton to have his hurricane account printed in the newspaper and acted as Hamilton's liaison. Conversely, even if Knox did these things, it does not mean he had any role in actually producing the newspaper.

Hugh Knox on Illegitimate Children

It has been argued that Alexander Hamilton attended the "school of a Jewess"[18] because the church schools would not accept illegitimate children.[19] If this was generally true, it was not so universally.

Hugh Knox believed that it was "as just to blame a man for being born blind as a child for being born with a corrupt nature" and that "no infant shall ever be everlastingly punished purely for original corruption." Thus, Knox believed that an illegitimate child should not be blamed for the circumstances of his birth and that everyone would be judged by the "just and righteous God" for their own actions rather than those of their parents.[20] Knox also contended that illegitimate children should be baptized and argued that not doing so would "to all intents and purposes" leave them and their descendants as "unbaptized heathens . . . to be treated with and addressed just as we would the wild Indians."[21]

Of course, Hugh Knox "happily directed" Hamilton's studies, "delighted with the unfolding of his mind," and "took a deep interest in his welfare."[22] Knox assisted Hamilton in his move to North America[23] and they continued to correspond for many years. He obviously did not care about Alexander Hamilton's illegitimacy.

Hugh Knox on the Law of Nature

In his *Discourses on the Truth of Revealed Religion and Other Important Subjects*, published in London in 1768, Hugh Knox wrote that God's laws are not just found in the Bible, but are also found in "the law of nature," a concept American revolutionaries would espouse as well. Knox continued, "Our duty is written, as it were, with sun beams. We are everywhere surrounded with a light which will leave us utterly speechless and excuseless if we shut our eyes against it or neglect to regulate our steps by its lucid rays."[24]

A few years later, Hamilton would take some of Knox's words and use them to argue for American rights. In *The Farmer Refuted*, Hamilton wrote, "The sacred rights of mankind are not to be rummaged for, among old parchments, or musty records. They are written, as with a sun beam, in the whole volume of human nature, by the hand of the divinity itself; and can never be erased or obscured by mortal power."[25]

Hugh Knox on Blacks and Slavery

Also in his *Discourses on the Truth of Revealed Religion*, Hugh Knox empathized with the "unfortunate creatures," the "poor, unhappy people who by some means . . . have lost their natural liberty." Knox argued that blacks "are of the same common nature with yourselves; that they are human creatures, reasonable beings, possessed of precious, immortal souls; souls as capable of religion and eternal happiness as our own." Knox believed that free men "ought to raise in our breasts some feelings of compassion for the unhappy condition of our poor heathen slaves." Knox contended that the "dullness and stupidity imputed to negroes is owing partly to their mean abject condition and partly to the unacquaintedness with our language, manners and

customs," and "that they want not, in general, a genius and capacity for learning." Knox pointed out that the whites of the West Indies had failed to edu-
cate their slaves and that "it is easy to conclude who must one day answer for
this."[26]

Years later, Hamilton again would repeat Hugh Knox's thoughts and even
use some of his words. In *A Full Vindication of the Measures of the Congress*,
Hamilton argued, "All men have one common original: they participate in
one common nature, and consequently have one common right. No reason
can be assigned why one man should exercise any power, or pre-eminence
over his fellow creatures more than another."[27] Arguing in favor of giving
slaves "their freedom with their muskets" if they fought for the patriot cause
during the War for Independence, Hamilton again repeated some of Knox's
ideas: "I frequently hear it objected to the scheme of embodying negroes that
they are too stupid to make soldiers. This is so far from appearing to me a
valid objection that I think their want of cultivation (for their natural faculties
are probably as good as ours) joined to that habit of subordination which they
acquire from a life of servitude, will make them sooner became soldiers than
our white inhabitants."[28]

Despite his progressive opinions about blacks and slavery, Hugh Knox's
primary interest was in educating these slaves and treating them better rather
than emancipating them. In fact, Knox owned thirteen slaves when he and
Hamilton knew each other on St. Croix,[29] and he failed to emancipate any of
them upon his death.[30] Nevertheless, Knox probably provided Hamilton with
his earliest and certainly his deepest exposure thus far to the intellectual and
religious arguments against slavery.

Hugh Knox on Drunkenness and Christianity

On other moral and religious topics, Hamilton learned from Knox's *Discourses* about "the folly and danger of drunkenness, and the way to avoid it,"[31]
and that "charity or Christian love" is "the most eminent among the graces"
and even "the mother of the graces."[32]

As his later life and writings attest, Hamilton embraced the ideas espoused
by Hugh Knox and, as John C. Hamilton reported, "the topics of their conversation opened to him an early glimpse of those polemical controversies
which have called forth the highest efforts of intellect."[33]

Hugh Knox Helps Anne Lytton Venton

After an absence of about six years, Anne Lytton Venton and her daughter returned to St. Croix from Philadelphia in 1779.[34]

H. U. Ramsing had already noted in his essay that "as early as 1779, Hugh Knox warmly assisted Ann Venton in her case against the probate court."[35]

It would seem that Knox did more than just help. Anne Lytton Venton herself explained, "The best of men Mr. Knox has unrequested contributed largely to our support since our arrival."[36] Evidently, Knox supported Venton financially as well as giving her legal assistance. Whether he provided this support from his own pocket or the church's charity fund is not known.

Dr. Hugh Knox

In addition to nurturing the spiritual wellbeing of his flock, Knox as a medical doctor tended to their physical health as well.

In 1765, Hugh Knox wrote, "My many, long, & grievous infirmities, as well as my taste & inclination, have led me for many years past to medical & physical enquiries; I have a pretty good collection of books on these sciences, & have often ventured to present & give gratuitous advice to many of my people with good success; but have never ventured to practise—first, because of the fatigue which a practitioner must endure in this place,—and secondly & chiefly from a sense of incapacity, & a fear of doing hurt thro' ignorance."[37]

However, when Hugh Knox applied for a medical license on St. Croix in 1775, it was noted that he had for "17 years practiced as a doctor on the Dutch Island [Saba]." He received his medical license on St. Croix in January 1776.[38]

Actually, Hugh Knox had been practicing medicine on St. Croix even before receiving his license.[39]

Hugh Knox's "Old Friends" in "America"

In 1784, Hugh Knox wrote to Alexander Hamilton about his "secret pride in having advised you to go to America, & in having recommended you to some of my old friends there."[40] These are the letters of introduction that Knox wrote to Elias Boudinot, William Livingston, John Rodgers, John Mason, "and other gentlemen of distinction."[41]

How did Hugh Knox know these men?

John Rodgers was a Presbyterian minister who in the 1750s helped Knox start a school and recommended him to the College of New Jersey.[42]

John Mason, however, immigrated from Scotland to New York in 1761,[43] after Knox had left to Saba. Unless the two had known each other in Scotland before they moved to America, it does not appear that Knox and Mason knew each other personally. One assumes, however, that they had corresponded. Knox, of course, was well known from his published works and other ministers surely wrote to him seeking his advice and thoughts. Alternatively, Hugh Knox could have given Hamilton generic letters of introduction not addressed to anyone in particular, one of which Hamilton gave to the stranger John Mason.

But what about Elias Boudinot and William Livingston? Did they know Hugh Knox personally? Did they correspond with Knox? Or were they complete strangers?

Although there is no record of it, Hugh Knox may have met Elias Boudinot back in the 1750s through their mutual friend, the Reverend Aaron Burr. Knox had studied under Burr at the College of New Jersey and considered "President Burr" to be his "worthy and excellent friend."[44] The Boudinots were also friends with Burr around this time and in fact had met with Burr to discuss young Elias Boudinot's interest in attending college.[45] Through his Presbyterian friends in New York and New Jersey, Knox surely knew that Boudinot had previously been a visitor at Elizabethtown's grammar school[46] and had in 1772 become a trustee of the College of New Jersey.[47] Knowing that Boudinot's support could help Hamilton get into both the grammar school and the College of New Jersey, Hugh Knox relied on his international reputation, mutual acquaintances, and perhaps a previous friendship in introducing the unknown Alexander Hamilton to Elias Boudinot.

Hugh Knox also wrote a letter of introduction for Hamilton to William Livingston. There is no evidence that Knox and Livingston had ever met or corresponded, but Livingston like Knox and Boudinot had been a good friend of Rev. Aaron Burr[48] and had known Burr when Knox was his student in the 1750s.[49] If William Livingston and Hugh Knox did not know each other in the 1750s, each had surely heard of the other and they continued to hear more about each other over the next two decades as they both gained in fame and reputation.

It is possible that Hugh Knox addressed these letters of introduction to no one in particular and relied upon his international reputation in promoting Hamilton's entrance into school. More likely, though, Knox did in fact know Elias Boudinot and William Livingston and that they knew and respected him. Knox's letters of introduction for Hamilton thus carried the weight that was needed to not only get him into school but to introduce him to new friends who would promote his interest for years to come.

Hugh Knox's Death and Obituary

On October 9, 1790, Hugh Knox passed away on St. Croix. His obituary appeared in *The Royal Danish American Gazette* on October 13, 1790:

On Saturday the 9th Instant, departed this Life, the Reverend Doctor HUGH KNOX, aged 63, Pastor of the Presbyterian Church, and Physician; Eminent in, and an ornament to the former Profession, Judicious and successful in the latter.—A Tender and affectionate Husband, the best of Fathers, and a sincere, faithful, and firm friend, and an Universal lover of Mankind—Possessed of every Virtue which made him beloved and respected here, and we doubt not, happy hereafter— 19 years was he a residenter in this Island, during which time he was anxiously employed in Promoting the Public and Private good of this Community, His whole life, when his Precarious Health wou'd permit, was a busy scene of Public and Private exertions for the welfare of his Fellow-creatures, and we flatter ourselves that his Christian endeavours have not been void of success.—Christian Fortitude and Resignation mark'd his last illness, and he met Death with a smile—his value was too well known to dwell longer on it here, and suffice it to say, that he was one of GOD's noblest Works.[50]

Hugh Knox's Last Will and Testament

On October 1, 1790, just eight days before his death, Hugh Knox, "being infirm in body & apprehending a speedy & perhaps sudden dissolution," made out his "last will and testament." A copy of the will is found in the probate record of Knox's estate:

In the Name & fear of God Amen

I Hugh Knox, Clerik Minister of the Gospel in this Island of St. Croix, being infirm in Body & apprehending a speedy & perhaps sudden Dissolution but being of a sound Mind and memory, think it Expedient to make this as my last Will & Testament.

1st I commit my Body to the Dust, whence it came & desire it may be buried in the plainest & least expensive manner having ever been an Enemy to expensive Funerals which are of no use to the Dead & often deprive the Survivers of that, which they much need and Request it of my Heirs & Relations to wear no Badges of what the World calls Mourning, as they are too often a Makery [mockery] of the Dead & rather Signals of Rejoicing.

2dly I commend my Soul to God, who gave it with an humble Reliance on his infinite mercy thro Christ the Redeemer of a lost & guilty World.

3dly As to the small Portion of wordly [worldly] Interest, with which God hath been pleased to Endow me, I will that it should be disposed of in the following manner to wit:

1st That Twenty Pieces of Eight shall be paid to the Danish Church & Hospital

2dly After the Debts due to the Estate of Hugh & Mary Knox / which are Nearly all contained in the Book Containing said Debts / are collected & realized and the three Heirs of Mary Knox have been paid their Nett Sixth parts of the whole Estate, agreeable to the Tenor of Hugh & Mary Knoxes Will, now confirmed by the King, it is my Will that the Residue, whether in House, Furniture, Slaves, Bonds or Book debts may be either sold or divided as the Executors & Dealing Masters of this my last Will shall deem it most expedient for the Interest & advantage of the Heirs & the Nett Proceeds equally divided among my three Children Peter John Knox, Ann Towers & my youngest Son Hugh Knox now in America or the lawfull Heirs of their Bodies   But

3dly As it may & probably will happen, that some of my children may have had more from the Estate at my Death than their motherly Portion shall have amounted to / as my accounts against them will make appear / my Will is that such Surplus of Surplusses shall be taken from their Fatherly Portion & equally divided amongst them in such manner, that every child shall have a like upon the whole dividend of the joint Estates, only with the Reservations of Legacies in the 4th & 5th Articles below specified as

4^{thly} As my youngest Son Hugh is yet a Child and has the whole Course of his Education to go through before he can be capable of Earning a livelyhood, I will & desire, that out of the Nett Proceeds of my whole Interest Five Hundred Pieces of Eight over & above his Fatherly Portion shall be allowed him and put to Interest by his Guardians to be employed toward his Education.

5^{thly} as to my Servants, who are now with me or who may Continue with me till my Death, I would willingly shew them some mark of my favour, and therefore will that Nannette who has been dry Nurse to my Son Hugh & House Keeper for me since my Wife's Death, shall be made free on the following Conditions. Either first, that she works out 6 years after my Death & punctually pays Twenty Five Pieces of Eight pr year to my Executors & my son Hughs Guardians for his use. or Secondly if she can get any Person to purchase her freedom, such Person may immediately obtain her freedom on paying down to said Executors & Guardians the Sum of one Hundred & Fourty Pieces of Eight, but that shall be under the Countroul of none but such Executors & Guardians. To Molly my washer Women [woman] I will & bequeath Fifty Pieces of Eight for her faithfull Services & to all my other Negroes, who shall be with me when I die, to each I bequeath five Pieces of Eight to drink to my Health after I am dead & to Encourage them to cry for the loss of so good a Master.

and for the Execution & fullfilment of this my last Will I do will & ordain / agreeable to His Majesties most Gracious ordinance of   / as my Executors & Dealing Masters, the following Gentlemen in whose integrity I repose a perfect Confidence Mr. Arthur Cooper, Mr. John Sempill, Mr. John Rodger & Mr. John Towers and also as Guardian to my Youngest Son Hugh & to these four Gentlemen I most willingly allow not only all Necessary Expenses, but also four pct for incassating [collecting] the Debts due to the Estate. Wittness my Hand & Sealed, Saint Croix this first day of october, 1790.

Hugh Knox

Signed, sealed in the Presence of H. Schultz

Daniel McFarlane[51]

Hugh Knox's Children

In his will, Hugh Knox listed "my three children Peter John Knox, Ann Towers & my youngest son Hugh Knox now in America."

When Alexander Hamilton knew Knox on St. Croix in 1772, Hugh Knox had one son and two daughters.[52]

Presumably, the son was Peter John Knox and one of the daughters was Ann Knox, who married James Towers.[53] The other daughter, who Hamilton had known but is not listed in Knox's will, must have been Knox's "very promising child," Rebecca Knox, who died in December 1773.[54]

The other son listed in the will, Hugh Knox Jr., who Hamilton did not know on St. Croix, was born on December 19, 1781.[55]

Hugh Knox's Provisions Regarding His Slaves

Despite bequeathing fifty pieces of eight to one slave and five pieces each to the others upon his death, all of Knox's slaves according to his will were to remain enslaved. Only one of his slaves was allowed to purchase her freedom.

It is interesting how Hugh Knox gave generous gifts to his slaves and even offered one of them her freedom for a price, yet he still treated them as property and clearly did not want to deprive his children of their inheritance. This dichotomy between kindness towards slaves on the one hand and condescension on the other probably says more about the time and place in which Hugh Knox lived rather than anything about Knox personally.

Notes

1. John C. Hamilton, *The Life of Alexander Hamilton* 1:3–4; John C. Hamilton, *History of the Republic* 1:42.
2. Hugh Knox to Jacob Green, January 22, 1772, in the *Simon Gratz Autograph Collection* 0250A, Case 9, Box 11.
3. *Christiansted Skiftebrevsprotokoller for Borgere og Plantere* 36:161r–v, 508v–509r.
4. Hugh Knox to the Privy Council, October 28, 1771, in *St. Croix Indkomne skrivelser til Generalguvernøren og Det sekrete Råd 1771* 382–383.
5. *St. Croix Secrete Råd Forhandlingsprotokoller 1771–1774* 41v.
6. Affidavits concerning Hugh Knox, November 30, December 7, 12, 1771, in the *Harold Larson Papers* Box 4; Hugh Knox to Jacob Green, January 22, 1772, in the *Simon Gratz Autograph Collection* 0250A, Case 9, Box 11; Ramsing, "Alexander Hamilton

Og Hans Modrene Slaegt" 263; Ramsing, *Alexander Hamilton's Birth and Parentage* 45–46; Mitchell, "The Man who Discovered Hamilton" 105.
Knox planned to move from Saba to St. Croix on May 1, 1772 (Hugh Knox to Jacob Green, January 22, 1772, in the *Simon Gratz Autograph Collection* 0250A, Case 9, Box 11), but there is no record of the date he actually moved.

7. *The Massachusetts Gazette; and the Boston Weekly News-Letter*, October 29, 1772, Supplement p2 cl.

8. *St. Croix Matrikel 1772* 9; ibid. *1773* 10; Oxholm, *Map No. 2*.

9. *St. Croix Matrikel 1772* 9.

10. Hugh Knox to unknown, March 2, 1759, in the *Simon Gratz Autograph Collection* 0250B, Box 159.
It is not known whether this daughter was Ann Knox, later Ann Towers, (see page 214) or Knox's "very promising child," Rebecca Knox, who died in December 1773 (*The Royal Danish American Gazette*, December 29, 1773, p2 c3).

11. *Christiansted Skiftebrevsprotokoller for Borgere og Plantere* 36:161r–v, 508v–509r.

12. *Christiansted Skiftebrevsprotokoller for Borgere og Plantere* 35:729r, 733r.

13. *Christiansted Skiftebrevsprotokoller for Borgere og Plantere* 36:508v–509r.

14. *Christiansted Skiftebrevsprotokoller for Borgere og Plantere* 36:161r–v.

15. *Christiansted Skiftesager på Enkeltpersoner* 38.61.180 image 187b.

16. Ramsing, "Alexander Hamilton Og Hans Modrene Slaegt" 263–264; Ramsing, *Alexander Hamilton's Birth and Parentage* 46.

17. Mitchell, *Alexander Hamilton: Youth to Maturity* 31; Chernow, *Alexander Hamilton* 36; Newton, *Alexander Hamilton: The Formative Years* 52.

18. John C. Hamilton, *The Life of Alexander Hamilton* 1:3; John C. Hamilton, *History of the Republic* 1:42.

19. Bobbé, "The Boyhood of Alexander Hamilton" 7; Lewisohn, *St. Croix Under Seven Flags* 150; Randall, *Alexander Hamilton: A Life* 18; Chernow, *Alexander Hamilton* 17.

20. Knox, *A Letter to the Rev. Mr. Jacob Green* 59.

21. Hugh Knox to Jacob Green, October 16, 1766, in the *Jacob Green Correspondence and Papers*.

22. John C. Hamilton, *The Life of Alexander Hamilton* 1:3–4; John C. Hamilton, *History of the Republic* 1:42.

23. See pages 209–211.

24. Knox, *Discourses on the Truth of Revealed Religion and Other Important Subjects* 2:243. See also Knox, *A Discourse . . . On Occasion of the Hurricane* 2–4.

25. Alexander Hamilton, *The Farmer Refuted*, February 1775, in *The Papers of Alexander Hamilton* 1:122.

26. Knox, *Discourses on the Truth of Revealed Religion and Other Important Subjects* 2:163–166 and 175.

27. Alexander Hamilton, *A Full Vindication of the Measures of the Congress*, December 1774, in *The Papers of Alexander Hamilton* 1:47.

28. Alexander Hamilton to John Jay, March 14, 1779, *The Papers of Alexander Hamilton* 2:18.

29. *St. Croix Matrikel 1772* 9; ibid. *1773* 9. See also Hugh Knox's advertisement offering a reward for the return of a runaway slave in *The Royal Danish American Gazette*,

September 19, 1772, p1 c2.

30. See pages 211–214.

31. Knox, *Discourses on the Truth of Revealed Religion and Other Important Subjects* 2:325–347. See also Knox, *A Discourse . . . On Occasion of the Hurricane* 1–2.

32. Knox, *Discourses on the Truth of Revealed Religion and Other Important Subjects* 2:296.

33. John C. Hamilton, *The Life of Alexander Hamilton* 1:4. See also John C. Hamilton, *History of the Republic* 1:42.

34. Ramsing, *Alexander Hamilton's Birth and Parentage* 31, 33; Newton, *Alexander Hamilton: The Formative Years* 525 note 59.

35. Ramsing, *Alexander Hamilton's Birth and Parentage* 47.

36. Anne Lytton Venton to James Towers, October 18, 1779, in *Christiansted Skiftebrevsprotokoller for Borgere og Plantere* 33:669r.

37. Hugh Knox to Jacob Green, September 24, 1765, in the *Simon Gratz Autograph Collection* 0250B, Box 159.

38. *St. Croix Reskriptprotokol* images 17a, 239b–240a; Danske Kancelli, *Vestindiske Sager 1773–1786* 104r–v; Carøe, *Den Danske Lægestand: Doktorer Og Licentiater, 1479–1788* 71.

39. *Christiansted Skiftebrevsprotokoller for Kgl. Betjente 1771–1777* 114–115; *St. Croix Accounts 1772–1779* 38, in *St. Croix Diverse Regnskabsprotokoller* 55.12.63 image 103a.

40. Hugh Knox to Alexander Hamilton, July 28, 1784, in *PAH* 3:573.

41. Mulligan, "Narrative"; Troup, "Narrative"; John C. Hamilton, *The Life of Alexander Hamilton* 1:7; John C. Hamilton, *History of the Republic* 1:45.

42. Miller, *Memoirs of the Rev. John Rodgers* 97, 102–103.

43. Miller, *Memoirs of the Rev. John Rodgers* 163–164; Van Vechten, *Memoirs of John M. Mason* 1.

44. Hugh Knox to Jacob Green, August 29, 1768, in the *Jacob Green Correspondence and Papers*.

45. Elias Boudinot to his parents, December 23, 1761, in the *Society Collection*; Boyd, *Elias Boudinot* 15.

46. Hatfield, *History of Elizabeth, New Jersey* 520. Boudinot was no longer a visitor at Elizabethtown's grammar school when Hamilton arrived (Mitchell, *Alexander Hamilton: Youth to Maturity* 494 note 75).

47. Hatfield, *History of Elizabeth, New Jersey* 589.

48. Livingston, *A Funeral Elogium on the Reverend Mr. Aaron Burr*; Sedgwick, *A Memoir of the Life of William Livingston* 113.

49. William Livingston to Aaron Burr, May 29, 1754, quoted in Sedgwick, *A Memoir of the Life of William Livingston* 78.

50. *The Royal Danish American Gazette*, October 13, 1790, p1 c1–2.

51. *Christiansted Skiftesager på Enkeltpersoner* 38.61.180 19r–23v.

52. *St. Croix Matrikel 1772* 9.

53. *St. John's Anglican Church, Christiansted, St. Croix, Marriage Registry 1761–1787* page 15.

54. *The Royal Danish American Gazette*, December 29, 1773, p2 c3.

55. Dexter, *Biographical Sketches of the Graduates of Yale College* 5:408.

The Great Hurricane of 1772

The great hurricane of 1772 is a central feature in Hamilton biographies, but details of the hurricane itself are hard to come by. Hamilton bios focus on how the hurricane devastated St. Croix and thereby affected Hamilton's life. More scientific books track the hurricane and give brief synopses of how hard it hit each island in an attempt to estimate its course and strength. But no one has accumulated accounts of this hurricane from the various islands and compiled them into one narrative.

On the evening of August 30, 1772, a steady breeze started blowing over the eastern Leeward Islands. The wind "continued to increase" throughout the night and by morning it "raged with inconceivable fury and violence" as a powerful hurricane entered the West Indies. Antigua, two hundred miles east of St. Croix, was one of the first islands to feel the wrath of this "dreadful tempest" when it arrived on August 31 between "one and two o'clock in the morning." The wind "continued increasing till five in the morning when it blew a hurricane" and "darkness prevailed for more than an hour after sun rise." At "eight o'clock the fury of the tempest in some measure abated, but it was only to collect new redoubled violence, and to display itself, with ten fold terror, for the space of 4 hours." This "most dreadful storm . . . was not properly assuaged till five in the afternoon." "Everyone" on the island "suffered in a greater or less[er] degree." In the capital city of St. John's, many houses were "carried into the harbour" and "above a third of the town" was "entirely destroyed." Most of the remaining houses had their interiors "torn in pieces" and became "uninhabitable." "Very few, if any, of the houses in St. John's have entirely escaped" and "some persons were buried in the ruins of their houses." On the island as a whole, "not one house in ten is said to be standing" and the remaining were "materially damaged." Both the town hospital at St. John's and the naval hospital at English Harbor were "blown to the ground," whereby eleven patients and one nurse "perished." The "church, courthouse, barracks, and most, if not all, the public buildings are greatly injured." Meanwhile, "all the buildings, windmills, works, etc.," on the plantations were "levelled with the ground" and the sugar cane was all "torn up by the roots." In sum, the island was "totally laid in ruins." Moreover, "the effects of this tempest was not less fatal on sea than upon land" as "all the vessels in the different harbours (with very few exceptions . . .) were either sunk, overset, or driven ashore." In total, "three men of war, two frigates, and sixty odd merchant-men" were "lost." Even the ships of the royal navy, anchored at "that secure place English Harbour," were "driven from their moorings and suffered greatly." The total cost of the damage, according to various reports, "cannot be estimated." Additionally, "several persons were killed and a considerable number wounded and maimed." On the whole, this hurricane was "more violent and destructive" than any other "known to have happened there in the memory of the oldest person in that island" and was "more violent and dreadful than perhaps ever before happened in the memory of man, and unparalleled (I believe) in its effects by any recorded in the annals of history."[1]

Guadeloupe, sixty miles south of Antigua, escaped the worst of it, but even there "much damage" was "done to the plantations" and as many as twenty-six "sail of vessels" were "drove ashore."[2] Sixty miles even farther south, Dominica "had but the tail" of the hurricane and therefore "the storm was not so severe" as elsewhere. Nevertheless, at least "eighteen vessels" there were also "drove ashore and lost."[3]

The hurricane wreaked devastation as it moved west, passing over Montserrat, Nevis, St. Kitts, St. Eustatius, Saba, and St. Martin. It reached St. Kitts at nine o'clock on the morning of August 31, at which time "the flood gates of Heaven seemed to have burst open." The wind blew out of the northeast and "continued with unremitting fury" for two hours as "horror and dismay seized all ranks & conditions, and destruction seemed suspended by a thread over the heads of all." The residents received a reprieve for one hour as the eye of the storm passed directly overhead and "the sun began to shine." Then, "the storm began again from the southward, with redoubled vigour, and proved by far more dreadful than the first." This even more "severe" gale lasted another two hours and included what felt like "a severe shock of an earthquake" but did less "mischief" because the first half of the storm "scarcely left anything" for the second part "to destroy." By the time the hurricane ended around two o'clock in the afternoon, most of the island's houses, churches, windmills, and boiling houses were destroyed. "Some houses were shoved . . . from the foundations without falling; others were turned upside-down; some were whirled into the street, others not a vestige of them left behind." All of the island's sailing vessels, thirty in total, were "parted from their anchors," driven ashore, and "wrecked." At least four whites and twenty blacks were killed. Many more were injured. All the trees were "disrobed of their foliage," grasses and vegetables were "entirely destroyed," "sugar canes, in many places, were twisted out by the root, others disjointed, and some for whole acres swept entirely away," and the "roads were rendered impassible either by floods, gullies, or huge trees laid across them." Some residents of St. Kitts estimated the loss at no less than half a million pounds sterling, others put it at "more than a million," still others "computed" it at "two millions currency," while others thought the loss "can scarce be computed." "In short, everyone who had anything to lose was a sufferer." It was believed that "the island will not be able to recover the loss sustained by that hurricane in the course of 50 years."[4]

The nearby islands of Nevis and Montserrat were also "sadly shattered" as "scarcely a house" was "left standing." At least four ships were "lost at Nevis" and seven more were forced ashore.[5]

On St. Eustatius, twenty miles northwest of St. Kitts, the hurricane "spread such terror and destruction as is not remembered by the oldest man now living among us; it destroyed almost everything that impeded its course." Two ships "foundered at their anchors, and every person on board perished." The remaining ships in the harbor were lost and their crews were thought to have "perished." Those who lived "upon the hill" were "the greatest sufferers" as "not less than 400 houses were blown down . . . or rendered untenable," some of which were "taken up bodily by the force of the wind and removed 10 or 20 yards from where they formerly stood" while the others were "carried into the sea." All the plantation houses, "except one or two," were also knocked down. The Jewish synagogue was "blown down" and the roof of the Dutch church "was blown into the sea," but the English church "lost but a quarter of its roof." The damage along the shore was "almost inconceivable" as many houses were "carried into the sea" and the flooding from the "deluges of rain" swamped the streets and left "so much rubbish" and "dirt" that people had to "come through the upper story windows" to exit those houses that remained standing. All the ships were driven out of the harbor, "many known to be lost, many returned dismasted, and many not heard of." In sum, "nothing but destruction and desolation" as "vast numbers of the inhabitants have lost their lives, and those who have survived have scarcely a covering to their heads." The damage was estimated at a million pieces of eight, or about £160,000 sterling.[6]

On the island of Saba, twenty miles northwest of St. Eustatius, about "180 houses," nearly all on the island, were "blown down, the cattle carried away from their stakes, and the people in a most wretched condition." Additionally, "two ships" were "lost on the back of that island, and every person on board perished."[7] Another thirty miles to the north, on the island of St. Martin, there remained "scarce a house standing, all their plantations destroyed."[8]

After devastating those islands, the tropical cyclone gained intensity as it spun its way westward over the warm Caribbean waters. After raining "considerably" during the day of August 31, the hurricane reached St. Croix just after sunset. From about seven in the evening until ten o'clock at night, the wind "blew violently from the north, raising the sea on the south side of the island about 12 or 14 feet above its usual standard." The air "had a suffocating, sulphureous smell." The "tempest" then stopped for nearly an hour as the eye of the storm passed directly over St. Croix. During this intermission, the air became so "calm" that one "might carry a lighted candle along the streets" without fear of it being extinguished. Just before eleven p.m., the wind "began to blow with redoubled violence," this time from "the southwest," until "near three o'clock in the morning." This second assault did even "more damage than the first." Amid the "tenfold darkness" that accompanied the storm that night, heavy rain fell, "perpetual lightning" flashed, and "fiery meteors" flew "about it in the air."[9] In sum, this was, according to one report, the "most dreadful & violent hurricane . . . ever known in the memory of the oldest man among us."[10] Another report claimed "that the late storm has not had its equal among these islands for two centuries past" and was the "most dreadful known among these islands since their first settlement."[11] An official proclamation even declared this to be "more violent and dreadful than perhaps ever before happened in the memory of man, and (as he believed) unparalleled in its effects by any recorded in the annals of history."[12]

The direct hit of this "unparalleled" hurricane devastated St. Croix. According to one report, "The sea swelled up 70 feet above the usual height, tore all the houses near the shore to pieces, and ruined them even to the foundations; beams, planks and stones flew through the air like feathers." Four hundred and sixty houses in Christiansted and sixty-three on the plantations "were thrown down." It was reported that "not one Negro-house" remained "standing in the island." In one section of Christiansted, all "but 6 or 7 houses" were destroyed, the remaining were "much damaged." A number of these houses had "been carried several yards" and dropped "in the middle of the streets." In Frederiksted, there were "but three houses left standing." The hospitals in both Christiansted and Frederiksted lay in "ruins." In Christiansted, the Anglican church and Hugh Knox's Presbyterian church were both destroyed, a third church "suffered inconceivably," a fourth "lost a little of one gable, some windows and doors," and the Quaker meeting house "was taken up and carried near 100 feet, and set down again without much damage." The Danish, Dutch, and Catholic churches, however, stood firm. In total, "about one half of the buildings" on St. Croix were "thrown down and blown away." Even the stronghold of Fort Christiansvaern suffered damage, enabling the escape of two imprisoned thieves "well practiced in all manner of roguery." The heavy wind and rain also caused mud and rock slides. Sea water flooded low-lying areas, including much of Christiansted. "The sea swelled in such a rapid manner" that in one instance "it overtook above 250 persons who ran up to the mountains to save themselves." "All the trees were rooted up, which occasioned holes of four, five and six feet in the ground." The island's "magazines, stores, and provisions" were "quite ruined." The plantations "were ruined in such a manner that it is impossible for them to be cultivated next year" because "all the trees" and "several heavy stones" were "lying in the plantations" so that "it will require above a twelvemonth's time to clear the plantation and to bring them into a situation able to be cultivated again." "All the ships at the different harbours" with a couple of exceptions, "about 42 sail" in total, "were cast ashore and driven fifty or a hundred yards on the land" and "wrecked." Their "valuable cargoes" were "destroyed" and the "crews dashed to pieces by the merciless waves." Meanwhile, inbound ships with much needed provisions were lost at sea.[13]

The 1772 matrikel lists dozens of houses that were blown down by the hurricane and not yet repaired months later. On one Christiansted street, twelve houses in a row were destroyed and not yet rebuilt.[14] The damage on St. Croix totaled an estimated 1,911,651 rigsdalers and 56 skillings,[15] or about

£300,000 sterling, but this total apparently did not include the damage suffered by ships in port and their cargos. Accordingly, other estimates came in with higher totals. One estimated the loss at one million pounds sterling[16] while a second asserted a similar sum of five million dollars.[17]

The human cost was just as great. "Many perished in the seas, many on shore, and others survived to see themselves ruined in a night."[18] According to an early tally, seven whites were killed in Christiansted alone, along with three free blacks and six slaves. Two whites and four slaves were also "dangerously wounded."[19] An updated estimate had twelve whites dead in Christiansted, plus "many Negroes killed in town and country."[20] A third update reported in excess of thirty total dead on the whole of the island, but that number daily increased as the "wounded and bruised" continued "dropping off the mortal stage."[21] Adding in those who died aboard sunken ships, the total was certainly much higher.

The storm left St. Croix in "almost universal desolation." Most of the residents were left "without a shift of cloaths . . . nor an house to put their heads in." The few houses that survived the hurricane were now crowded with "20 or 30 persons in them." This "lately blooming, fertile, flourishing" country became a "poor, distressed, miserable, helpless island." The "cistern water" became tainted during the storm and a week later still tasted "so strong of sulphur and nitre that it is scarce fit for use." The hurricane left the island with a "dearth and scarcity of provisions." And with most of the island's ships destroyed or driven ashore, St. Croix's harbors were "entirely bare" and there was a total "deadness of trade." With "a scarcity of all the necessaries of life and little hope of a supply," mass starvation was imminent if provisions could not be produced or imported quickly.[22]

Just forty miles north of St. Croix, the "very destructive" and "violent" hurricane accompanied by "heavy rain" and a storm surge of "70 feet above its usual height" did "considerable damage" to St. John, St. Thomas, and Tortola, "tearing up their canes, destroying houses," driving ashore a "great number of vessels," and killing "a number of whites as well as blacks."[23] One merchant from Tortola summarized, "The once rich, fertile, and flourishing West Indies are now as barren as rocks; our shipping are dashed to pieces, and many on dry land; our plantations ruined, and several merchants reduced to poverty in one night's time. Many lives are lost."[24]

Over the next few days, the hurricane continued its trek westward. After

St. Croix, the hurricane proceeded to Puerto Rico, where the storm lasted over six hours and did considerable damage.[25] It then hit Hispaniola, where "all the vessels" at the northwestern port of Cape Nicolas Mole were driven "from their anchors" towards the "rocks" but a fortuitous shift in the wind "drove them on the opposite shore, being a sandy beach, from whence they were all got off without much damage, except a brig."[26] The hurricane continued on to Cuba, where on September 3 the north side of the island "met with a hard gale of wind attended with thunder and lightning" and the south side "met with a violent hurricane" and a "heavy sea."[27] That same day, the hurricane's outer bands struck Jamaica with a storm "more terrible than any that ever happened in the memory of the oldest inhabitant." Most of the island was hit with "deluges of rain, which flooded the rivers to an incredible height, tore up several bridges, and drowned a good many cattle, sheep, and some negroes." At St. Ann's Bay on the north side of the island, where "the wind was chiefly felt," one ship was "drove out" of the harbor, dismasted, "set on fire by lightning, and soon after blew up."[28] The following day, Cape San Antonio at the west end of Cuba "met with a very violent gale of wind, the severity of which continued about 4 hours, veering all round the compass."[29] At this point, after travelling over the large and mountainous islands of Puerto Rico, Hispaniola, and Cuba, the hurricane had dissipated and its trail of devastation ended.

Notes

1. *The Gentleman's Magazine and Historical Chronicle* 42:590; *The Royal Danish American Gazette*, September 9, 1772, p1 c3; ibid. September 19, 1772, p2 c2–3; *The Pennsylvania Journal; and the Weekly Advertiser*, October 7, 1772, p1 c3; *The New-York Journal; or, The General Advertiser*, October 8, 1772, p2 c1; ibid. October 29, 1772, Supplement p2 c2; *The London Chronicle*, November 5–7, 1772, p7 c3; ibid. November 10–12, 1772, p2 c1; *The St. James's Chronicle Or, the British Evening-Post* [London], November 7–10, 1772, p1 c3; *The Middlesex Journal, or Universal Evening-Post* [London], November 28 – December 1, 1772, p2 c2; *The Dublin Journal*, December 1–3, 1772, p1 c3; Knox, *A Discourse . . . On Occasion of the Hurricane* 17n; Southey, *Chronological History of the West Indies* 2:409; *Minutes of the Provincial Council of Pennsylvania* 10:57; Oliver, *The History of the Island of Antigua* 1:cxxi.
2. *The Massachusetts Gazette; and the Boston Weekly News-Letter*, October 29, 1772, Supplement p2 c2; *The Middlesex Journal, or Universal Evening-Post* [London], November 10–12, 1772, p4 c2.
3. *The Pennsylvania Journal; and the Weekly Advertiser*, October 7, 1772, p1 c3 and p3

c1–2; *The Daily Advertiser* [London], November 7, 1772, p1 c2; *The Middlesex Journal, or Universal Evening-Post* [London], November 10–12, 1772, p4 c2.

4. *An Account of the Late Dreadful Hurricane, Which happened On the 31st of August, 1772* 3–5, 7, and 10; *The Royal Danish American Gazette*, September 19, 1772, p2 c3; *The Boston Evening-Post*, October 5, 1772, p1 c3; *The Pennsylvania Journal; and the Weekly Advertiser*, October 7, 1772, p3 c1–2; *The Boston Evening-Post*, October 12, 1772, p2 c3; *The Gazetteer and New Daily Advertiser* [London], November 2, 1772, p4 c2; *The St. James's Chronicle Or, the British Evening-Post* [London], December 1–3, 1772, p4 c4; Knox, *A Discourse . . . On Occasion of the Hurricane* 17n; Southey, *Chronological History of the West Indies* 2:411.

Despite claims that St. Kitts "will not be able to recover the loss sustained by that hurricane in the course of 50 years," it was soon reported that "a surprising vegetation . . . has since made the island assume a more comfortable aspect, and our hopes of the next crop are risen in proportion" (*An Account of the Late Dreadful Hurricane, Which happened On the 31st of August, 1772* 10). Two and a half months after the hurricane, it was said that "the island was in a fair way of making a great quantity of sugars this year, the canes being very fine and green; and that a great number of the houses which had been blown down in the late hurricane were rebuilt; and they were in hopes in a little time to complete the whole, as they hourly expected ships from England with building materials" ("Letters" dated November 16, 1772, in *The Daily Advertiser* [London], January 15, 1773, p1 c1). Similarly, just a month after the hurricane, one resident of Antigua wrote that "the seasonable weather we have had since the hurricane affords us now a fine prospect for next crop" and that "we have had a good many arrivals from America, which have relieved us much; and I hope we shall be ourselves again soon" (Letter from Antigua, October 10, 1772, in *The London Evening Post*, January 2–5, 1773, p4 c4). Nevertheless, one can argue that St. Kitts and the other islands never fully recovered from "the loss sustained by that hurricane," but this was due to a larger trend, i.e., a shift in the production of sugar from the smaller islands to larger ones like Jamaica and Cuba along with the declining importance of sugar and the West Indies in general.

5. *The Pennsylvania Journal; and the Weekly Advertiser*, October 7, 1772, p1 c2–3 and p3 c1–2; *The Boston Evening-Post*, October 12, 1772, p2 c3; Knox, *A Discourse . . . On Occasion of the Hurricane* 17n.

6. *The Royal Danish American Gazette*, September 9, 1772, p1 c3; ibid. September 23, 1772, p2 c1; *The Pennsylvania Journal; and the Weekly Advertiser*, October 7, 1772, p2 c2; *The Boston Evening-Post*, October 12, 1772, p2 c3. See also Knox, *A Discourse . . . On Occasion of the Hurricane* 17n.

7. *The Pennsylvania Journal; and the Weekly Advertiser*, October 7, 1772, p1 c3; *The St. James's Chronicle Or, the British Evening-Post* [London], November 12–14, 1772, p3 c1. Whereas these two accounts report that "182 houses were destroyed" and "180 houses blown down," Hugh Knox wrote that "out of about 180 dwelling-houses on Saba, it is said, only about 30 stand, and these much injured" (Knox, *A Discourse . . . On Occasion of the Hurricane* 17n; see also *The Royal Danish American Gazette*, September 12, 1772, p2 c3). Another account had "but one house remains on Saba" (*The Providence Gazette; and Country Journal*, October 24, 1772, p2 c2).

8. *The General Evening Post* [London], November 24–26, 1772, p3 c2; Southey, *Chronological History of the West Indies* 2:411.

9. Knox, *A Discourse . . . On Occasion of the Hurricane* 16n–17n and 18; Alexander Hamilton's Hurricane Account, in *The Royal Danish American Gazette*, October 3, 1772, p2 c2–3, and reprinted in *The Papers of Alexander Hamilton* 1:35; *The Morning Chronicle, and London Advertiser*, November 16, 1772, p2 c3; Millás, *Hurricanes of the Caribbean and Adjacent Regions* 237.
   The "tenfold darkness" was partly the result of the thin crescent moon sinking below the horizon just three hours after sunset.

10. *Proceedings of the St. Croix Burgher Council, 1767–1780* 468.

11. Knox, *A Discourse . . . On Occasion of the Hurricane* title page and 17n.

12. *An Account of the Late Dreadful Hurricane, Which happened On the 31st of August, 1772* 50. See also *The Royal Danish American Gazette*, September 9, 1772, p1 c2–3; *The Pennsylvania Journal; and the Weekly Advertiser*, October 7, 1772, p1 c1, p2 c3 – p3 c1.

13. Knox, *A Discourse . . . On Occasion of the Hurricane* 16n, 17n–18n, and 19; *The Royal Danish American Gazette*, September 9, 1772, p1 c1 and c2–3; ibid. October 14, 1772, p1 c1; ibid. October 24, 1771, p1 c1; ibid. June 5, 1773, p1 c1; *The Pennsylvania Journal; and the Weekly Advertiser*, October 7, 1772, p1 c1 and p2 c3 – p3 c1; *The Massachusetts Gazette; and the Boston Weekly News-Letter*, October 29, 1772, Supplement p2 c1; *The Morning Chronicle, and London Advertiser*, November 16, 1772, p2 c4; *The Gazetteer and New Daily Advertiser* [London], December 12, 1772, p4 c2; *The Gentleman's Magazine and Historical Chronicle* 42:590; Millás, *Hurricanes of the Caribbean and Adjacent Regions* 237.
   For more than a dozen depositions regarding ships lost or damaged on St. Croix, see *Christiansted Notarialprotokoller 1766–1776* 188r–199r. For auctions of stranded and damaged ships and their inventories, see *The Royal Danish American Gazette*, September 9, 1772 ff.; *Christiansted Auktionsprotokol 1772–1774* 115ff.

14. *St. Croix Matrikel 1772* 13.

15. *St. Croix Orkansager 1772–1827* 8.

16. Knox, *A Discourse . . . On Occasion of the Hurricane* 16n. Regarding the estimated damage of one million pounds sterling, Hugh Knox acknowledged that the losses "are indeed inexpressibly great" but hoped that "this estimation . . . is a little beyond the truth" (ibid.).

17. *The Gentleman's Magazine and Historical Chronicle* 42:590.

18. *The Royal Danish American Gazette*, September 9, 1772, p1 c2–3.

19. *The Royal Danish American Gazette*, September 9, 1772, p1 c3.

20. *The Pennsylvania Journal; and the Weekly Advertiser*, October 7, 1772, p2 c3 – p3 c1.

21. Knox, *A Discourse . . . On Occasion of the Hurricane* 16n.

22. Knox, *A Discourse . . . On Occasion of the Hurricane* 16, 17n, and 19; Alexander Hamilton's Hurricane Account, in *The Royal Danish American Gazette*, October 3, 1772, p2 c2–3, and reprinted in *The Papers of Alexander Hamilton* 1:35; *The Essex Gazette*, October 20, 1772, p1 c3.

23. *The Daily Advertiser* [London], November 19, 1772, p1 c1; *The Pennsylvania Journal; and the Weekly Advertiser*, December 2, 1772, p3 c1; *The St. James's Chronicle Or, the*

British Evening-Post [London], December 3–5, 1772, p3 c2; *The Gentleman's Magazine and Historical Chronicle* 42:590; Southey, *Chronological History of the West Indies* 2:411.

24. *The Public Register: Or, Freeman's Journal* [Dublin], December 17–19, 1772, p2 c3.

25. Ortiz, *Eighteenth-Century Reforms in the Caribbean* 144.

26. *The Pennsylvania Gazette*, October 14, 1772, p3 c1.

27. *The Pennsylvania Packet, and the General Advertiser*, November 9, 1772, p2 c3.

28. *The Westminster Journal; and London Political Miscellany*, November 7–14, 1772, p3 c4; Long, *The History of Jamaica* 3:620–621.

29. *The Pennsylvania Journal; and the Weekly Advertiser*, November 4, 1772, p2 c3.

Where Did Alexander Hamilton Live While Attending Grammar School in Elizabethtown, New Jersey?

When Alexander Hamilton arrived on mainland North America in the autumn of 1772 to pursue his education, he enrolled in Francis Barber's grammar school in Elizabethtown (now Elizabeth), New Jersey. He studied at this school, which was later known as the Elizabethtown Academy, from his arrival in October or November 1772 until he started college in September 1773.[1]

Since the grammar school in Elizabethtown had no dormitories, out-of-town students were advised that "boarding may be had in reputable families on reasonable terms."[2]

According to John C. Hamilton, his father Alexander Hamilton during his stay in Elizabethtown lived with William Livingston,[3] an esteemed New York lawyer who had come to New Jersey to retire.

Where in Elizabethtown did William Livingston live?

William Livingston Moves to Elizabethtown in April–May 1772

William Livingston had been living in 1771 and early 1772 in a New York City house he rented from David Clarkson. On March 18, 1772, Livingston paid £100 to Clarkson "for house rent for house he lived in to the first May 1772."[4]

On April 6 and 13, 1772, William Livingston advertised in *The New-York Gazette* his plan "to remove into the province of New-Jersey by the first of May" and informed the public that letters can be sent "to him at Elizabeth-Town."[5]

In late April or early May 1772, William Livingston and his family moved into an Elizabethtown house he rented from Jacob De Hart. A year later, on May 4, 1773, William Livingston paid John De Hart £25 for "one years house rent in behalf of Jacob De Hart."[6]

Thus, when Alexander Hamilton arrived in Elizabethtown in October or

November 1772 and moved in with the Livingstons, they lived in this house rented from Jacob De Hart.

Where in Elizabethtown was this house located?

Jacob De Hart's Two Houses

Jacob De Hart owned two houses in Elizabethtown. One was just south of the stone bridge over the Elizabeth River, at present-day South Broad Street and Pearl Street. The other was a few blocks to the northwest on the west side of the Elizabeth River, at present-day Cherry Street and Rahway Avenue. The former location was just three-tenths of a mile from Elizabethtown's grammar school. The latter was about six-tenths of a mile from the school.[7]

Descriptions of both houses can be found in contemporary newspapers. Just days after Jacob De Hart's wife Abigail passed away on June 10, 1770,[8]

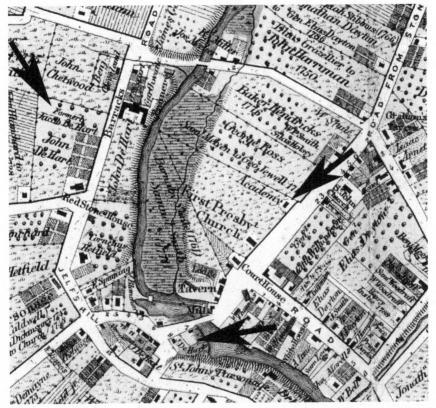

Meyer, *Map of Elizabeth Town, N.J. at the Time of the Revolutionary War.*

De Hart advertised his house for lease. This house, apparently the one on the west side of the river at present-day Cherry Street and Rahway Avenue, was described as a "large, convenient, and well situated dwelling-house . . . suitable for a gentleman, or any business, with out-houses, a good orchard and garden."[9]

In February 1771, this house was again advertised for lease along with "another house and lot of ground of the said Jacob Dehart, situated in a very pleasant part of the town, and suitable for any kind of business." This second house was apparently the one south of the river at present-day South Broad Street and Pearl Street.[10]

William Livingston could have rented either of these houses from Jacob De Hart. The house on the west side of the river at present-day Cherry Street and Rahway Avenue appears to have been the larger of the two. It was farther away from the center of town, but closer to Livingston's property northwest of town, where he was planning to build a new house. The house at present-day South Broad Street and Pearl Street was not as large but was closer to the center of town.

It was one of these two houses that William Livingston rented from Jacob De Hart and in which Alexander Hamilton lived for ten or eleven months while attending Elizabethtown's grammar school. Unfortunately, there is no record which of the two houses William Livingston rented and, given the available information, it cannot be determined with certainty which of these two houses Hamilton and the Livingstons lived in.

With a wife and nine surviving children, most of whom lived with their parents and those who did not presumably visiting often, and taking in at least one boarder, i.e., Alexander Hamilton, it makes sense that William Livingston would have rented the larger of the two houses. Being closer to his property northwest of town, where Livingston was to start building a new house that undoubtedly would need his attention, probably also influenced his decision.

Thus, it would seem that William Livingston more likely rented the "large, convenient, and well situated dwelling-house . . . suitable for a gentleman, or any business, with out-houses, a good orchard and garden" on the west side of the Elizabeth River, at present-day Cherry Street and Rahway Avenue, and that it was in this house that Alexander Hamilton lived for ten or eleven months while attending Elizabethtown's grammar school.

Liberty Hall

As mentioned, William Livingston owned property northwest of Eliza-bethtown, on which he planned to build a new house for his permanent residence. When Livingston moved into the house he rented from De Hart, construction on this house a mile and a half to the northwest of town, to be called Liberty Hall, had not yet begun. William Livingston hired a master artisan in December 1772 to help design the house. Livingston planned to start building in the spring of 1773 and hoped to take up residence that autumn. Construction took longer than expected and he did not move into Liberty Hall until April 1774.[11]

On April 28, 1774, a grand event marked the opening of Liberty Hall: the marriage of John Jay to William Livingston's daughter Sarah.[12] By this time, Alexander Hamilton was in school at King's College in New York City. Perhaps, as a close friend of the Livingstons, he came back to Elizabethtown to attend the wedding of John Jay and Sarah Livingston at Liberty Hall.

Notes

1. Newton, *Alexander Hamilton: The Formative Years* 69.
2. *The New-York Gazette; and the Weekly Mercury*, December 23, 1771, p3 c3.
3. John C. Hamilton, *The Life of Alexander Hamilton* 1:8; John C. Hamilton, *History of the Republic* 1:46.
4. David Clarkson receipt to William Livingston, March 18, 1772, in *William Livingston Papers*.
5. *The New-York Gazette; and the Weekly Mercury*, April 6, 1772, p3 c4, and April 13, 1772, p4 c3.
6. William Livingston receipt to John De Hart, May 4, 1773, in the *William Livingston Papers*; *The Papers of William Livingston* 1:5.
7. Meyer, *Map of Elizabeth Town, N.J. at the Time of the Revolutionary War*.
8. *Documents Relating to the Colonial History of the State of New Jersey* 19:390n.
9. *The New-York Gazette; and the Weekly Mercury*, June 18, 1770, p3 c3; *The New-York Gazette; or, the Weekly Post-Boy*, June 18, 1770, p3 c3.
10. *The New-York Gazette; and the Weekly Mercury*, February 18, 1771, p3 c3.
11. William Livingston to Paparel Bloodgood, December 9, 1772 in *The Papers of William Livingston* 1:363–364; ibid. 5–6 and 364 note 2.
12. *Rivington's New-York Gazetteer*, May 5, 1774, p3 c1; *The New-York Gazette; and the Weekly Mercury*, May 9, 1774, p2 c4.

Alexander Hamilton's Classmates at the Grammar School in Elizabethtown, New Jersey

According to son John C. Hamilton, Alexander Hamilton studied at the grammar school of Elizabethtown, New Jersey, alongside "Jonathan Dayton, afterwards speaker of the House of Representatives; Brockholst Livingston, subsequently a judge of the Supreme Court of the United States, and others who became of note."[1]

Was John C. Hamilton correct about Jonathan Dayton and Brockholst Livingston attending grammar school with Alexander Hamilton? Can anyone else be identified as Alexander Hamilton's classmate in Elizabethtown?

Henry Brockholst Livingston

Henry Brockholst Livingston, the son of William Livingston, could not have been Alexander Hamilton's schoolmate at the grammar school of Elizabethtown in 1772–73. Brockholst enrolled at the College of New Jersey at Princeton in 1770 and as a freshman won a "premium" at the September 1771 commencement for "extempore exercises in the Latin language."[2] He graduated from the College of New Jersey in September 1774. At the "public commencement," he delivered an "English oration on liberty."[3]

Thus, Brockholst Livingston could not have attended the grammar school in Elizabethtown with Alexander Hamilton since he attended the College of New Jersey in Princeton at the time. However, it is likely that Brockholst visited his family during breaks and that Hamilton and Brockholst Livingston met during Hamilton's time living in Elizabethtown.

Jonathan Dayton

Jonathan Dayton, the son of Elias Dayton of Elizabethtown, may have been Hamilton's classmate in grammar school, as John C. Hamilton asserted. Jonathan Dayton graduated from the College of New Jersey in 1776.[4] If he attended college for the usual four years, he would have already left Elizabeth-town by the time Hamilton arrived. It is possible, however, that Dayton did not enter the College of New Jersey until September 1773 and graduated after just three years. Although the college generally prohibited pupils from study-ing at an advanced pace, they may have granted early diplomas in 1776 to students who were entering the army, as Jonathan Dayton did. Like with Brockholst Livingston, even if Jonathan Dayton did not attend grammar school alongside Hamilton, the two surely would have met whenever Dayton came home to visit his family and friends.

John Lawrence Livingston

There is one youth who definitely attended the grammar school in Eliza-bethtown alongside Alexander Hamilton. On May 5, 1773, Francis Barber billed "Mast^r John Livingston," the son of William Livingston, £1 5s for "1 quarters instruction" and another 7s 6d for "wood & cash for house clean-ing." The total of £1 12s 6d was received in full by Francis Barber on May 12.[5]

A second receipt shows that Francis Barber billed "Mast^r John L. Living-ston" £1 5s on August 5, 1773, for "1 quarters instruction," which was paid on August 21.[6]

Thus, for the two quarters ending in May and August 1773, Alexander Hamilton and John Lawrence Livingston were classmates at Francis Barber's grammar school in Elizabethtown. It is possible that John Lawrence Living-ston's attendance at this school lasted more than just these two quarters, but no record of this has been found. If so, perhaps John Lawrence Livingston was Hamilton's classmate during the entirety of Hamilton's attendance at the grammar school in Elizabethtown.

It is possible that John C. Hamilton or his source had misheard or misre-membered that it was John Lawrence Livingston and not his brother Henry Brockholst Livingston who attended the grammar school of Elizabethtown with Alexander Hamilton.

Classmates, Housemates, and Walking Companions

Alexander Hamilton and John Lawrence Livingston were more than just schoolmates. During his stay in Elizabethtown, Alexander Hamilton lived with the Livingston family.[7] Thus, Alexander Hamilton and John Lawrence Livingston must have frequently walked together to and from school.

About John Lawrence Livingston

John Lawrence Livingston was born in July 1762, making him about eight years younger than Hamilton. In the spring of 1780, New Jersey Governor William Livingston obtained for his son John Lawrence an appointment as midshipman in the navy. In March 1781, the *Saratoga* with John Lawrence Livingston aboard was chasing another ship when the wind became "so exceeding violent" that the ship was "with great probability supposed to have been lost." For years, William Livingston hoped that his son was still alive, perhaps having been taken to Algiers, but "no reliable news was ever received" regarding the *Saratoga* or John Lawrence Livingston.[8]

Notes

1. John C. Hamilton, *History of the Republic* 1:45. See also John C. Hamilton, *The Life of Alexander Hamilton* 1:8.
2. *The Pennsylvania Gazette*, October 3, 1771, p3 cl.
3. *The Pennsylvania Journal; and the Weekly Advertiser*, October 12, 1774; *General Catalogue of Princeton University* 97.
4. *General Catalogue of Princeton University* 99.
5. Francis Barber receipt to John Livingston, May 12, 1773, in the *William Livingston Papers*.
6. Francis Barber receipt to John Livingston, August 11, 1773, in the *William Livingston Papers*.
7. John C. Hamilton, *The Life of Alexander Hamilton* 1:8; John C. Hamilton, *History of the Republic* 1:45.
8. *The New York Genealogical and Biographical Record* 41:307; *The Correspondence and Public Papers of John Jay* 3:384.

Was Alexander Hamilton "girl crazy and brimming with libido"? Hamilton's letter to Catharine "Kitty" Livingston

widely held trope regarding Alexander Hamilton is that he actively pursued women left and right. During the American Revolution, the dashing and attractive young man on the rise supposedly earned a reputation as a tomcat. One Hamilton biographer, for instance, remarked that by 1780 Hamilton had already made "a career of dalliance that was at once gallant, predatory and oddly guarded."[1]

Alexander Hamilton to Catharine "Kitty" Livingston

One piece of evidence biographers point to as proof of Hamilton's lascivious pursuits is a letter he wrote on April 11, 1777, to Catharine "Kitty" Livingston, who was about two years his senior. In this letter, Hamilton wrote:

Though I am perfectly willing to harmonize with your inclination, in this respect, without making the cynical inquiry, whether it proceed from sympathy in the concerns of the public, or merely from female curiosity, yet I will not consent to be limited to any particular subject. I challenge you to meet me in whatever path you dare; and if you have no objection, for variety and amusement, we will even sometimes make excursions in the flowery walks, and roseate bowers of Cupid. You know, I am renowned for gallantry, and shall always be able to entertain you with a choice collection of the prettiest things imaginable. I fancy my knowlege of you affords me a tolerably just idea of your taste, but lest I should be mistaken I shall take it kind, if you will give me such intimations of it, as will remove all doubt, and save me the trouble of finding it out with certainty myself. This will be the more obliging, as, without it, I should have a most arduous task on my hands, at least, if connoisseurs in the sex say true, according to whose representations, contrary to the vulgar opinion, woman is not a simple, but a most complex, intricate and enigmatical being.

After knowing exactly your taste, and whether you are of a romantic, or discreet temper, as to love affairs, I will endeavour to regulate myself by it. If you would choose to be a goddess, and to be worshipped as such, I will torture my imagination for the best arguments, the nature of the case will admit, to prove you so. You shall be one of the graces, or Diana, or Venus, or something surpassing them all. And after your deification, I will cull out of every poet of my acquaintance, the choicest delicacies, they possess, as offerings at your Goddesships' shrine. But if, conformable to your usual discernment, you are content with being a mere mortal, and require no other incense, than is justly due to you, I will talk to you like one [in] his sober senses; and, though it may be straining the point a little, I will even stipulate to pay you all the rational tribute properly applicable to a fine girl.

But amidst my amorous transports, let me not forget, that I am also to perform the part of a politician and intelligencer. This however will not take up much time, as the present situation of things gives birth to very little worth notice, though it seems pregnant with something of importance. The enemy, from some late movements, appear to be brooding mischief, which must soon break out, but I hope it will turn to their own ruin. To speak plainly, there is reason to believe, they are upon the point of attempting some important entreprize. Philadelphia in the opinion of most people, is their object. I hope they may be disappointed.

Of this, I am pretty confident, that the ensuing campaign will effectually put to death all their hopes; and establish the success of our cause beyond a doubt. You and I, as well as our neighbours, are deeply interested to pray for victory, and its necessary attendant peace; as, among other good effects, they would remove those obstacles, which now lie in the way of that most delectable thing, called matrimony;—a state, which, with a kind of magnetic force, attracts every breast to it, in which sensibility has a place, in spite of the resistance it encounters in the dull admonitions of prudence, which is so prudish and perverse a dame, as to be at perpetual variance with it.[2]

Hamilton Biographers Opine

Hamilton biographers have much to say about this letter.

James T. Flexner noted, "Unless we assume a previous heavy flirtation, which the entire context of Hamilton's communication seems to exclude, the young man is trying to pounce on the older woman with the suddenness of a tiger."[3]

Ron Chernow delved even deeper into Hamilton's psyche:

One thing grew crystal clear at Morristown: Hamilton was girl crazy and brimming with libido. Throughout his career, at unlikely moments, he tended to grow flirtatious, almost giddy, with women. No sooner had he joined Washington's staff than he began to woo his old friend Catherine Livingston, daughter of his former patron, William Livingston, now the first governor of an independent New Jersey. In an April 11 letter to Kitty, Hamilton struck the note of badinage favored by young rakes of the day. . . . That Hamilton was being more than playful with Kitty Livingston is shown in his declaration in the letter that the end of the Revolution would "remove those obstacles which now lie in the way of that most delectable thing called matrimony."[4]

Based on the above excerpt from Hamilton's letter and the analyses of biographers, one could very well conclude that Hamilton, in his letter to Kitty Livingston, was on a romantic crusade with courtship in mind. But a further analysis of the letter and a deeper understanding of its context cast doubts on this conclusion.

Hamilton was Encouraged to Write to Kitty

The above excerpt from Hamilton's letter to Kitty, which is often quoted, was preceded by a more mundane paragraph, which biographers often neglect to quote or even mention. Hamilton opened his letter to Kitty with:

I take pleasure in transmitting you a letter, committed to my care, by your Sister Miss Suky, and in executing a promise, I gave her, of making an advance towards a correspondence with you. She says you discover,

in all your letters to her, a relish for politics, which she thinks my situation qualifies me better for gratifying, than would be in her power;
and from a desire to accommodate you in this particular, as well as to
get rid of what she calls a difficult task to herself, and to give me an
opportunity of enjoying the felicity which must naturally attend it, she
wishes me to engage on the footing of a political correspondent.[5]

Thus, Susanna "Suky" Livingston had written a letter to her sister and
asked Hamilton, as an aide-de-camp to General Washington, to transmit it
to her. Suky also encouraged Hamilton to write to Kitty. The purpose of
Hamilton opening this correspondence, according to what Suky told him,
was to discuss politics. But Hamilton undoubtedly assumed that Suky had
more than just a political correspondence in mind. He must have thought
that Suky was trying to initiate a correspondence between him and Kitty for
the purpose of a courtship.

Even if Suky did not have this in mind, why wouldn't a young bachelor
make the most of the opportunity provided him? Yes, Hamilton was willing
to be Kitty's political correspondent, but he was also open to the idea that he
could be something more, but he left that decision to Kitty.

The Romantic Era

It will be noticed that at this early stage of their potential courtship, Hamilton wrote nothing about his love or affection for Kitty. Hamilton struck a
playful tone that touched upon the topics of love and marriage, asking Kitty
what she thought about the possibility of going down that path, but without
expressing any affection for her. He likened Kitty to a "goddess" if she chose
to be one or "a fine girl" as he knew her to be, but he never actually expressed
any emotions for her. Just compare the nature of this letter to those Hamilton
wrote to Elizabeth Schuyler during their courtship and those to her family
during that time, which contain much less bravado but noticeably more
warmth and affection.[6]

In this letter to Kitty, Hamilton wrote in a style meant to impress rather
than one meant to convey one's feelings. This flirtatious, over-the-top style
was all the rage during this period. It often included allusions to love, sexual
desires, matrimony, and intercourse. Among the most popular novels of the

time was Laurence Sterne's *The Life and Opinions of Tristram Shandy, Gentleman*, which was thought to be "the dirtiest novel in English."[7] The gentlemen and ladies of society participated wholeheartedly in this good-natured fun. Martha Daingerfield Bland described how "General Washington," a man known for his Stoic composure, "throws of[f] the Hero" whenever he joins a riding party "and takes on the chatty agreable companion—he can be down right impudent sometimes." And the women loved it. "Such impudence," Bland told her sister-in-law, "as you and I like."[8] Similarly, Angelica Church wrote to Elizabeth Hamilton in 1795 with the wish that Alexander Hamilton "shall not talk politics to us. A little of his agreeable nonsense will do us more good."[9]

As men were expected, in appropriate situations, to write and speak in this style and women appreciated it and often reciprocated, Alexander Hamilton put his brilliant mind, quick wit, and able pen to the task of mastering this form of communication. Accordingly, Alexander Hamilton would later explain to Angelica Church, "I seldom write to a lady without fancying the relation of lover and mistress. It has a very inspiring effect."[10] And this was exactly how Hamilton had written to Kitty Livingston.

Hamilton Knew Kitty Livingston

It will be recalled that Alexander Hamilton had lived with William Livingston in Elizabethtown, New Jersey, back in 1772–73.[11] During this time, Hamilton befriended Suky and Kitty, as presumably they were both living with their father. Accordingly, Hamilton knew Kitty well and must have known that she enjoyed this style of banter. In fact, in his letter to Kitty, Hamilton wrote of "my knowlege of you" and how he already knew about Kitty's "usual discernment."

Moreover, Hamilton must have expected that Kitty would tell Suky and perhaps her father, William Livingston, about what he had written to her. Perhaps Kitty would even show them the letter. Knowing this, Hamilton would never have written anything inappropriate. Although the letter might seem overly forthcoming to modern ears, this was the kind of writing that would not have embarrassed the author if it were to be shown to others. Accordingly, Hamilton's letter should not be seen as a love letter. Rather, it was written as a work of literature designed to amuse and impress the recipient.

A Wonderful Piece of Literature

Some previous Hamilton biographers have noted correctly the context in which this letter was written. Mary Jo Kline wrote, "Alexander Hamilton's courtship of 'Kitty' Livingston should not be taken seriously. . . . Catharine enjoyed flirting and flattery."[12] James T. Flexner noted, "Susanna (Suky) encouraged Hamilton to write her sister Catherine. . . . The general tone of this epistle is in keeping with the flirtatious idioms of the time. A parody of pretentious metaphors, it makes fun both of the writer and the recipient. . . . As for the bantering generalizations concerning the opposite sex, they were an accepted convention, perhaps because they served as a nonphysical and impersonal way of keeping in the foreground that the communication was a sexual one. Both women and men teased each other with presumably witty allegations unflattering to their correspondent's gender."[13] However, these biographers are in the minority, and in the case of Flexner, despite noting that this was the style of the era and that Suky initiated the conversation between Hamilton and Kitty, he still concluded, as noted earlier, that Hamilton was a "young man . . . trying to pounce on the older woman with the suddenness of a tiger."[14]

Thus, one who reads the Hamilton biographies by James T. Flexner, Ron Chernow, and most other authors is left with the impression that Alexander Hamilton was "girl crazy and brimming with libido" and that he pursued Kitty Livingston like a "young man . . . trying to pounce on the older woman with the suddenness of a tiger."

But the reality is quite different. Alexander Hamilton was writing to an old friend in the style of the time. A mutual friend had encouraged Hamilton to write to Kitty Livingston, which he did, under the assumption that the purpose was to see if a romantic relationship could develop. Alexander Hamilton's offer to go on "excursions in the flowery walks, and roseate bowers of Cupid" was not an attempt to "pounce" on Kitty Livingston. Rather, if Hamilton was not just writing in the style of the time and in fact was serious about pursuing a romantic relationship with Kitty, his letter should then be seen as an offer to become better acquainted with courtship in mind. This would be akin in today's world to asking someone out on a first date. This could lead to something more, but it might not, and it is merely an expression of interest rather than of love or desire. Accordingly, Hamilton's letter is full of the boastful, flirtatious language that was popular at the time, but made no mention of any affection for Kitty or a desire to marry her, for it was way too early in their relationship, which did not even exist yet, to express such feelings except in broad terms of the other gender.

Desiring to write the most sensational and tantalizing narratives, it is clear that many Hamilton biographers simply go too far when writing about Alexander Hamilton's letter to Kitty Livingston. It is nothing more than a wonderful piece of literature, if one enjoys the flirtatious, over-the-top style of the day, as Hamilton knew Kitty would.

Notes

1. Emery, *Alexander Hamilton: An Intimate Portrait* 54.
2. Alexander Hamilton to Catharine Livingston, April 11, 1777, in *The Papers of Alexander Hamilton* 1:225–227.
3. Flexner, *The Young Hamilton* 151.
4. Chernow, *Alexander Hamilton* 93.
5. Alexander Hamilton to Catharine Livingston, April 11, 1777, in *The Papers of Alexander Hamilton* 1:225–227.
6. For instance, see Alexander Hamilton to Margarita Schuyler, February 1780, in *The Papers of Alexander Hamilton* 2:269–271; Alexander Hamilton to Elizabeth Schuyler, March 17, 1780, in ibid. 2:285–287.
7. Brady, "Tristram Shandy: Sexuality, Morality, and Sensibility" 41.
8. Martha Daingerfield Bland to Frances Bland Randolph, May 12, 1777, in *Proceedings of the New Jersey Historical Society* 51:152.
9. Allan McLane Hamilton, *The Intimate Life of Alexander Hamilton* 164.
10. Alexander Hamilton to Angelica Church, December 6, 1787, in *The Papers of Alexander Hamilton* 4:374–376.
11. John C. Hamilton, *The Life of Alexander Hamilton* 1:8; John C. Hamilton, *History of the Republic* 1:45.
12. Kline, *Alexander Hamilton: A Biography in His Own Words* 1:54.
13. Flexner, *The Young Hamilton* 149.
14. Flexner, *The Young Hamilton* 151.

The Tomcat Fully Refuted

Alexander Hamilton's 1777 letter to Catharine "Kitty" Livingston is not the only example from the American Revolution period supposedly showing him to be "girl crazy and brimming with libido." On January 1, 1780, a Captain Smythe wrote:

> Mrs. Washington has a mottled tom-cat, (which she calls, in a complimentary way, 'Hamilton,') with thirteen yellow rings around his tail, and that his flaunting it suggested to the Congress the adoption of the same number of stripes for the rebel flag.[1]

Repeat and Embellish

This anecdote about Martha Washington naming a tomcat Hamilton has been repeated and embellished in dozens of Hamilton biographies and has become one of the most popular Hamilton anecdotes. A few examples will demonstrate the evolution of this story.

In 1902, Gertrude Atherton wrote about Alexander Hamilton in her book *The Conqueror*:

> The Lady-in-chief made such a pet of him that he was referred to in the irreverent Tory press as "Mrs. Washington's Tom-cat."[2]

Not only did Atherton report the story as true, she changed a number of details. Instead of a tomcat named Hamilton, she had Hamilton being called "Mrs. Washington's Tom-cat." She also had the story being printed in the Tory press, a detail not mentioned in the original source. In her timeline, she had this story taking place in 1777 instead of 1780. Granted, Gertrude Atherton's *The Conqueror* was a work of historical fiction, but this book had much influence upon future generations of Hamilton biographers.

In 1946, Nathan Schachner wrote in his Hamilton biography:

His reputation as a gallant spread far beyond the confines of the camp.
A Tory newspaper managed to weave Hamilton's notoriety and the
proposed new American flag into a single withering sneer. "Mrs. Washington," it reported, "has a mottled tom-cat (which she calls, in a complimentary way, 'Hamilton') with thirteen yellow rings around its tail,
and that his flaunting it suggested to the Congress the adoption of the
same number of stripes for the rebel flag."[3]

Despite quoting the original source, Schachner like Atherton placed this
story in 1777 instead of 1780 and had it printed in a Tory newspaper. He also
used this tale as proof of Hamilton's "notoriety" and "reputation as a gallant,"
something not mentioned in the original.

In 1999, Thomas Fleming wrote in *Duel*:

Martha Washington, in one of her droller moments, had nicknamed
the house pet, a bigheaded, extremely amorous tomcat, "Hamilton"—
a glimpse of his reputation as a ladies man in those days.[4]

Fleming, like his predecessors, reported this story as true. The mottled
tomcat had by this time become a "bigheaded, extremely amorous tomcat."
Moreover, the tomcat was named Hamilton, not "in a complimentary way"
as originally reported, but because of his "reputation as a ladies man."

In 2004, Ron Chernow wrote in his Hamilton bio:

Not for nothing did Martha Washington nickname her large lascivious
tomcat "Hamilton."[5]

With each new Hamilton biography, this tomcat apparently grows larger
and more lustful.

Sealing the fate of this story in the public mind, *Hamilton: An American
Musical* contains the lines:

Burr: Martha Washington named her feral tomcat after him.
Hamilton: That's true.[6]

Not only is the story repeated, with the tomcat being "feral," but even Alexander Hamilton says the story is true. If Hamilton says it is true, then it must be. Right?

In a book about the musical, *Hamilton*-creator Lin-Manuel Miranda explained:

> This is most likely a tale spread by John Adams later in life. But I like Hamilton owning it. At this point in the story he is at peak cockiness.[7]

The story of Martha Washington's tomcat has thus become so universally accepted that the original source has been all but forgotten. Somehow, it has become a story that was spread by John Adams, which no previous biographer mentioned.

In sum, this story has been repeated in dozens of Hamilton biographies as if it were undoubtedly true. They write that Martha Washington had a tomcat and that this tomcat was "extremely amorous," "lascivious," and "feral." They write that for this reason the tomcat was named Hamilton or that Hamilton was called a tomcat. On top of this, they write that it was reported in the Tory press during the American Revolution. Some even believe that the tale was "most likely . . . spread by John Adams later in life."

Returning to the Original Source

As will be recalled, the original tomcat anecdote was written by Captain Smythe on January 1, 1780. A look at Captain Smythe's entire entry will cast this story in its proper context:

> Thirteen is a number peculiarly belonging to the rebels. A party of naval prisoners lately returned from Jersey, say, that rations among the rebels are thirteen dried clams per day; that the titular Lord Stirling takes thirteen glasses of grog every morning, has thirteen enormous rum-bunches on his nose, and that (when duly impregnated) he always makes thirteen attempts before he can walk; that Mr. Washington has thirteen toes on his feet, (the extra ones having grown since the Declaration of Independence,) and the same number of teeth in each jaw; that the Sachem Schuyler has a top-knot of thirteen stiff hairs, which

erect themselves on the crown of his head when he grows mad; that
Old Putnam had thirteen pounds of his posteriors bit off in an encoun-
ter with a Connecticut bear, ('twas then he lost the *balance* of his
mind;) that it takes thirteen Congress paper dollars to equal one penny
sterling; that Polly Wayne was just thirteen hours in subduing Stony
Point, and as many seconds in leaving it; that a well-organized rebel
household has thirteen children, all of whom expect to be generals and
members of the High and Mighty Congress of the "thirteen United
States" when they attain thirteen years; that Mrs. Washington has a
mottled tom-cat, (which she calls, in a complimentary way, 'Hamilton,') with thirteen yellow rings around his tail, and that his flaunting
it suggested to the Congress the adoption of the same number of stripes
for the rebel flag.[8]

Are any of the above anecdotes true? Did George Washington really have
thirteen toes, the extras having grown since the Declaration of Independence?
Did Lord Stirling really have thirteen rum-bunches on his nose? Did Philip
Schuyler really have thirteen hairs on his head? Did Israel Putnam really have
thirteen pounds of his posterior bit off by a bear? Did Martha Washington
really have a cat with thirteen stripes on its tail? Did the idea of having thirteen stripes on the American flag really come from this cat?[9]

A Satirical Tomcat

Obviously, this entire entry by Captain Smythe was a piece of sarcasm. It
was all a joke. No one in 1780 would have believed any of these stories. No
one today should believe them either.

Hamilton a Known Tomcat

Admitting that the story was satire and that Martha Washington had no
tomcat, Captain Smythe still wrote about a tomcat being named Hamilton.
It would seem then that the British in 1780 knew Hamilton was a tomcat.

Moreover, the tale was reportedly published in the "Tory press." Again, it
appears that everyone knew that Hamilton was an "extremely amorous," "lascivious," "feral tomcat."

First Publication

This story first appeared for public consumption in 1860 in Frank Moore's *Diary of the American Revolution.*[10] In sharing the story, that book cites "Smythe's Journal."[11] The book's "list of authorities" shows that this was the "Diary of Captain Smythe, of the Royal Army."[12] In other words, this was a private journal or diary of a British officer. "Smythe's Journal" was not a "Tory press" or newspaper. Thus, the tomcat story did not appear in the Tory press nor was it disseminated to the public in 1780.

Hamilton Still a Known Tomcat

Admitting that the story was satire, that Martha Washington had no tomcat, that the story did not appear in the press in 1780, and was not published until 1860, it is still a fact that this tale written in 1780 likens Hamilton to a "tomcat."

Thus, despite all the misreporting regarding this anecdote, it still appears like Hamilton was widely known on both sides as an "extremely amorous," "lascivious," "feral tomcat."

Tomcat Defined

According to modern dictionaries, a tomcat is defined formally as "a male domestic cat" but informally as "a sexually aggressive man; a womanizer."[13]

Which of these two definitions did Captain Smythe have in mind? Was Smythe's fictional "mottled tom-cat" just a male domestic cat? Or was Smythe's "mottled tom-cat" a "sexually aggressive" male cat?

To answer this question, today's definition of "tomcat" is irrelevant. Rather, the meaning of the word circa 1780 needs to be determined.

According to *The Oxford English Dictionary*:

In 1760 was published an anonymous work 'The Life and Adventures of a Cat', which became very popular. The hero, a male or 'ram' cat, bore the name of Tom, and is commonly mentioned as 'Tom the Cat'. . . . Thus Tom became a favourite allusive name for a male cat . . . and people said 'this cat is a Tom' or a 'Tom cat'.[14]

THE

L I F E

AND

ADVENTURES

OF A

C A T.

By the late Mr. FIELDING.

LONDON:

Printed for JOHN SEYMOUR, in Pater-
Nofter-Row.
M.DCC.LX.

C H A P. IV.

Tom *the Cat is born of poor but
honeft parents. His mother dies
in child-bed, his brothers and fifters,
to the number of nine are fent a-
drift, and drowned.*

The Oxford English Dictionary gives further examples of the word tomcat being used in literature. At least through 1881, tomcat simply meant a male cat and had no sexual connotation.[15]

Likewise, *Chambers's Etymological Dictionary of the English Language* of 1867, 1882, 1900, and 1904 defined tomcat as "a male cat, esp. when full grown."[16] There was no mention of the male cat being lustful nor was there a second definition referring to a "sexually aggressive man; a womanizer."

Similarly, *Webster's Handy Dictionary* of 1879 and 1905 and *Webster's Collegiate Dictionary* of 1917 defined "tomcat" simply as "a male cat."[17] Again, there was no reference to the cat being lustful or a second definition of a "sexually aggressive man; a womanizer."

According to *The Oxford English Dictionary*, the earliest reference they could find for tomcat with a sexual connotation was in 1927 for the verb form, meaning "to pursue women promiscuously for sexual gratification."[18]

Merriam Webster's Dictionary also gives a date of 1927 for tomcat meaning "to seek sexual gratification promiscuously."[19]

Thus, when Captain Smythe made up a story about a tomcat in 1780, the word tomcat meant "a male cat" and nothing more. The term tomcat had no sexual connotation at that time. Accordingly, Captain Smythe never meant for Hamilton to be seen as an "extremely amorous," "lascivious," "feral tomcat." In fact, Smythe wrote that Martha Washington named the tomcat Hamilton "in a complimentary way." The tomcat story was never meant to disparage Hamilton.

The Tomcat Fully Refuted

To summarize:

- Martha Washington did not have a tomcat named Hamilton and probably did not even have a tomcat at all. Certainly, she did not call Alexander Hamilton a tomcat.
- The tomcat story was a satirical tale written in 1780 by Captain Smythe in his private journal.
- Captain Smythe did not call Hamilton a "tomcat" nor did he imply that a tomcat was named after him because of his reputation with the ladies.

- The tomcat story first appeared in print in 1860.
- The word "tomcat" had no sexual connotation when the story was written in 1780 or when it was first published in 1860.

In other words, Alexander Hamilton was no tomcat.

Notes

1. "Smythe's Journal," January 1, 1780, excerpted in Moore, *Diary of the American Revolution* 2:250.
2. Atherton, *The Conqueror* 163.
3. Schachner, *Alexander Hamilton* 92.
4. Fleming, *Duel* 16.
5. Chernow, *Alexander Hamilton* 126.
6. Miranda, "A Winter's Ball."
7. Miranda and McCarter, *Hamilton: The Revolution* 70.
8. "Smythe's Journal," January 1, 1780, excerpted in Moore, *Diary of the American Revolution* 2:250.
9. The Grand Union Flag with thirteen stripes made its first appearance in December 1775, long before Alexander Hamilton and Martha Washington first met.
10. Moore, *Diary of the American Revolution* 2:250.
11. "Smythe's Journal," January 1, 1780, excerpted in Moore, *Diary of the American Revolution* 2:250.
12. Moore, *Diary of the American Revolution* 1:vi.
13. Google search: 'Define tomcat.'
14. *The Oxford English Dictionary* 18:212.
15. *The Oxford English Dictionary* 18:212.
16. *Chambers's Etymological Dictionary of the English Language* 1867:524; 1882:523; 1900:523; 1904:523.
17. *Webster's Handy Dictionary* 1879:280; 1905:280; *Webster's Collegiate Dictionary* 1917:1011.
18. *The Oxford English Dictionary* 18:212.
19. *Merriam-Webster's Collegiate Dictionary* 2004:1315.

Did James McHenry Attend
Alexander Hamilton's Wedding?

James McHenry's presence at the wedding of Alexander Hamilton to Elizabeth Schuyler is well known. Ron Chernow wrote, "Hamilton had few people to invite to the wedding. . . . Except for James McHenry, Hamilton's friends on Washington's staff were too busy with wartime duties to attend."[1] Broadus Mitchell asserted that not only did McHenry attend the wedding but he also served as Hamilton's "best man."[2] McHenry reportedly also penned a poem for the newlyweds,[3] which is often cited as proof that he attended the wedding.

Dating James McHenry's Poem

The sole source for the story of James McHenry attending Hamilton's wedding and writing a poem to celebrate the occasion is Bernard C. Steiner's *The Life and Correspondence of James McHenry*, published in 1907. According to Steiner, "In September [1780], Hamilton married General Philip Schuyler's daughter and McHenry went to Albany for the wedding and wrote the following verses to his friend on the morning after the ceremony."[4] After sharing McHenry's poem, Steiner then included Hamilton's reply to McHenry thanking him for his poetry.[5]

Neither McHenry's poem nor Hamilton's reply has been found since Steiner included them in his McHenry biography. So the only source for the contents and dates of these items is Steiner's book.

According to Steiner, as noted above, the wedding of Alexander Hamilton and Elizabeth Schuyler took place in September 1780. The poem, as printed by Steiner, is undated. Hamilton's reply to McHenry bears a date of "Sep. 12. [1780]." In other words, Hamilton's reply is dated September 12 but no year was written. Steiner apparently added the "[1780]" because that is the year the wedding took place and he thought the poem and reply were related to that event. Accordingly, if the year was not written on the reply and was added by Steiner, it is possible that the poem and Hamilton's reply were not written in 1780.

McHenry's Poem Related to Hamilton's Wedding?

As is well known, the wedding of Alexander Hamilton and Elizabeth Schuyler took place in Albany on December 14, 1780,[6] not in September 1780 as Bernard Steiner had written. If Hamilton wrote to McHenry on September 12, 1780,[7] or some other year, to thank him for his poetry, McHenry's verses have nothing to do with Hamilton's wedding. And if the poem has nothing to do with the wedding, no evidence was presented by Steiner or by anyone else placing McHenry at the wedding.

Perhaps Steiner was correct about these two items being related to Hamilton's wedding but simply gave the wrong date in his book. Indeed, the editors of *The Papers of Alexander Hamilton* asserted, "Steiner, after stating that H was married in September, 1780, incorrectly dates this letter September 12, 1780."[8] This supposes that Steiner somehow misread or changed both the month and the day of Hamilton's letter. It requires ignoring the date of a letter that Steiner had in hand but believing that the poem and reply were connected to the wedding which Steiner had three months too early.

Furthermore, neither the poem nor Hamilton's reply mentions the wedding.[9] Hamilton did not even mention his new wife in his reply to McHenry.

In other words, there is no evidence that McHenry's poem and Hamilton's reply have anything to do with the wedding. In fact, the available evidence—the date given by Steiner—says that they did not.

It is possible, however, that Bernard Steiner had another source placing McHenry at the wedding, even though he did not cite the source and had the wrong date. So even if McHenry's poem and Hamilton's reply had nothing to do with Hamilton's nuptials, the story of McHenry attending Hamilton's wedding cannot be dismissed outright.

Where was James McHenry on Hamilton's wedding day?

Determining James McHenry's location on the date of Alexander Hamilton's wedding—December 14, 1780—would be the clearest way to settle this matter. If only it were that simple. . . .

Unfortunately, there are no extant letters written by James McHenry in the *James McHenry Papers* at the Library of Congress on this date or for several weeks before or afterward,[10] nor have any drafts by him for Lafayette, for whom he served as an aide, been found for the period between September 1780 and January 1781.[11] Other than the poem by McHenry and Hamilton's reply, there is no reference to McHenry during this period in *Founders Online*, which includes the correspondence of Washington, Hamilton, Adams, Jefferson, Madison, and Franklin.[12] Nor has anything been found about McHenry's whereabouts during this period in the writings of Nathanael Greene, Lafayette, Philip Schuyler, John Jay, the delegates to Congress, and numerous other contemporaries.

After several years and countless hours of searching through biographies of related persons, volumes of collected papers, contemporaneous newspapers, and library collections, here is the best information that has been collected so far regarding James McHenry's whereabouts around the time of Hamilton's wedding:

- James McHenry apparently was with Lafayette at the "Light Camp near Totowa, on the Passaic," in New Jersey, on November 19, 1780.[13]
- The Marquis de Chastellux wrote that James McHenry travelled with him from the light camp to Washington's headquarters at the Dey Mansion in Preakness (now Wayne), New Jersey, on November 23.[14]
- McHenry was at Lafayette's "Head Quarters" in Morristown, New Jersey, on December 28, 1780.[15]

No record has been found of McHenry traveling with Lafayette, Chastellux, and others to and from Philadelphia in November and December 1780, despite numerous accounts of this journey.[16] On the other hand, nothing has been found placing McHenry with the army in New York or New Jersey or traveling to Albany. In sum, nothing has been found regarding McHenry between November 23 and December 28, 1780.

Without knowing James McHenry's location during this period, one cannot say with certainty whether or not he attended the wedding of Alexander Hamilton and Elizabeth Schuyler in Albany on December 14, 1780. While it cannot be proven that McHenry did not attend, there is no evidence he was there.

Without any evidence to support the story, one must conclude that James McHenry probably did not attend Hamilton's wedding. But if one wants to believe he was there, one should write that McHenry *possibly* or *reportedly* attended the wedding but should not present it as a certainty.

Until someone finds long-lost evidence revealing McHenry's whereabouts on the date of Hamilton's wedding, the uncertainty must remain.

Notes

1. Chernow, *Alexander Hamilton* 148.
2. Mitchell, *Alexander Hamilton: Youth to Maturity* 206 and 558 note 91.
3. Poem by Major James McHenry, date unknown but listed as December 14–15, 1780, in *The Papers of Alexander Hamilton* 2:522–524.
4. Steiner, *The Life and Correspondence of James McHenry* 29–30.
5. Steiner, *The Life and Correspondence of James McHenry* 30–31.
6. *The Papers of Alexander Hamilton* 2:521.
7. Hamilton was in New Bridge, New Jersey, on September 12, 1780 (*The Papers of Alexander Hamilton* 2:426).
8. *The Papers of Alexander Hamilton* 2:524.
9. McHenry's poem does have one reference to "last night," but it is not known if this refers to an actual event nor is it known when the poem was written so it is not clear that this refers to the wedding. Moreover, the full line "Last night I sought. . . ." refers to something that the author [McHenry] had done, not the reader [Hamilton]. The poem does talk about "you embosomed with your Queen" and "thus ye lay the happiest pair," but even if these are meant literally it does not necessarily refer to Hamilton's wedding or that the wedding took place "last night."
10. *James McHenry Papers.*
11. *Lafayette in the Age of the American Revolution* Vol. 3.
12. *Founders Online.*
13. Lafayette to Benjamin Franklin, November 19, 1780, duplicate in James McHenry's hand, in *Lafayette in the Age of the American Revolution* 3:228–230. One assumes this copy was made at the time, but it is possible that it was made later.
14. Chastellux, *Travels in North America* 103–105, 275 note 1.
15. James McHenry to Mr. Von Riper, in *Anthony Wayne Papers* 11:86. McHenry gives his location as "Head Quarters," but the contents of the letter make it clear he was in or near Morristown.
16. For instance, see Chastellux, *Travels in North America* 106–223; Gottschalk, *Lafayette and the Close of the American Revolution* 153–161.

Alexander Hamilton Visits Saratoga
in December 1780

O
n February 9, 1781, Alexander Hamilton wrote to Quartermaster General Timothy Pickering to request "a couple of the best Continental horses that can be found" because "the bad condition of my horses and the scarcity of forage in Camp induced me to leave them at Saratoga."[1]

When was Alexander Hamilton in Saratoga, New York? There is no mention of Hamilton visiting Saratoga around this time in any of the Hamilton biographies.

The Papers of Alexander Hamilton has a footnote regarding Hamilton's remark about leaving his horses in Saratoga: "H had been in upstate New York in December, 1780, for his marriage to Elizabeth Schuyler at her father's house in Albany."[2]

That's great, but it does not explain when Hamilton visited Saratoga or why he was there.

In fact, Hamilton may have visited Saratoga at two different times.

Early December 1780

On November 22, 1780, Alexander Hamilton informed George Washington, "My peculiar situation will in any case call me away from the army in a few days."[3] Hamilton was talking about his plan to go to Albany, where he would marry Elizabeth Schuyler.

On November 27, 1780, Alexander Hamilton at headquarters at the Dey Mansion in Preakness, New Jersey, wrote one short letter to Timothy Pickering[4] and drafted twelve letters for Washington.[5] Hamilton would not draft another letter for Washington for more than a month.

The following day, November 28, 1780, George Washington went to Morristown, New Jersey, where he "made some necessary regulations . . . and visited the Hospitals."[6] Hamilton did not travel with Washington, evidenced by the fact that he did not draft any of Washington's letters on this trip. More-over, Morristown lies about 18 miles southwest of Preakness whereas Hamil-ton was planning to ride north to Albany.

It is therefore safe to assume that Hamilton left Preakness, New Jersey, for Albany on or just after November 28, 1780. From Preakness, it would have taken Hamilton three or four days to travel the approximately 140 miles to Albany, putting his arrival around December 1 or 2.

So why did Alexander Hamilton and Elizabeth Schuyler wait until De-cember 14 to get married? Why did they not get married right after Hamilton arrived in Albany?

On December 2, 1780, Philip Schuyler wrote to the President of Congress from Saratoga [Schuylerville].[7] Thus, when Hamilton arrived in Albany, Philip Schuyler was in Saratoga. And Schuyler was not alone in Saratoga. A few weeks earlier, on November 12, 1780, Philip Schuyler wrote to Hamilton from Saratoga and noted that "Mrs. Schuyler joins me in the most affection-ate wishes."[8] One assumes that Catherine Schuyler was still with her husband in Saratoga when Hamilton arrived in Albany in early December. The lack of "wishes" from Elizabeth Schuyler indicates that she did not travel from Al-bany to Saratoga with her parents. So when Hamilton arrived in Albany around December 1 or 2, his fiancée was there to greet him, but her parents were away and therefore the wedding had to wait.

So what did Hamilton do after arriving in Albany in early December 1780?

Perhaps he sent the Schuylers a note and then waited in Albany for them to return. Alternatively, Hamilton may have taken to his horse and rode up to Saratoga to fetch his future in-laws. If so, Hamilton presumably traveled with Philip and Catherine Schuyler back to Albany for the wedding. Perhaps Elizabeth also traveled with Alexander Hamilton to and from Saratoga. And perhaps this is when Hamilton left his horses "at Saratoga."

Late December 1780

At sunrise on December 29, 1780, Philip Schuyler, the Marquis de Chas-tellux, and others loaded into "five different sledges" and rode up to Sara-toga.[9] Chastellux did not record who else joined the "party." Chastellux re-turned to Albany on December 31.[10] Philip Schuyler stayed in Saratoga.[11]

Alexander Hamilton is next found in Fishkill on January 9.[12] Accordingly, he must have left Albany around January 7. Thus, it is possible that Alexander Hamilton, with or without his bride, traveled with Schuyler and Chastellux to Saratoga in late December. And perhaps his horses were among those who pulled the "five different sledges," and he left them in Saratoga because of "the bad condition of my horses and the scarcity of forage in Camp."

Which Trip? Or Both?

Unfortunately, there is no evidence regarding which trip Hamilton made. It is possible that he made both. Either way, it is clear that Hamilton visited Saratoga in December 1780, a fact missing from all the Hamilton biographies.

Notes

1. Alexander Hamilton to Colonel Timothy Pickering, February 9, 1781, in *The Papers of Alexander Hamilton* 26:408–409.
2. *The Papers of Alexander Hamilton* 26:408–409.
3. Alexander Hamilton to George Washington November 22, 1780, in *The Papers of Alexander Hamilton* 2:509–510.
4. Alexander Hamilton to Timothy Pickering, November 27, 1780, in *The Papers of Alexander Hamilton* 2:513.
5. *The Papers of Alexander Hamilton* 2:514–516.
6. George Washington to the President of Congress [Samuel Huntington], November 28, 1780, in *The Writings of George Washington* [Fitzpatrick] 20:418–420.
7. Philip Schuyler to the President of Congress [Samuel Huntington], December 2, 1780, in *Papers of the Continental Congress*, Item 153, pages 551–554.
8. Philip Schuyler to Alexander Hamilton, November 12, 1780, in *The Papers of Alexander Hamilton* 2:498–500.
9. Chastellux, *Travels in North America* 210–217.
10. Chastellux, *Travels in North America* 217–223.
11. Chastellux, *Travels in North America* 221.
12. Alexander Hamilton to George Fisher, January 9, 1781, in *The Papers of Alexander Hamilton* 2:528.

Alexander Hamilton's Journey from Yorktown to Albany in October–November 1781

O n the morning of October 17, 1781, the British army in Yorktown, Virginia, surrounded by the joint American-French army, waved the white flag of defeat. Negotiations for the British surrender commenced that day. The following day, October 18, Alexander Hamilton wrote to his wife, "Tomorrow Cornwallis and his army are ours. In two days after I shall in all probability set out for Albany, and I hope to embrace you in three weeks from this time."[1] If Hamilton stuck to this schedule, he would have left Yorktown on October 21 and planned to be in Albany around November 9. Certainly by October 27, Hamilton had left Yorktown, as George Washington reported to Philip Schuyler.[2]

Little was previously known regarding Hamilton's route and timeline from Yorktown to Albany. On December 6, Philip Schuyler reported to James Duane that Hamilton, "absent from his wife for some time, . . . thought of nothing but reaching her the soonest possible, and indeed he tired his horses to accomplish it and was obliged to hire others to come on from Red Hook."[3] This establishes that Hamilton reached Albany by December 6 and had traveled through Red Hook, New York, a town about 50 miles south of Albany.

That is all that can be found in the Hamilton biographies regarding his journey. There is no mention of Hamilton's route from Yorktown to Red Hook. No one writes about when Hamilton reached Red Hook or Albany.

Two more pieces of the puzzle have been found in the *Public Papers of George Clinton*, published in 1899–1914. For decades, these two scraps of information went unnoticed by Hamilton biographers.

Alexander Hamilton in Philadelphia

On November 6, 1781, Secretary of Foreign Affairs Robert R. Livingston wrote to New York Governor George Clinton, "I enclose you a List of Prisoners, Stores, etc. taken at York. Coll. Hamilton leaves me no time to add anything, but my desire to hear from you what passes in our state."[4]

Clearly, Hamilton was with Livingston when he wrote this letter. In fact, as will be seen below, it appears that Livingston gave this letter to Hamilton to deliver to Clinton. Although the letter as published does not give their location, a quick look through other sources reveals that Livingston was in Philadelphia.[5] Thus, Hamilton was in Philadelphia on November 6, 1781.

The above letter also makes it clear that Hamilton was in a hurry to continue northward. Likewise, Hamilton later apologized to Richard Kidder Meade for having "neglected to prepare what I promised you at Philadelphia. The truth is, I was in such a hurry to get home that I could think of nothing else."[6] According to this, it would seem that Hamilton did not stay long in Philadelphia. One therefore must assume that Hamilton arrived in Philadelphia on November 6 or perhaps a day or two earlier and then departed the city on November 6 to continue his journey northward.

Alexander Hamilton in Poughkeepsie

On November 9, 1781, Governor George Clinton wrote from Poughkeepsie to Patrick Barber, the father of Francis Barber, who had been Hamilton's teacher at the grammar school in Elizabethtown. Patrick Barber had written to Clinton to inquire regarding reports that his two sons serving in the army had been wounded at Yorktown, both of them having served under Hamilton in the assault on Redoubt Ten.[7] Clinton reported to Barber, "Yesterday evening Colo. Hamilton, who was immediately from Yorktown, called upon me, who assured me that tho the accounts of their being wounded was true, they had nothing to apprehend from the wounds they received. The Colo's [Francis Barber's] was a slight touch of a bayonet in his lips, the Major's [William Barber's] was a cannon ball that grazed his side & took out some flesh & tho' a very narrow escape it does not prove a dangerous wound."[8]

Thus, according to this letter, Alexander Hamilton was in Poughkeepsie the evening of November 8, 1781.

Updated Route and Timeline

It is now clear that Alexander Hamilton traveled from Yorktown to Philadelphia to Poughkeepsie to Red Hook and finally to Albany. His exact route between those cities, however, remains unknown.

The timeline of Hamilton's journey also remains somewhat unclear. Hamilton planned to leave Yorktown on October 21 and he certainly did by October 27. He was in Philadelphia on November 6 and was eager to continue his journey. This, however, raises some questions. It is a ride of about three hundred miles from Yorktown to Philadelphia. Hurrying along, this should take perhaps six days and definitely not more than ten. (Tench Tilghman left Yorktown on October 20 by ship to deliver news of the American victory to Congress. He reached Philadelphia on October 24.) Either Hamilton left Yorktown closer to October 27, which was later than he expected, he traveled slower than full speed, or he spent some time in Philadelphia despite all evidence he was in a hurry to move on.

From Philadelphia, the timeline and route is much clearer. Hamilton presumably left Philadelphia on November 6 and arrived in Poughkeepsie on the evening of November 8, traveling the 150 miles in just three days. From Poughkeepsie, Hamilton rode through Red Hook, where his horses tired out and he hired new ones, and then continued on to Albany. Depending on when Hamilton left Poughkeepsie and how long it took him to hire new horses in Red Hook, he should have reached Albany around November 11, about two days later than he had predicted before setting out from Yorktown.

All this hard riding to reach his wife in Albany left Hamilton in a miserable condition. On December 29, 1781, he wrote to Nicholas Fish, "I have been very sick—I am still alternately in and out of bed. How are you after your Southern fatigues?"[9] This again suggests that Hamilton traveled as quickly as possible from Philadelphia to Poughkeepsie to Red Hook to Albany, and perhaps also traveled as fast as possible from Yorktown to Philadelphia, though the uncertain timeline raises some questions regarding that leg of the trip.

Notes

1. Alexander Hamilton to Elizabeth Hamilton, October 18, 1781, in *The Papers of Alexander Hamilton* 2:683.
2. George Washington to Philip Schuyler, October 27, 1781, in *The Writings of George Washington* [Fitzpatrick] 23:280.
3. Philip Schuyler to James Duane, December 6, 1781, in *James Duane Papers*; quoted in Mitchell, *Alexander Hamilton: Youth to Maturity* 261; Mitchell, *Alexander Hamilton: The Revolutionary Years* 283; Flexner, *The Young Hamilton* 369; Newton,

Alexander Hamilton: The Formative Years 503.

4.   Robert R. Livingston to George Clinton, November 6, 1781, in *Public Papers of George Clinton* 7:486.

5.   Robert R. Livingston to Benjamin Franklin, November 2, 1781, in *Founders Online*; Robert R. Livingston to John Adams, November 20, 1781, in *Founders Online*.

6.   Alexander Hamilton to Richard Kidder Meade, March 1782, in *The Papers of Alexander Hamilton* 3:69–71.

7.   Newton, *Alexander Hamilton: The Formative Years* 482, 484, 718 note 48.

8.   George Clinton to Patrick Barber, November 9, 1781, in *Public Papers of George Clinton* 7:459.

9.   Alexander Hamilton to Nicholas Fish, December 29, 1781, in *The Papers of Alexander Hamilton* 2:684.

Alexander Hamilton's Participation in the Newburgh Conspiracy Reexamined

Throughout the War for Independence, the Continental Congress and the various states were unable or unwilling to provide for the needs of the army. The soldiers often went without clothing, without food, and without pay. Some in Congress wanted to do justice for the men who sacrificed so much for their country, but the national government lacked the power of taxation and therefore never had enough money to provide for the soldiers.

Upset at the neglect of them and fearing that the end of the war would mean being sent home without receiving what they were owed, discontent within the army rose. Soldiers mutinied. Many talked of refusing to disband after peace was declared. Some even threatened to revolt against Congress.

General Washington sympathized with his men. A look at his writings reveals that much of his correspondence dealt not with military matters but with the inability of the continental and state governments to properly provide for the army. Despite this, Washington believed strongly in civilian control of the army.

In March 1783, an anonymous "Address to the Officers" circulated through the army camp at New Windsor, New York. It called for a meeting to discuss the demands of the soldiers and to decide how to pursue their rightful claims.[1] Fearing a mutiny or a coup against himself or Congress, Washington canceled the unauthorized meeting and called one of his own.[2] At Washington's meeting, which took place at the New Windsor Cantonment, Washington pledged to do all he could to help the men of the army and urged them to be patient.[3] Washington was at his best. He begged the assembled crowd, "Gentlemen, you will permit me to put on my spectacles, for I have not only grown gray, but almost blind in the service of my country." Upon hearing these words and recognizing the sacrifice General Washington made for his country and fellow Americans, many officers were brought to tears and the so-called Newburgh Conspiracy evaporated.[4]

Hamilton advising Washington

By early 1783, Washington and Hamilton had not written to each other for more than a year. In February, Hamilton broke the silence, providing his former boss with valuable information regarding the growing unrest in the army, of which the Commander-in-Chief was not aware. Hamilton then advised Washington:

The claims of the army urged with moderation, but with firmness, may operate on those weak minds which are influenced by their apprehensions more than their judgments; so as to produce a concurrence in the measures which the exigencies of affairs demand. They may add weight to the applications of Congress to the several states. . . . But the difficulty will be to keep a complaining and suffering army within the bounds of moderation. This Your Excellency's influence must effect. In order to it, it will be adviseable not to discountenance their endeavours to procure redress, but rather by the intervention of confidential and prudent persons, to take the direction of them. . . . Your Excellency should preserve the confidence of the army without losing that of the people. This will enable you in case of extremity to guide the torrent, and bring order perhaps even good, out of confusion.[5]

Hamilton as a conspirator?

Some believe that this letter shows Hamilton encouraging Washington and the army to pressure and even threaten Congress into establishing funds for the continental government. For example, Ron Chernow writes, "Hamilton was coaxing Washington to dabble in a dangerous game of pretending to be a lofty statesman while covertly orchestrating pressure on Congress. The letter shows Hamilton at his most devious, playing with combustible forces."[6]

But Washington did not see things this way. Replying to Hamilton, Washington wrote that he was "pursuing the suggestions of your letter, which I am happy to find coincides with my own practice for several months past, & which was the means of directing the business of the army into the channel it now is, leaves me under no great apprehension of its exceeding the bounds of reason & moderation, nothwithstanding the prevailing sentiment in the army is, that the prospect of compensation for past services will terminate with the war."[7]

Thus, according to Washington, he and Hamilton were in complete agreement that the course to follow was to push for a funding system and try to keep the anger of the army within "the bounds of reason & moderation."

On March 12, Washington again wrote to Alexander Hamilton:

> After the arrival of a certain Gentleman, who shall be nameless at present, from Philadelphia, a storm very suddenly arose with unfavourable prognostics. . . . There is something very misterious in this business. It appears, reports have been propagated in Philadelphia, that dangerous combinations were forming in the army; and this at a time when there was not a syllable of the kind in agitation in camp. . . . From this, and a variety of other considerations, it is firmly believed, by some, the scheme was not only planned but also digested and matured in Philadelphia; but in my opinion shall be suspended till I have a better ground to found one on.[8]

Was there a conspiracy originating in Philadelphia? If so, Washington refused to believe it without further evidence. Was Hamilton a conspirator? If so, Washington did not say so.

In fact, Washington asked Hamilton to continue on the same course he had been pursuing so far.

> Let me beseech you therefore, my good Sir, to urge this matter earnestly, and without further delay. . . . To prevail on the delegates of those states through whose means these difficulties occur, it may, in my opinion, with propriety be suggested to them, if any disastrous consequences should follow, by reason of their delinquency, that they must be answerable to God & their country for the ineffable horrors which may be occasioned thereby.[9]

So who did Washington blame for the "ineffable horrors" that may result? Definitely not Hamilton. In fact, he relied on Hamilton to "urge this matter earnestly." Instead, Washington blamed "the delegates of those states through whose means these difficulties occur," i.e., those who refused to give the national government the power to tax.

Upon receiving this letter, Hamilton replied, "I am happy to find you co-incide in opinion with me on the conduct proper to be observed by yourself. I am persuaded more and more it is that which is most consistent with your own reputation and the public safety."[10] Yet again, Hamilton and Washington were in complete agreement and were working together to prevent "danger-ous combinations."

For the next month, Hamilton and Washington corresponded about how to promote the funding system and keep the army in check.[11]

On April 4, after the Newburgh Conspiracy was quelled, Washington in-formed Hamilton, "Some men (& leading ones too) in this army, are begin-ning to entertain suspicions that Congress, or some members of it," were using them "as mere Puppits to establish Continental funds." Washington warned Hamilton "that the army . . . is a dangerous instrument to play with."[12] The critics cite this as proof that Washington was disappointed with Hamilton's playing with the army to promote a stronger national government. As Ron Chernow comments, "Washington must have seen that Hamilton, for all his brains and daring, sometimes lacked judgment and had to be supervised care-fully."[13]

But Washington had not accused Hamilton of playing with the army. Washington wrote his warning generally and never implied that Hamilton was one of those men under suspicion. In fact, in his letter, Washington called out "the Financier," Robert Morris, as the one "suspected to be at the bottom of this scheme," but he apparently did not believe that accusation.[14] Wash-ington made no mention of Hamilton being involved in any way.

Less than two weeks later, on April 16, George Washington apologized to Alexander Hamilton. "My last letter to you was written in a hurry, when I was fatigued. . . . Possibly, I did not on that occasion express myself (in what I intended as a hint) with so much perspicuity as I ought—possibly too, what I then dropped, might have conveyed more than I intended; for I do not, at this time, recollect the force of my expression." Washington then noted, "To Mr. Morris . . . or rather to Mr. G[ouverneur] M[orris] is ascribed, in a great degree, the ground work of the superstructure which was intended to be raised in the Army by the Anonymous Addresser."[15] Yet again, Washington did not accuse Hamilton of being involved in this conspiracy nor did he say that others had mentioned him as a conspirator. Rather, it was Gouverneur

Morris who stood accused of encouraging the discontented. But this accusation against Morris came not from Washington himself but from the very men who had threatened a mutiny against Washington and an overthrow of Congress and who now argued that they had been used as "Puppits." Perhaps Morris had indeed encouraged these men. Or perhaps these men were trying to shift the blame in an attempt to exonerate themselves.

At this point, there is no evidence Hamilton was involved in any conspiracy. Some members of Congress had been accused of using the army as "Puppits," but those were unsubstantiated accusations and only Robert Morris and Gouvernour Morris had been named as possible conspirators. No one pointed a finger at Hamilton.

Historiography: 1820

In 1820, a man going by the name of John Montgars, who claimed to have "been employed, for several years, upon a history of the United States," was investigating the Newburgh Conspiracy. Montgars wrote that "a letter was received by the Commander-in-Chief from a Mr. Hardy [or Harvie], of Virginia, then a member of Congress, advising him that a conspiracy of the very worst character, having for object the demolition of our free constitutions, and the destruction of the General's authority, was in embryo, and would soon show itself in some overt act; and that Robert and Gouverneur Morris and Alexander Hamilton, &c, were at the bottom of the plan."[16]

Here is the first accusation against Hamilton of not only encouraging a conspiracy to overthrow Washington and the civilian government but that he was "at the bottom of the plan." Yet again, the two Morrises also stood accused of being "at the bottom of the plan" alongside Hamilton.

Who was this John Montgars? Was he a trustworthy, non-biased historian, as he claimed? And what was the source for his information?

It turns out that Montgars invented this story, or at the least he never provided any evidence to support it. Timothy Pickering, Nicholas Fish, John Brooks, David Cobb, Ebenezer Huntington, James Thacher, and others all said that they were eyewitnesses to the events that day or talked to people who were and that Washington received no such letter from a Hardy, Harvie, or anyone else implicating Hamilton and the Morrises.[17]

Furthermore, it just so happens that this John Montgars was none other than John Armstrong,[18] Montgars being an anagram for Armstrong with one "r" removed. Armstrong was one of the worst offenders in the Newburgh Conspiracy. He had written the anonymous "Address to the Officers,"[19] though he denied it for decades, leading a number of historians to believe that someone else, possibly Gouverneur Morris, had been the author. Armstrong had also been an aide to Major General Horatio Gates, an old rival of Washington who had falsely accused Hamilton in 1777 of having "stealingly copied" a letter he had received from Thomas Conway that was critical of Washington.[20] It was Gates who probably would have become commander-in-chief had Washington been overthrown or forced to resign. Thus, the long-lasting enmity between Gates and Armstrong on one side and Hamilton and Washington on the other reappeared during the Newburgh Conspiracy. Armstrong renewed this rivalry in 1820 as he tried to change the narrative of the affair in which he was involved.

With Montgars's identity revealed and his account refuted by other eye-witnesses, there is good reason to believe that Armstrong as one of the con-spirators was attempting to shift the blame off himself and onto Washington's supporters, i.e., Hamilton and the Morrises. Certainly, Armstrong's accusa-tions against Hamilton and others remain meager and unsubstantiated.

Historiography: 1970

This is how things stood for the next 150 years. John Armstrong was known as the author of the "Address to the Officers" and one of the leaders of the conspiracy. The idea that Hamilton and the Morrises were involved in the Newburgh Conspiracy was occasionally mentioned, but was not believed by most because the evidence was meager and unreliable. Just read any Hamilton biography written prior to 1970. Few, if any, mention Hamilton's involvement in any sort of conspiracy. In fact, the term "Newburgh Conspiracy" was rarely used in Hamilton bios prior to 1970. Thus, up until 1970, for all intents and purposes, Hamilton was given no role in the Newburgh Conspiracy and was not only completely innocent, but was often commended for being a great help to Washington in preventing a disaster by warning him and providing him with solid advice.[21]

Then, in 1970, Richard Kohn wrote an essay called "The Inside History of the Newburgh Conspiracy."[22] In this essay, Kohn argued that Hamilton and the Morrises organized the Newburgh Conspiracy. Ever since, this version of history has become mainstream and Kohn's essay is cited by nearly all who write on this subject.

Kohn's essay is far too long—34 pages—and complex to quote here in full or to provide the relevant excerpts. Here, however, are a few short quotes from the essay that provide the gist of Kohn's argument:

"This is speculation."

"My speculation."

"could imply."

"imply to me."

"does not imply."

"in no way implies."

"There is no direct evidence."

"circumstantial evidence."

"The evidence . . . is circumstantial."

"The evidence cited, as I admitted, was circumstantial."

"The exact nature of the group and its plans will probably never be known."

"no proof."

"strong hints."

"an educated guess."

"cannot be gauged with certainty."

There it is. The argument that Hamilton was a leading participant in the Newburgh Conspiracy is based on speculation, implications, circumstantial evidence, and hints.

Even Richard Kohn admitted, in a footnote, that he cannot prove his case because the conspiracy was "an event that never even happened, using evidence that probably never existed, or was immediately destroyed."[23]

Hamilton as a Hero

Although Armstrong, Kohn, and their historical heirs accuse Hamilton of being involved in the Newburgh Conspiracy, there are a number of undeniable facts showing Hamilton to be blameless and even deserving of credit:

- Hamilton forewarned Washington.
- Washington and Hamilton agreed on the course to pursue.
- Washington followed Hamilton's advice.
- Washington encouraged Hamilton to continue on the same course he had been pursuing in Congress.
- Hamilton and the two Morrises became leading advisers to Washington after the conspiracy ended, which Washington would not have allowed if he believed they encouraged a conspiracy to overthrow the civilian government and replace it with a military one.

As the man to warn and advise Washington and one who fought for truth and justice throughout the affair, Hamilton deserves the utmost credit, second only to Washington, for his role in quelling this conspiracy.

It is a real shame that Alexander Hamilton has been portrayed by so many biographers and historians as a villain or as an unsuspecting contributor to the Newburgh Conspiracy when, in reality, he was one of the heroes who helped Washington save the infant United States of America from impending collapse.

Notes

1. *The Writings of George Washington* [Sparks] 8:555–558.
2. *The Writings of George Washington* [Sparks] 8:558.
3. *The Writings of George Washington* [Sparks] 8:558–563.
4. Pickering, *The Life of Timothy Pickering* 1:431; *The Writings of George Washington* [Sparks] 8:564–565.
5. Alexander Hamilton to George Washington, February 13, 1783, in *The Papers of Alexander Hamilton* 3:253–255.
6. Chernow, *Alexander Hamilton* 177.
7. George Washington to Alexander Hamilton, March 4, 1783, in *The Papers of Alexander Hamilton* 3:278.
8. George Washington to Alexander Hamilton, March 12, 1783, in *The Papers of Alexander Hamilton* 3:286.
9. George Washington to Alexander Hamilton, March 12, 1783, in *The Papers of Alexander Hamilton* 3:287.
10. Alexander Hamilton to George Washington, March 17, 1783, in *The Papers of Alexander Hamilton* 3:291.
11. *The Papers of Alexander Hamilton* 3:304–305, 305–307, 307–309, 309–311.
12. George Washington to Alexander Hamilton, April 4, 1783, in *The Papers of Alexander*

Hamilton 3:315–316.

13. Chernow, *Alexander Hamilton* 179–180.

14. George Washington to Alexander Hamilton, April 4, 1783, in *The Papers of Alexander Hamilton* 3:315–316.

15. George Washington to Alexander Hamilton, April 16, 1783, in *The Papers of Alexander Hamilton* 3:329–330.

16. Pickering, *The Life of Timothy Pickering* 1:407, 409.

17. Pickering, *The Life of Timothy Pickering* 1:415, 416, 417–418, 430–431, 431–433, 435–436.

18. Pickering, *The Life of Timothy Pickering* 1:407, 421–422.

19. Pickering, *The Life of Timothy Pickering* 1:419, 425; *The Writings of George Washington* [Sparks] 8:555.

20. Horatio Gates to George Washington, December 8, 1777, in *The Writings of George Washington* [Sparks] 5:487.

21. For some examples, see Bancroft, *A History of the United States* 1:87–88; Lodge, *Alexander Hamilton* 41; Mitchell, *Alexander Hamilton: Youth to Maturity* 306–308; Mitchell, *Alexander Hamilton: The Revolutionary Years* 288–298.

22. Kohn, "The Inside History of the Newburgh Conspiracy."

23. Kohn, "The Inside History of the Newburgh Conspiracy" 189 note 4.
    Richard Kohn followed up his 1970 essay with another in 1974, coauthored by C. Edward Skeen, entitled "The Newburgh Conspiracy Reconsidered," and repeated the same arguments in a 1975 book, *Eagle and Sword: The Beginnings of the Military Establishment in America.*

Acknowledgments

This book would not have been possible without the assistance of a number of people.

Foremost on the list of those who helped make this book possible is Professor Daniel Hopkins, who not only spent countless hours translating documents written in Gothic Danish script, a task few could perform, but also shared his thoughts, critiques, and expertise regarding eighteenth century St. Croix and the West Indian collections at the Rigsarkivet. Most of the translations in this work come from Prof. Hopkins. To point out a couple of laudable examples, Prof. Hopkins translated the records regarding Rachel Faucett's extramarital affair and the court proceedings regarding her divorce from John Michael Lavien. Indeed, I found Professor Hopkins only after discovering the record of the extramarital affair and the name of Rachel Faucett's paramour because Prof. Hopkins has written extensively on the cadastre (division and recording of land ownership) and cartography of St. Croix[1] and happens to be an expert on the person with whom Rachel had her affair. After translating the documents related to the affair, Professor Hopkins has since translated dozens more documents for me, most notably the divorce court record. As an expert on eighteenth century St. Croix and the island's records, Prof. Hopkins has also provided great insights into life, business, government operations, and record keeping on St. Croix.

I would also like to thank Mads Langballe Jensen, who took time out of his busy schedule to translate some Gothic Danish manuscripts for me. It was Jensen's initial translation of some of the extramarital affair records that led me to Prof. Hopkins.

Douglas Hamilton also deserves much credit for his contributions to this work. Whenever I have a question regarding Hamilton family history and genealogy, Doug is the person to whom I turn. But his interest in Hamilton extends far beyond just the family tree and he is always eager to learn and provide feedback about the latest Hamilton research and literature.

Next, I'd like to thank the many archives with whom I have done research, including but not limited to the Rigsarkivet (Danish National Archives); the Library of Congress; U.S. National Archives; U.K. National Archives; the New York Public Library, including the Manuscripts, Archives and Rare Books Division; Columbia Library, including the Rare Book and Manuscripts Library; the New-York Historical Society; the Morgan Library; the Historical Society of Pennsylvania; the Presbyterian Historical Society; the National Archives of Scotland; the Nationaal Archief (National Archives of the Netherlands); the British Library; the Bodleian Library; and the Massachusetts Historical Society. Each has been the source of valuable information and has been a pleasure to work with.

I'd like to thank Rhiannon Markless (www.legalarchiveresearch.com) and Susan Moore (www.susanmooreresearch.co.uk) for locating and photographing documents at my request within the collections of the U.K. National Archives.

I would also like to thank the above Susan Moore along with Mariana Oller, the Associate Curator of Special Collections at Wellesley College and Chair of the Alexander Hamilton Awareness Society, for inspecting John Faucett's deposition and analyzing the handwriting of the various parts, including John Faucett's signature.

Thank you to Christine Eickelmann, Research Associate at University of Bristol Department of Archaeology and Anthropology, for sharing her Nevis research as it pertains to the Gurley and Iles families.

Thank you to Nicola Redway, local historian on Bequia, who contacted me after I had written on my blog DiscoveringHamilton.com about James Hamilton on Bequia and St. Vincent. Nicola graciously shared her research about James Hamilton on both those islands, particularly Bequia, and kindly did some additional research for me regarding Ingram, Iles, Gurley, and Peters on St. Vincent. In addition, we have discussed the various possibilities regarding why and how Hamilton came to be on Bequia and later St. Vincent, a discussion that I hope has improved my analysis on the subject.

Many thanks to those who reviewed and critiqued the manuscript of this book prior to publication, including the previously mentioned Douglas Hamilton; Sophie Schiller, poet and author of historical fiction set in the West Indies (sophieschiller.blogspot.com); Nicole Scholet de Villavicencio, President of the Alexander Hamilton Awareness Society; Rand Scholet, founder of the Alexander Hamilton Awareness Society; and Sergio Villavicencio, Vice President and Communications Director of the Alexander Hamilton Awareness Society.

Of course, I thank my family for supporting this ongoing project since before anyone, including myself, knew where it would lead.

Notes

1. Among Prof. Daniel Hopkins's writings on the subject are Hopkins, *The Danish Cadastral Survey of St. Croix*; Hopkins, "An Extraordinary Eighteenth-Century Map of the Danish Sugar-Plantation Island St. Croix"; Hopkins, "An Early Map and the Cadastral Survey of St. Croix, Danish West Indies 1734-41."

Bibliography

A Collection of the Facts and Documents Relative to the Death of Alexander Hamilton. Ed. William Coleman. New York, 1804.

A History of Columbia University, 1754–1904. New York: Columbia University Press, 1904.

Account of the Islands of Grenada & Tobago. 1776. Rhodes House, Bodleian Library, MSS. W. Ind. r. 4.

Acts of the Privy Council, Colonial Series. Hereford and London: His Majesty's Stationery Office, 1908–1912.

Addison, W. Innes. *The Snell Exhibitions: From the University of Glasgow to Balliol College, Oxford.* Glasgow: James MacLehose & Sons, 1901.

Afskrifter og Ekstrakter af St. Croix Sekrete Råd Sekretprotokoller [Copies and Extracts of St. Croix Privy Council Secret Registers]. 1744-1754. Rigsarkivet, Copenhagen, Denmark.
https://www.sa.dk/ao-soegesider/da/other/index-creator/100/1647669/20202744

Alexander Hamilton Papers. Library of Congress, Washington, DC.
https://www.loc.gov/collections/alexander-hamilton-papers/about-this-collection

An Account of the Late Dreadful Hurricane, Which happened On the 31st of August, 1772. Also The Damage done on that Day In the Islands of St. Christopher and Nevis, Attempted to be Ascertained. St. Christopher: Thomas Howe, 1772.

Anthony Wayne Papers. Historical Society of Pennsylvania.
https://discover.hsp.org/Record/ead-0699

Atherton, Gertrude. *A Few of Hamilton's Letters, including His Description of the Great West Indian Hurricane of 1772.* New York: Macmillan, 1903.

Atherton, Gertrude. *The Conqueror: Being the True and Romantic Story of Alexander Hamilton.* New York: The Macmillan Company, 1902.

Atherton, Gertrude. "The Hunt for Hamilton's Mother." *The North American Review* Vol. 175, No. 549 (August 1902): 229–242.

Bancroft, George. *A History of the United States, from the Discovery of American Continent to the Present Time.* Boston: Little, Brown and Company, 1834–74.

Bequia ou Becouya, la plus Septentrionale des Granadilles. Leve en 1763.

Blackstone, William. *Commentaries on the Laws of England.* Oxford: Clarendon Press, 1765–1769.

Bobbé, Dorothie. "The Boyhood of Alexander Hamilton." *American Heritage* Vol. 6, No. 4 (June 1955): 4–9 and 96–99.

Boyd, George Adams. *Elias Boudinot: Patriot and Statesman, 1740–1821.* Princeton: Princeton University Press, 1952.

Brady, Frank. "Tristram Shandy: Sexuality, Morality, and Sensibility." *Eighteenth-Century Studies* Vol. 4, No. 1 (Autumn, 1970): 41-56.

Byres, John. *Plan of the Island of Bequia Laid Down by Actual Survey.* London: J. Bayly, 1776. https://www.loc.gov/resource/g5122b.ct003663/

Byres, John. *References to the Plan of the Island of St. Vincent, As surveyed from the Year 1765 to 1773.* London: S. Hooper, 1777.

Calendar of State Papers, Colonial Series, America and West Indies. 1661–1739. London: His/Her Majesty's Stationery Office, 1880–1994.

Caribbeana, Being Miscellaneous Papers Relating to the History, Genealogy, Topography, and Antiquities of the British West Indies. Ed. Vere Langford Oliver. London: Mitchell Hughes and Clark, 1910–1919.

Carøe, Kristian. *Den Danske Lægestand.* København og Kristiania: Gyldendalske Boghandel Nordisk Forlag, 1904–1922.

Chambers's Etymological Dictionary of the English Language. London: W. & R. Chambers, 1867, 1882, 1900, and 1904.

Chastellux, Marquis de. *Travels in North America in the Years 1780, 1781 and 1782.* Trans. Howard C. Rice Jr. Chapel Hill: University of North Carolina Press, 1963.

Chernow, Ron. *Alexander Hamilton.* New York: Penguin, 2004.

Christiansted Auktionsprotokol [Auctions Register]. 1736–1899. Rigsarkivet, Copenhagen, Denmark.
https://www.sa.dk/ao-soegesider/da/other/index-creator/114/195283/20201429

Christiansted Byfogedens Sager [Sheriff's Files]. 1755–1800. Rigsarkivet, Copenhagen, Denmark.
https://www.sa.dk/ao-soegesider/en/other/index-creator/114/195283/20204641

Christiansted Bytingsprotokoller [Municipal Court Registers]. 1734–1895. Rigsarkivet, Copenhagen, Denmark.
https://www.sa.dk/ao-soegesider/da/other/index-creator/114/195283/20200825

Christiansted Domprotokoller [Registers of Judgments]. 1756–1887. Rigsarkivet, Copenhagen, Denmark.
https://www.sa.dk/ao-soegesider/da/other/index-creator/114/195283/20200829

Christiansted Embedsarkiver for Byfogeden [Office Archives for the Sheriff]. 1756–1828. Rigsarkivet, Copenhagen, Denmark.
https://www.sa.dk/ao-soegesider/da/other/index-creator/114/195283/20204645

Christiansted Fogedprotokoller [Bailiff Registers]. 1744–1896. Rigsarkivet, Copenhagen, Denmark.
https://www.sa.dk/ao-soegesider/en/other/index-creator/114/195283/20201405

Christiansted Gæsteretsprotokoller [Guest Court Records]. 1758–1810. Rigsarkivet, Copenhagen, Denmark.
https://www.sa.dk/ao-soegesider/da/other/index-creator/114/195283/20200827

Christiansted Notarialprotokoller [Notarial Registers]. 1746–1884. Rigsarkivet, Copenhagen, Denmark.
https://www.sa.dk/ao-soegesider/da/other/index-creator/114/195283/20201425

Christiansted Panteprotokoller [Register of Mortgages]. 1736–1844. Rigsarkivet, Copenhagen, Denmark.
https://www.sa.dk/ao-soegesider/da/other/index-creator/114/195283/20201411

Index 1765–1801:
https://www.sa.dk/ao-soegesider/da/other/index-creator/115/195283/20201415
Christiansted Registrerings og Vurderingsprotokoller for Borgere og Plantere [*Registers of Inventories and Appraisals for Citizens and Planters*]. 1761–1799. Rigsarkivet, Copenhagen, Denmark.
https://www.sa.dk/ao-soegesider/da/other/index-creator/114/195283/20200833
Christiansted Retsdokumenter [*Legal Documents*]. 1740–1862. Rigsarkivet, Copenhagen, Denmark.
https://www.sa.dk/ao-soegesider/da/other/index-creator/109/194974/20196362
Christiansted Sager vedr. Arrest- og Eksekutionsforretninger [*Cases of Attachment and Enforcement*]. 1758–1822. Rigsarkivet, Copenhagen, Denmark.
https://www.sa.dk/ao-soegesider/da/other/index-creator/114/195283/20200831
Christiansted Skiftebrevsprotokoller for Borgere og Plantere [*Registers of Probate Records for Citizens and Planters*]. 38.46.1–36. 1736–1790. Rigsarkivet, Copenhagen, Denmark.
https://www.sa.dk/ao-soegesider/da/other/index-creator/115/195283/20200839
Christiansted Skiftebrevsprotokoller for Kgl. Betjente [Registers of Probate Letters Concerning Civil Servants]. 1734–1797. Rigsarkivet, Copenhagen, Denmark.
https://www.sa.dk/ao-soegesider/da/other/index-creator/114/195283/20200841
Christiansted Skiftesager på Enkeltpersoner [*Probate Files of Individuals*]. 1748–1857. Rigsarkivet, Copenhagen, Denmark.
https://www.sa.dk/ao-soegesider/da/other/index-creator/114/195283/20200851
Christiansted Testamentprotokoller [*Registers of Wills*]. 1740–1845. Rigsarkivet, Copenhagen, Denmark.
https://www.sa.dk/ao-soegesider/da/other/index-creator/114/195283/20201421
Christiansted Tingsvidneprotokoller [*Registers of Sworn Testimony*]. 1758–1845. Rigsarkivet, Copenhagen, Denmark.
https://www.sa.dk/ao-soegesider/da/other/index-creator/114/195283/20201389
CO 152. "Colonial Office and predecessors: Leeward Islands, Original Correspondence." U.K. National Archives, Kew, United Kingdom.
https://discovery.nationalarchives.gov.uk/details/r/C4343
CO 186. "Colonial Office and Predecessors: Nevis Sessional Papers." U.K. National Archives, Kew, United Kingdom.
https://discovery.nationalarchives.gov.uk/details/r/C4377
CO 243. "Colonial Office and Predecessors: St. Christopher (St. Kitts), Nevis and Anguilla: Miscellanea." U.K. National Archives, Kew, United Kingdom.
https://discovery.nationalarchives.gov.uk/details/r/C4434
CO 288. "Colonial Office and Predecessor: Tobago Sessional Papers." U.K. National Archives, Kew, United Kingdom.
https://discovery.nationalarchives.gov.uk/details/r/C4479
Cronenberg, Johann and Johann Christoph Jaeger von Jaegersberg. *Charte Over Eilandet St. Croix udi America*. 1750. Manuscript Map No. A/18–49. Nautical Charts Department Archive, Copenhagen, Denmark.
Cruger, Henry and John. *Waste* [*Account*] *Book, 1762–1768*. New-York Historical Society.

http://bobcat.library.nyu.edu/primo_library/libweb/action/dlDisplay.do?vid=NYHS&institution=NYHS&docId=nyu_aleph001616011

Cuninghame, Topographized by Timothy Pont, A.M., 1604–1608, with Continuations and Illustrative Notices by the Late James Dobie. Ed. John Shedden Dobie. Glasgow: John Tweed, 1876.

Customs Journals of Arrivals & Clearances of Vessels [Toldboger], Christiansted and Frederiksted, St. Croix. 1742–1799. U.S. National Archives, College Park, Maryland, RG55 Entry 460 and T39 Rolls 1–16.

Danske Folkekirke, St. Croix, Kirkeboger [Danish National Church, St. Croix, Church Books]. 1740–1860. Rigsarkivet, Copenhagen, Denmark. https://www.sa.dk/ao-soegesider/da/other/index-creator/104/797196/17116762

Danske Kancelli [Danish Chancellery], *Vestindiske Sager [West India Files].* 1699–1799. Rigsarkivet, Copenhagen, Denmark. https://www.sa.dk/ao-soegesider/da/other/index-creator/114/638/19977154 https://www.sa.dk/ao-soegesider/da/other/index-creator/114/638/19977539

Day, Stacey B. *Edward Stevens: Gastric Physiologist, Physician and American Statesman.* Montreal: Cultural and Education Productions, 1969.

Dexter, Franklin Bowditch. *Biographical Sketches of the Graduates of Yale College with Annals of the College History, Vol. V. June, 1792–September, 1805.* New York: Henry Holt and Company, 1911.

Documents Relating to the Colonial History of the State of New Jersey. Vol. 19. Ed. William Nelson. Paterson: The Press Printing and Publishing Co., 1897.

Dookhan, Isaac. *A History of the Virgin Islands of the United States.* Jamaica: Canoe Press, 1994.

Eickelmann, Christine. *Montpelier Estate, St John Figtree, Nevis: Contrasting Legacies on a Sugar Plantation.* https://seis.bristol.ac.uk/~emceee/otherwork.html

Eickelmann, Christine. *The Mountravers Plantation Community, 1734 to 1834.* https://seis.bristol.ac.uk/~emceee/mountraversplantationcommunity.html

Emery, Noemie. *Alexander Hamilton: An Intimate Portrait.* New York: G. P. Putnam's Sons, 1982.

Fish, Lester Warren. *The Fish Family in England and America.* Vermont: The Tuttle Publishing Company, 1948.

"Five Ways to Compute the Relative Value of a UK Pound Amount, 1270 to Present." *MeasuringWorth.* https://www.measuringworth.com/calculators/ukcompare/

Fleming, Thomas. *Duel: Alexander Hamilton, Aaron Burr, And The Future Of America.* New York: Basic Books, 1999.

Flexner, James Thomas. *The Young Hamilton: A Biography.* Boston: Little, Brown and Company, 1978.

Foster, Joseph. *Alumni Oxonienses: The Members of the University of Oxford.* Oxford: James Parker & Co., 1891.

Founders Online. https://founders.archives.gov/

General Catalogue of Princeton University, 1746–1906. Princeton: 1908.

Giellerup, Carl Ludvig, and von Friis. *Grundtegning over Christiansværnsfort med narmeste Omgivelser [Drawing of Fort Christiansvaern with the Closest Surroundings].* 1836. Rigsarkivet, Copenhagen, Denmark.

https://www.sa.dk/ao-soegesider/en/billedviser?epid=20104124#282933,55098953

Gottschalk, Louis. *Lafayette and the Close of the American Revolution*. Chicago: University of Chicago Press, 1998.

Haagensen, Reimert. *Beskrivelse over Eylandet St. Croix i America i Vest-Indien*. Copenhagen: 1758.

Haagensen, Reimert. *Description of the Island of St. Croix in America in the West Indies*. Trans. Arnold R. Highfield. St. Croix: Virgin Islands Humanities Council, 1995.

Hamilton, Allan McLane. *The Intimate Life of Alexander Hamilton*. New York: Charles Scribner's Sons, 1910.

Hamilton, George. *A History of the House of Hamilton*. Edinburgh: J. Skinner & Co., 1933.

Hamilton, James A. *Reminiscences of James A. Hamilton*. New York: Charles Scribner & Co., 1869.

Hamilton, John C. *History of the Republic as Traced in the Writings of Alexander Hamilton and of his Contemporaries*. Vol. 1–6. New York: D. Appleton & Company, 1857–60.

Hamilton, John C. *The Life of Alexander Hamilton*. Vol. 1. New York: Halsted & Voorhies, 1834.

Harold Larson Papers. Columbia University, Rare Book & Manuscript Library.

Hartog, Johannes. *History of St. Eustatius*. Central U.S.A. Bicentennial Committee of the Netherlands Antilles, 1976.

Hatfield, Edwin F. *History of Elizabeth, New Jersey*. New York: Carlton & Lanahan, 1868.

Hesselberg, Engelbret. "Detailed description of the negro insurrection planned on the island of St. Croix in the year 1759." Trans. Waldemar Westergaard. "Account of the Negro Rebellion on St. Croix, Danish West Indies, 1759." *The Journal of Negro History* Vol. 11, No. 1 (January 1926): 50–61.

Hoff, Henry B. and F. Kenneth Barta. "De Windt Families of the West Indies." *The Genealogist* Vol. 6, No. 1 (Spring 1985): 104–127.

Hollandske Kirke, Sint Eustatius, Kirkeboger [*Dutch Reformed Church, St. Eustatius, Church Books*]. 1709–1791. Nationaal Archief [National Archives], The Hague, Netherlands.
https://familysearch.org/search/catalog/220125

Hopkins, Daniel. "An Early Map and the Cadastral Survey of St. Croix, Danish West Indies 1734-41." *Cartographica: The International Journal for Geographic Information and Geovisualization* Vol. 29 Nos. 3–4 (Autumn/Winter 1992): 1–19.

Hopkins, Daniel. "An Extraordinary Eighteenth-Century Map of the Danish Sugar-Plantation Island St. Croix." *Imago Mundi* Vol. 41 (1989): 44–58.

Hopkins, Daniel. *The Danish Cadastral Survey of St. Croix, 1733–1754*. 1987. Louisiana State University, Phd Dissertation.

Humphrey, David C. *From King's College to Columbia*. New York: Columbia University Press, 1976.

Jacob Green Correspondence and Papers, Oct. 16, 1766 – Oct. 30, 1787. Presbyterian Historical Society, MS G824.

James McHenry Papers. Library of Congress, Washington, DC.
https://lccn.loc.gov/mm78032177

James Duane Papers. New-York Historical Society.

Johnson, Samuel. *A Dictionary of the English Language.* Third Edition. Dublin: W. G. Jones, 1768.

Journal of the Commissioners for Trade and Plantations. 1704–1782. London: His Majesty's Stationery Office, 1920–1937.

Kline, Mary-Jo. *Alexander Hamilton: A Biography in His Own Words.* Vol. 1. New York: Newsweek, 1973.

Knox, Hugh. *A Discourse Delivered on the 6th of September, 1772, In the Dutch Church of St. Croix. On Occasion of the Hurricane which happened on the 31st day of August.* St. Croix: Daniel Thibou, 1772.

Knox, Hugh. *A Letter to the Rev. Mr. Jacob Green, of New Jersey, Pointing out some Difficulties in the Calvinistick Scheme of Divinity, Respecting Free Will, Divine Decrees, Particular Redemption, &c. and requesting a Solution of them.* London: G. Keith, 1770.

Knox, Hugh. *Discourses on the Truth of Revealed Religion and Other Important Subjects.* London: Thomas Cadell, 1768.

Kohn, Richard H. *Eagle and Sword: The Beginnings of the Military Establishment in America.* New York: The Free Press, 1975.

Kohn, Richard H. "The Inside History of the Newburgh Conspiracy: America and the Coup d'Etat." *The William and Mary Quarterly* Third Series, Vol. 27, No. 2 (April 1970): 187–220.

Kohn, Richard H., and C. Edward Skeen. "The Newburgh Conspiracy Reconsidered." *The William and Mary Quarterly* Third Series, Vol. 31, No. 2 (April 1974): 273–298.

Lafayette in the Age of the American Revolution: Selected Letters and Papers, 1776–1790. Ed. Stanley J. Idzerda. Ithaca: Cornell University Press, 1977–83.

Larson, Harold. "Alexander Hamilton: The Fact and Fiction of his Early Years." *The William and Mary Quarterly* Third Series, Vol. 9, No. 2 (April 1952): 139–151.

Lewisohn, Florence. *St. Croix Under Seven Flags.* Hollywood, FL: Dukane Press, 1970.

Livingston, William. *A Funeral Elogium on the Reverend Mr. Aaron Burr, Late President of the College of New-Jersey.* New York: Hugh Gaine, 1757.

Lodge, Henry Cabot. *Alexander Hamilton.* Boston: Houghton, Mifflin and Company, 1898.

Long, Edward. *The History of Jamaica.* London: T. Lowndes, 1774.

McDonald, John. *A Sermon on the Premature and Lamented Death of General Alexander Hamilton.* Albany: John Barber, 1804.

Medicinalvæsenet på de vestindiske [West Indian Medical Administration], *Indkomne breve og koncepter til udgåede skrivelser [Letters received and drafts for letters sent].* 1753–1854. Rigsarkivet, Copenhagen, Denmark. https://www.sa.dk/ao-soegesider/da/other/index-creator/119/195231/20201123

Merriam-Webster's Collegiate Dictionary. Eleventh Edition. Springfield, Mass.: Merriam-Webster, 2004.

Merrill, Gordon C. *The Historical Geography of St. Kitts and Nevis, the West Indies.* Mexico: Pan American Institute of Geography and History, 1958.

Meyer, Ernest L. *Map of Elizabeth Town, N.J. at the Time of the Revolutionary War, 1775–1783.* New York: J. Schedler, 1879.

http://library.princeton.edu/njmaps/counties/union.html

Millás, José Carlos. *Hurricanes of the Caribbean and Adjacent Regions, 1492–1800.* Miami: Academy of the Arts and Sciences of the Americas, 1968.

Miller, John C. *Alexander Hamilton and the Growth of the New Nation.* New York: Harper & Row, 1959.

Miller, Samuel. *Memoirs of the Rev. John Rodgers, D. D. Late Pastor of the Wall-Street and Brick Churches, in the City of New-York.* New York: Whiting and Watson, 1813.

Minutes of the Provincial Council of Pennsylvania. Vol. X. Harrisburg: Theo. Fenn & Co., 1852.

Miranda, Lin-Manuel. "Alexander Hamilton." *Hamilton: An American Musical.* 2015. https://genius.com/Original-broadway-cast-of-hamilton-alexander-hamilton-lyrics

Miranda, Lin-Manuel. "A Winter's Ball." *Hamilton: An American Musical.* 2015. https://genius.com/Original-broadway-cast-of-hamilton-a-winters-ball-lyrics

Miranda, Lin-Manuel, and Jeremy McCarter. *Hamilton: The Revolution.* New York: Grand Central Publishing, 2016.

Mitchell, Broadus. *Alexander Hamilton: The Revolutionary Years.* New York: Thomas Y. Crowell Company, 1970.

Mitchell, Broadus. *Alexander Hamilton: Youth to Maturity, 1755–1788.* New York: The Macmillan Company, 1957.

Mitchell, Broadus. "The Man who Discovered Hamilton." *Proceedings of the New Jersey Historical Society* Vol. 69, No. 2 (April 1951): 88–114.

Moore, Frank. *Diary of the American Revolution: From Newspapers and Original Documents.* New York: Charles Scribner, 1860.

Mulligan, Hercules. "Narrative of Hercules Mulligan of the City of New York," no date [1810–15]. *Alexander Hamilton Papers*, Library of Congress.

Munimenta Alme Universitatis Glasguensis. Records of the University of Glasgow From its Foundation Till 1727. Vol. 3. Glasgow: 1854.

Newton, Michael. *Alexander Hamilton: The Formative Years.* Phoenix: Eleftheria Publishing, 2015.

Newton, Michael. "The Story of James Ash." *DiscoveringHamilton.com.* September 13–20, 2018.
http://discoveringhamilton.com/james-ash-part-1/
http://discoveringhamilton.com/james-ash-part-2/

Newton, Michael. "The Story of Jemima Faucett, Alexander Hamilton's Long-Lost Aunt." *DiscoveringHamilton.com.* August 20 – September 4, 2018.
http://discoveringhamilton.com/jemima-faucett-part-1/
http://discoveringhamilton.com/jemima-faucett-part-2/
http://discoveringhamilton.com/jemima-faucett-part-3/

Newton, Michael. "Who was James Hendrie?" *DiscoveringHamilton.com.* October 8–22, 2018.
http://discoveringhamilton.com/james-hendrie-part-1/
http://discoveringhamilton.com/james-hendrie-part-2/
http://discoveringhamilton.com/james-hendrie-part-3/

Newton, Michael. "Why Were the Hamiltons on St. Eustatius in 1758? And Who Were Their Friends There?" *DiscoveringHamilton.com.* February 5–12, 2018.

http://discoveringhamilton.com/hamiltons-st-eustatius-1758-friends-part1/
http://discoveringhamilton.com/hamiltons-st-eustatius-1758-friends-part2/
Old Parish Registers. National Records of Scotland.
    https://www.nrscotland.gov.uk/research/guides/birth-death-and-marriage-records/old-parish-registers
Oliver, Vere Langford. *The History of the Island of Antigua.* London: Mitchell and Hughes, 1894–1896.
Ortiz, Altagracia. *Eighteenth-Century Reforms in the Caribbean: Miguel de Muesas, Governor of Puerto Rico, 1769–76.* Rutherford, N.J.: Fairleigh Dickinson University Press, 1983.
Ottley, C. R. *The Story of Tobago: Robinson Crusoe's Island in the Caribbean.* Trinidad and Jamaica: Longman Caribbean, 1973.
Oxholm, Peter Lotharius. *Charte over den Danske Øe St. Croix i America, forfærdiget i Aaret 1794, og udgivet i Aaret 1799* [Map of the Danish Island of Saint Croix in America, done in the year 1794, and published in the year 1799]. Copenhagen: G.N. Angelo, 1799. Rigsarkivet, Copenhagen, Denmark.
    https://www.sa.dk/ao-soegesider/en/other/index-creator/153/2354827/20104126
Oxholm, Peter Lotharius. *Map No. 2 Grundriss af Byen Christianstæd med derudi liggende Fort Christiansværn opmaælt i Aaret 1779.* Rigsarkivet, Copenhagen, Denmark.
    https://www.sa.dk/ao-soegesider/en/other/index-creator/153/2354827/20104126
Papers of the Continental Congress.
    https://www.fold3.com/title/63/continental-congress-papers
PC 1. "Privy Council and Privy Council Office: Miscellaneous Unbound Papers." U.K. National Archives, Kew, United Kingdom.
    https://discovery.nationalarchives.gov.uk/details/r/C11474
PC 2. "Privy Council Registers." U.K. National Archives, Kew, United Kingdom.
    https://discovery.nationalarchives.gov.uk/details/r/C11475
Pickering, Octavius. *The Life of Timothy Pickering.* Vol. 1. Boston: Little, Brown, & Company, 1867.
Pont, Timothy. *Topographical Account of the District of Cunningham, Ayrshire. Compiled about the Year 1600.* Glasgow: The Maitland Club, 1858.
Proceedings and Transactions of the Natural History Society of Glasgow, New Series, Volume II. Glasgow: Natural History Society, 1890.
Proceedings of the New Jersey Historical Society. Vol. 51. Newark: 1933.
Proceedings of the St. Croix Burgher Council, 1767–1780. U.S. National Archives, College Park, Maryland, RG55 Entry 863, Box 2030.
Public Papers of George Clinton. Ed Hugh Hastings. New York and Albany: 1899–1914.
Ramsing, Holger Utke. "Alexander Hamilton Og Hans Modrene Slaegt. Tidsbilleder fra Dansk Vest-Indiens Barndom." *Personalhistorik Tidsskirft* Vol. 10, No. 6 (1939): 225–270.
Ramsing, Holger Utke. *Alexander Hamilton's Birth and Parentage.* 1939. Trans. Solvejg Vahl. New York Public Library, 1951.
Randall, Willard Sterne. *Alexander Hamilton: A Life.* New York: HarperCollins, 2003.
Robertson, George. *Topographical Description of Ayrshire: More Particularly of Cunninghame: Together with a Genealogical Account of the Principle Families in that Bailiwick.*

Irving: Cunninghame Press, 1820.

Schachner, Nathan. *Alexander Hamilton*. New York: D. Appleton–Century Company, Inc., 1946.

Schmidt, Johan Christian. *Various Remarks Collected on and about the Island of St. Croix in America*. Trans. Svend E. Holsoe. St. Croix: Virgin Islands Humanities Council, 1998.

Sedgwick, Theodore Jr. *A Memoir of the Life of William Livingston*. New York: J. & J. Harper, 1833.

Simon Gratz Autograph Collection. The Historical Society of Pennsylvania.

Southey, Thomas. *Chronological History of the West Indies*. London: Longman, Rees, Orme, Brown, and Green, 1827.

St. Croix Bytings- & Ekstraretssager [*Municipal & Extraordinary Law Cases*]. 1761–1850. Rigsarkivet, Copenhagen, Denmark.
https://www.sa.dk/ao-soegesider/da/other/index-creator/109/194974/20196362

St. Croix Diverse Regnskabsprotokoller [*Miscellaneous Account Books*]. 1756–1850. Rigsarkivet, Copenhagen, Denmark.
https://www.sa.dk/ao-soegesider/da/other/index-creator/113/195864/20200905

St. Croix Diverse Regnskabssager [*Miscellaneous Account Files*]. 1756–1850. Rigsarkivet, Copenhagen, Denmark.
https://www.sa.dk/ao-soegesider/da/other/index-creator/113/195864/20200907

St. Croix Genparter af Testamenter [*Copies of Wills*]. 1749–1813. Rigsarkivet, Copenhagen, Denmark.
https://www.sa.dk/ao-soegesider/da/other/index-creator/109/194974/20196362

St. Croix Hovedboger [*Account Books*]. 1755–1917. Rigsarkivet, Copenhagen, Denmark.
https://www.sa.dk/ao-soegesider/da/other/index-creator/113/3348662/20205139

St. Croix Hovedboger [*Account Books*]. 1741–1918. U.S. National Archives, College Park, Maryland, RG55 Entry 251.

St. Croix Indkomne skrivelser til Generalguvernøren og Det sekrete Råd [*Letters sent to the Governor General and the Privy Council*]. 1754–1773. Rigsarkivet, Copenhagen, Denmark.
https://www.sa.dk/ao-soegesider/da/other/index-creator/100/194974/20200749

St. Croix Landstinget Domprotokoller [*Court of Appeals Registers of Judgments*]. 1760–1806. Rigsarkivet, Copenhagen, Denmark.
https://www.sa.dk/ao-soegesider/da/other/index-creator/114/195135/20297344

St. Croix Landstinget Justitsprotokol [*Court of Appeals Records*]. 1755–1806. Rigsarkivet, Copenhagen, Denmark.
https://www.sa.dk/ao-soegesider/da/other/index-creator/114/195135/20196490

St. Croix Mandtal o.a. dokumenter vedk. plantagernes optagelse [*St. Croix Census lists and other documents concerning the establishing of plantations*]. 1736–1747. Rigsarkivet, Copenhagen, Denmark.
https://www.sa.dk/ao-soegesider/da/other/index-creator/102/1647759/17226858

St. Croix Matrikel for Plantagerne [*Land Registers for Plantations*]. 1825. Rigsarkivet, Copenhagen, Denmark.
https://www.sa.dk/ao-soegesider/da/other/index-creator/106/2579017/20201031
https://www.sa.dk/ao-soegesider/da/other/index-creator/106/2579017/20201047

St. Croix Matrikels, Mandtals, Landlisters, and Kospkatlisters [*Land Registers, Census Lists, and Poll Tax Lists*]. 1736–1915. Rigsarkivet, Copenhagen, Denmark.
https://www.sa.dk/ao-soegesider/da/other/index-creator/102/1647759/17226858
https://www.sa.dk/ao-soegesider/da/other/index-creator/106/1647759/17226860
https://www.sa.dk/ao-soegesider/da/other/index-creator/106/3348662/17226869
The generic term "matrikel" is used in the text and notes to denote the various forms of tax, land, and census lists, but additional information is given if it is unclear which volume is being cited.

St. Croix Matrikels, Mandtals, Landlisters, and Kospkatlisters [*Land Registers, Census Lists, and Poll Tax Lists*]. 1756–1757. U.S. National Archives, College Park, Maryland, RG55 Entry 896 and M1884 Roll 37.

St. Croix Notarialsager [*Notarial Files*]. 1763–1776. Rigsarkivet, Copenhagen, Denmark.
https://www.sa.dk/ao-soegesider/da/other/index-creator/109/194974/20196362

St. Croix Ordrer og Instruktioner til de Militære Afdelinger [*Orders and Instructions for Military Departments*]. 1744–1806. Rigsarkivet, Copenhagen, Denmark.
https://www.sa.dk/ao-soegesider/da/other/index-creator/99/194974/17345466

St. Croix Orkansager [*Hurricane Files*]. 1772–1827. Rigsarkivet, Copenhagen, Denmark.
https://www.sa.dk/ao-soegesider/da/other/index-creator/107/194974/20196480

St. Croix Overretten Justitsprotokol [*Superior Court Registers*]. 1736–1755. Rigsarkivet, Copenhagen, Denmark.
https://www.sa.dk/ao-soegesider/da/other/index-creator/114/195135/20196490

St. Croix Panteprotokoller [*Mortgage Records*]. 1756–1776. U.S. National Archives, College Park, Maryland, RG55 Entry 825 and M1884 Roll 119.

St. Croix Regnskabsvæsen Sager [*Accounting Files*]. 1754–1917. Rigsarkivet, Copenhagen, Denmark.
https://www.sa.dk/ao-soegesider/da/other/index-creator/113/194974/20196400

St. Croix Reskriptprotokol [*St. Croix Register of Royal Ordinances*]. 1723–1779. Rigsarkivet, Copenhagen, Denmark.
https://www.sa.dk/ao-soegesider/da/other/index-creator/100/194974/20200737

St. Croix Secrete Råd Forhandlingsprotokoller [*Privy Council Proceedings Registers*]. 1755–1774. Rigsarkivet, Copenhagen, Denmark.
https://www.sa.dk/ao-soegesider/da/other/index-creator/100/194974/20200735

St. John's Anglican Church, Christiansted, St. Croix, Burial Registry 1761–1787.
https://www.familysearch.org/search/catalog/1860813

St. John's Anglican Church, Christiansted, St. Croix, Marriage Registry 1761–1787.
https://www.familysearch.org/search/catalog/1860813

St. Thomas Matrikels, Mandtals, Landlisters, and Kospkatlisters [*Land Registers, Census Lists, and Poll Tax Lists*]. 1688–1915. Rigsarkivet, Copenhagen, Denmark.
https://www.sa.dk/ao-soegesider/da/other/index-creator/106/1647701/17226838
https://www.sa.dk/ao-soegesider/da/other/index-creator/106/3348662/17226867
The generic term "matrikel" is used in the text and notes to denote the various forms of tax, land, and census lists, but additional information is given if it is unclear which volume is being cited.

St. Vincent Deed Books. 1770–1839. British Library, EAP688.
https://eap.bl.uk/collection/EAP688-1-1

Steiner, Bernard C. *The Life and Correspondence of James McHenry, Secretary of War under Washington and Adams*. Cleveland: Burrows Brothers Company, 1907.

Stern. Malcolm H. "A Successful Caribbean Restoration: The Nevis Story." *American Jewish Historical Quarterly* Vol. 61, No. 1 (September 1971): 19–32.

T 1. "Treasury: Treasury Board Papers and In-Letters." U.K. National Archives, Kew, United Kingdom. https://discovery.nationalarchives.gov.uk/details/r/C13738

Terrell, Michelle M. *The Jewish Community of Early Colonial Nevis: A Historical Archaeological Study*. Gainesville: University Press of Florida, 2005.

"The Annual RPI and Average Earnings for Britain." *Measuring Worth*. https://www.measuringworth.com/ukearncpi/

The Beekman Mercantile Papers, 1746–1799. Ed. Philip L White. New York: The New-York Historical Society, 1956.

"The Case of the Poor Distressed Planters, and other Inhabitants of the Islands of Nevis, and St. Christophers, in America." London: 1709.

The Correspondence and Public Papers of John Jay. Ed. Henry P. Johnston. New York: G. P. Putnam's Sons, 1890–93.

The Danish Laws: or, the Code of Christian the Fifth. Faithfully Translated for the Use of the English Inhabitants of the Danish Settlements in America. London: N. Gibson, 1756.

The Diary of John Baker. Ed. Philip C. Yorke. London: Hutchinson & Co., 1931.

The Edinburgh Magazine, or Literary Miscellany. Vol. XVII New Series. Edinburgh: J. Ruthven & Sons, 1801.

The Gentleman's Magazine and Historical Chronicle. Vol. 41. Ed. Sylvanus Urban. London: D. Henry, 1771.

The Gentleman's Magazine and Historical Chronicle. Vol. 42. Ed. Sylvanus Urban. London: D. Henry, 1772.

The Historical Society of Trinidad and Tobago. *Publications*. http://library2.nalis.gov.tt/gsdl/cgi-bin/library.cgi?site=localhost&a=p&p= about&c= hist3&l=en&w=utf-8

The History and Proceedings of the House of Commons from the Restoration to the Present Time. Vol. IV. London: Richard Chandler, 1742.

The Inscriptions in St. Peter's Church Yard, Philadelphia. Ed. Charles R. Hildeburn. Camden: Sinnickson Chew, 1879.

The Law Practice of Alexander Hamilton. Ed. Julius Goebel. New York: Columbia University Press, 1964–81.

The London Magazine Or, Gentleman's Monthly Intelligencer. Vol. XXII. For the Year 1753. London: R. Baldwin, 1753.

The Matriculation Albums of the University of Glasgow from 1728–1858. Ed. W. Innes Addison. Glasgow: James MacLehose and Sons, 1913.

The New York Genealogical and Biographical Record. Vol. 41. New York: New York Genealogical and Biographical Society, 1910.

The Oxford English Dictionary. Second Edition. Vol. 18. Oxford: Clarendon Press, 2001.

The Papers of Alexander Hamilton. Ed. Harold C. Syrett and Jacob E. Cooke. New York: Columbia University Press, 1961–1979.

The Tryal of John Barbot, Attorney at Law, for the Murder of Mathew Mills, Esq; At a Court of Oyer and Terminer and General Goal-Delivery, held at the Town of Basseterre, in and for the Island of St. Christopher; On Friday te 5th Day of January, 1753. London: John Whiston and Benjamin White, 1753.

The Writings of George Washington. Ed. Jared Sparks. Harper & Brothers, 1847.

The Writings of George Washington. Ed. John C. Fitzpatrick. Washington, D.C.: Government Printing Office, 1931–44.

Timothy Pickering Papers. Massachusetts Historical Society, Boston, MA. http://www.masshist.org/collection-guides/view/fa0256

Udmålingsattester mm. for hele St. Croix [Certificates of Surveys etc. for all of St. Croix]. 1750–1790. Rigsarkivet, Copenhagen, Denmark. https://www.sa.dk/ao-soegesider/da/other/index-creator/106/2579017/20200893

University of Pennsylvania Biographical Catalogue of the Matriculates of the College. Philadelphia: Avil Printing Company, 1894.

Van Vechten, Jacob. Memoirs of John M. Mason, D.D., S.T.P. with Portions of his Correspondence. New York: Robert Carter and Brothers, 1856.

Vestindisk-Guineisk Generaltoldkammeret [West India and Guinea Chamber of Customs]. Indkomne Vestindiske Breve [Incoming West Indian Letters]. 1760–1767. Rigsarkivet, Copenhagen, Denmark. https://www.sa.dk/ao-soegesider/da/other/index-creator/100/1210437/20201606

Vestindisk-Guineisk Generaltoldkammeret [West India and Guinea Chamber of Customs]. Vestindiske (og Guineiske) Kongelige Resolutioner [West Indian (and Guinean) Royal Resolutions]. 1754–1816. Rigsarkivet, Copenhagen, Denmark. https://www.sa.dk/ao-soegesider/da/other/index-creator/114/1210437/19593095

Vestindisk-Guineisk Kompagni [West India and Guinea Company]. Breve og Dokumenter fra Vestindien [Letters and documents from the West Indies]. 1674–1754. Rigsarkivet, Copenhagen, Denmark. https://www.sa.dk/ao-soegesider/en/other/index-creator/102/144093/20202270

Vestindisk-Guineisk Kompagni [West India and Guinea Company]. Kassebog for St. Croix [Cashier Books for St. Croix]. 1735–1755. Rigsarkivet, Copenhagen, Denmark. https://www.sa.dk/ao-soegesider/da/other/index-creator/102/1647806/20202898

Vestindisk-Guineisk Kompagni [West India and Guinea Company]. Hovedboger paa St. Croix [Account Books of St. Croix]. 1741–1755. Rigsarkivet, Copenhagen, Denmark. https://www.sa.dk/ao-soegesider/da/other/index-creator/113/1647759/20202822

Vestindisk-Guineisk Kompagni [West India and Guinea Company]. St. Croix Auktionsprotokol [Auctions Register]. 1734–1755. Rigsarkivet, Copenhagen, Denmark. https://www.sa.dk/ao-soegesider/da/other/index-creator/113/1647806/20202914

Vestindisk-Guineisk Kompagni [West India and Guinea Company]. St. Croix Rekognitionsboger [St. Croix Duties Books]. 1741–1752. Rigsarkivet, Copenhagen, Denmark. https://www.sa.dk/ao-soegesider/da/other/index-creator/102/1647806/20202906

Vestindisk-Guineisk Kompagni Direktionen [West India and Guinea Company Board of Directors]. Amerikansk og Afrikansk Kopibog [American and African Copybooks]. 1703–1754. Rigsarkivet, Copenhagen, Denmark. https://www.sa.dk/ao-soegesider/da/other/index-creator/102/144093/16519100

Vestindisk-Guineisk Kompagni Direktionen [West India and Guinea Company Board of Directors]. Protokoller [Minute Books]. 1697–1752. Rigsarkivet, Copenhagen,

Denmark.
https://www.sa.dk/ao-soegesider/da/other/index-creator/102/144093/20202172

Webster's Collegiate Dictionary. Springfield, Mass.: G. & C. Merriam Co., 1917.

Webster's Handy Dictionary. New York: Nelson & Phillips, 1879 and 1905.

Westergaard, Waldemar. *The Danish West Indies under Company Rule (1671–1754)*. New York: The Macmillan Company, 1917.

William Livingston Papers. Massachusetts Historical Society.

Works of Fisher Ames. Boston: T. B. Wait & Co., 1809.

Young, Sir William. *An Account of the Black Charaibs in the Island of St. Vincent's*. London: J. Sewell, 1795.

Index

Made in the USA
Coppell, TX
06 July 2020

30329870R00173